Newbery and Caldecott Medal Books:

1956-1965

edited by LEE KINGMAN

Newbery and Caldecott

Medal Books: 1956-1965

with Acceptance Papers, Biographies
& Related Material chiefly from the

HORN BOOK MAGAZINE

THE HORN BOOK, INCORPORATED · BOSTON · 1965

78839

Illustration from *Time of Wonder* by Robert McCloskey. Copyright © 1957 by Robert McCloskey. Reproduced by permission of THE VIKING PRESS, INC.

Illustration by Barbara Cooney from *Chanticleer and the Fox,* adapted by Barbara Cooney from Chaucer's *Canterbury Tales.* Copyright © 1958 by Barbara Cooney Porter. THOMAS Y. CROWELL COMPANY, PUBLISHERS. And to SIMON AND SCHUSTER, INC., New York, publishers of *The Canterbury Tales* translated by Robert Mayer Lumiansky, from which Barbara Cooney adapted her text.

Illustration from *Nine Days to Christmas* by Marie Hall Ets. Copyright © 1959 by Marie Hall Ets and Aurora Labastida. Reproduced by permission of THE VIKING PRESS, INC.

Illustration from *Baboushka and the Three Kings.* Copyright © 1960 by Ruth Robbins for the story; by Nicolas Sidjakov for illustrations. Reproduced by permission of PARNASSUS PRESS.

Illustration reproduced with the permission of CHARLES SCRIBNER'S SONS from *Once a Mouse,* pp. 22-23, by Marcia Brown. Copyright © 1961 Marcia Brown.

Illustration from *The Snowy Day* by Ezra Jack Keats. Copyright © 1962 by Ezra Jack Keats. Reproduced by permission of THE VIKING PRESS, INC.

Illustration from *Where the Wild Things Are.* Copyright © 1963 by Maurice Sendak. Reproduced by permission of HARPER & ROW, PUBLISHERS.

Illustration from *May I Bring a Friend?* by Beatrice Schenk de Regniers. Pictures copyright © 1964 by Beni Montresor. Used by permission of ATHENEUM PUBLISHERS. And also acknowledgment to WILLIAM COLLINS SONS & CO., LTD., for permission extending to England and the British Commonwealth.

To BEACON PRESS, Boston, for permission to use the quotation from *Fiction and the Unconscious* by Simon Lesser.

To FABER & FABER, LTD., London, for use of the quotation by Herbert Read in " Surrealism and the Romantic Principle " from *The Philosophy of Modern Art.*

To HARPER'S MAGAZINE for permission to reprint " Measure " by Salomon de la Selva.

To HOLT, RINEHART & WINSTON, INC., New York, and to ÉDITIONS ALBIN MICHEL, Paris, for permission to use the quotation from *Jean-Christophe* by Romain Rolland, translated by Gilbert Cannan.

To ALFRED A. KNOPF, INC., for the quotations from *Lucy Gayheart* by Willa Cather.

To THE MACMILLAN COMPANY for the quotation from *Between Man and Man* by Martin Buber, translated by Ronald Gregor Smith.

To SATURDAY REVIEW, New York, for the quotation by William Lipkind from "Fairy Tales: A Tradition for Excellence Today" from the May 12, 1962 issue; and for the quotation by Joseph Wood Krutch from "Challenge to an Unknown Writer" from the March 19, 1962 issue.

The editor wishes to thank the Children's Services Division of the American Library Association for the privilege of reprinting from *The Horn Book* the annual Newbery and Caldecott Acceptance papers for the years 1956-1965; and also Miss Helen R. Sattley and Miss Mildred L. Batchelder for their kind cooperation in preparation of this volume.

We also thank the authors and illustrators for permission to publish their addresses in this volume. We thank the authors of the biographies, written to accompany the Acceptance papers in *The Horn Book*, for permission to reprint the papers here, and a special thanks to Mr. Asa Bordages for writing a biography of Joseph Krumgold specially for this book.

We also wish to thank Mrs. Bonita E. Stecher for preparation of the list of Newbery and Caldecott Honor Books, and to Miss Elizabeth Burr, Supervisor, Cooperative Children's Book Center, Madison, Wisconsin, for giving us permission to publish the definitive list.

The editor especially wishes to thank Bertha Mahony Miller, Mary E. Manthorne, and Anne Robinson, former Business Manager of The Horn Book, Inc., for work previously done on this volume; to Miss Siri Andrews; and to the three contributors of articles, Miss Elizabeth H. Gross, Mrs. Carolyn Horovitz, and Miss Norma R. Fryatt for their willingness to enlarge their original articles when the scope of this volume was expanded to include a full decade.

To

FREDERIC G. MELCHER

Originator of the Newbery and Caldecott Medals, who raised
and enhanced the quality and stature of Children's Literature
by his imagination, vision and concern.

Contents

PREFACE   xvii

THE ORIGIN OF THE NEWBERY AND
    CALDECOTT MEDALS   1
by *Frederic G. Melcher*

TWENTY MEDAL BOOKS: In Perspective   3
by *Elizabeth H. Gross*

THE NEWBERY AWARDS: 1956-1965   11

1956   CARRY ON, MR. BOWDITCH   13
      by *Jean Lee Latham*
      BOOK NOTE: 13 • EXCERPT FROM THE BOOK: 14
      NEWBERY ACCEPTANCE SPEECH BY *Jean Lee Latham:* 16
      JEAN LEE LATHAM BY *Ellen Fulton:* 25

1957   MIRACLES ON MAPLE HILL   31
      by *Virginia Sorensen*
      BOOK NOTE: 31 • EXCERPT FROM THE BOOK: 32
      NEWBERY AWARD ACCEPTANCE BY *Virginia Sorensen:* 34
      MY FRIEND, VIRGINIA SORENSEN BY *Anna Marie Smith:* 43

1958   RIFLES FOR WATIE   50
       by *Harold Keith*
       BOOK NOTE: 50 · EXCERPT FROM THE BOOK: 51
       NEWBERY AWARD ACCEPTANCE BY *Harold Keith:* 53
       HAROLD KEITH BY *Fayette Copeland:* 63

1959   THE WITCH OF BLACKBIRD POND   69
       by *Elizabeth George Speare*
       BOOK NOTE: 69 · EXCERPT FROM THE BOOK: 70
       NEWBERY AWARD ACCEPTANCE
          BY *Elizabeth George Speare:* 72
       ELIZABETH GEORGE SPEARE BY *Helen Reeder Cross:* 78

1960   ONION JOHN   82
       by *Joseph Krumgold*
       BOOK NOTE: 82 · EXCERPT FROM THE BOOK: 82
       NEWBERY AWARD ACCEPTANCE BY *Joseph Krumgold:* 85
       JOSEPH KRUMGOLD BY *Asa Bordages:* 90

1961   ISLAND OF THE BLUE DOLPHINS   97
       by *Scott O'Dell*
       BOOK NOTE: 97 · EXCERPT FROM THE BOOK: 97
       NEWBERY AWARD ACCEPTANCE BY *Scott O'Dell:* 99
       SCOTT O'DELL BY *Maud Hart Lovelace:* 105

1962   THE BRONZE BOW   109
       by *Elizabeth George Speare*
       BOOK NOTE: 109 · EXCERPT FROM THE BOOK: 109
       REPORT OF A JOURNEY BY *Elizabeth George Speare:* 111

1963   A WRINKLE IN TIME   116
       by *Madeleine L'Engle*
       BOOK NOTE: 116   •   EXCERPT FROM THE BOOK: 117
       THE EXPANDING UNIVERSE BY *Madeleine L'Engle:* 119
       MADELEINE L'ENGLE BY *Hugh Franklin:* 124

1964   IT'S LIKE THIS, CAT   129
       by *Emily Neville*
       BOOK NOTE: 129   •   EXCERPT FROM THE BOOK: 130
       OUT WHERE THE REAL PEOPLE ARE BY *Emily Neville:* 131
       EMILY CHENEY NEVILLE BY *Glenn Neville:* 137

1965   SHADOW OF A BULL   140
       by *Maia Wojciechowska*
       BOOK NOTE: 140   •   EXCERPT FROM THE BOOK: 141
       SHADOW OF A KID BY *Maia Wojciechowska:* 142
       MAIA WOJCIECHOWSKA BY *Selden Rodman:* 147

       ONLY THE BEST   153
       by *Carolyn Horovitz*

       THE CALDECOTT AWARDS: 1956–1965   163

1956   FROG WENT A-COURTIN'   165
       illustrated by Feodor Rojankovsky
       text retold by John Langstaff
       FORMAT NOTE & BOOK NOTE: 165
       CALDECOTT AWARD ACCEPTANCE
       by Feodor Rojankovsky: 166
       UNFINISHED PORTRAIT OF AN ARTIST
       by Esther Averill: 171

1957   A TREE IS NICE   176
        illustrated by Marc Simont
        written by Janice Udry
        FORMAT NOTE & BOOK NOTE: 176
        CALDECOTT AWARD ACCEPTANCE *by* Marc Simont: 177
        MARC SIMONT *by* Elisabeth Lansing: 180

1958   TIME OF WONDER   187
        written and illustrated by Robert McCloskey
        FORMAT NOTE & BOOK NOTE: 187
        CALDECOTT AWARD ACCEPTANCE
        by Robert McCloskey: 188
        ROBERT MC CLOSKEY *by* Margaret McCloskey: 194
        BOB MC CLOSKEY, INVENTOR *by* Marc Simont: 196

1959   CHANTICLEER AND THE FOX   198
        adapted and illustrated by Barbara Cooney
        written by Geoffrey Chaucer
        FORMAT NOTE & BOOK NOTE: 198
        CALDECOTT AWARD ACCEPTANCE *by* Barbara Cooney: 199
        BARBARA COONEY *by* Anna Newton Porter: 203

1960   NINE DAYS TO CHRISTMAS   208
        illustrated by Marie Hall Ets
        written by Marie Hall Ets *and* Aurora Labastida
        FORMAT NOTE & BOOK NOTE: 208
        CALDECOTT AWARD ACCEPTANCE *by* Marie Hall Ets: 209
        MARIE HALL ETS *by* May Massee: 212

1961   BABOUSHKA AND THE THREE KINGS   217
       illustrated by Nicolas Sidjakov
       written by Ruth Robbins
       FORMAT NOTE & BOOK NOTE: 217
       CALDECOTT AWARD ACCEPTANCE *by* Nicolas Sidjakov: 218
       NICOLAS SIDJAKOV *by* Ruth Robbins: 221

1962   ONCE A MOUSE . . .   225
       written and illustrated by Marcia Brown
       FORMAT NOTE & BOOK NOTE: 225
       BIG AND LITTLE: CALDECOTT AWARD ACCEPTANCE
       by Marcia Brown: 226
       FROM CALDECOTT TO CALDECOTT
       by Helen Adams Masten: 232

1963   THE SNOWY DAY   238
       written and illustrated by Ezra Jack Keats
       FORMAT NOTE & BOOK NOTE: 238
       CALDECOTT AWARD ACCEPTANCE *by* Ezra Jack Keats: 239
       EZRA JACK KEATS *by* Esther Hautzig: 241

1964   WHERE THE WILD THINGS ARE   246
       written and illustrated by Maurice Sendak
       FORMAT NOTE & BOOK NOTE: 246
       CALDECOTT AWARD ACCEPTANCE *by* Maurice Sendak: 247
       MAURICE SENDAK *by* Leo Wolfe: 254

1965   MAY I BRING A FRIEND?   258
       illustrated by Beni Montresor
       written by Beatrice Schenk De Regniers
       FORMAT NOTE & BOOK NOTE: 258
       CALDECOTT AWARD ACCEPTANCE *by* Beni Montresor: 259
       BENI MONTRESOR *by* Velma V. Varner: 266

       PICTURE BOOKS TODAY   270
       by Norma R. Fryatt

   I. HONOR BOOKS — THE NEWBERY MEDAL   281

   II. HONOR BOOKS — THE CALDECOTT MEDAL   288

       INDEX OF TITLES MENTIONED   295

       INDEX BY AUTHOR OF BOOKS MENTIONED   297

Preface

IN EVERY BOOK there lies a paradox. First, the book is created by an author or artist out of imagination and talent. These intangible substances must be caught and tamed during the process of creation. But secondly, that book is created to be used in a very tangible existence, to be read, enjoyed, discussed, sometimes criticized, to be sold by bookstores, to be collected in a family's library, and circulated by public and school libraries. So in this volume we are concerned with the paradox of twenty books, which have been singled out of thousands and honored as Newbery and Caldecott award winners. We salute them all, and their creators, the authors and artists.

Because the process of creation in the realm of books is elusive, it is important to understand what each author strove to do and how he achieved it. The acceptance papers by the authors and illustrators give many clues as to why books are written, and what their authors hoped for them. The biographies explain the backgrounds of the authors and artists, backgrounds which often give expression to their work. The heart of our book is, therefore, in the papers and biographies.

But because books are to be used, we must come to an evaluation of their success for two reasons. First, the Newbery and Caldecott awards should serve as inspiration and guiding star to authors, artists, editors and publishers alike. Only the best should merit the award, for it is a heavy responsibility to be a superb inspiration. We would logically expect, therefore, each award to be given to a specific book, the *best* the author or illustrator has achieved so far in his career — not to a lesser book in recognition of previous work. If this does not seem to be the case, then it is inevitable that there will be questions, discussions, and criticisms.

The second reason we evaluate the success of the award books is because the most distinguished book in the world is useless — if it is not read. We would hope that the award books reach out to hundreds of thousands of readers, and become a part of their lives. If this does not seem to be the case, then surely there will be questions, discussions, and criticisms.

We would point out that those who suffer most over the procedures of award-giving are not usually authors, artists, and publishers, but undoubtedly are the members of the committee who must judge the books nominated for the awards. There must be many difficult decisions and agonizing re-appraisals. We would also point out that discussion and criticism in this book is not meant to undermine whatever judgment went into each particular decision of the award-giving committees. The discussion and criticism is for the purpose of study. How might even a good book have been strengthened so that it might appeal to more readers? What in the structure and character of a book seems unconvincing, and why?

Most important of all, we would point out that each critic brings to his criticism his own experience, his own prejudices, his own hopes for a book. If ten critics were given the ten Newbery award books and asked to evaluate them as to which were most meaningful and most successful in their experience, each list would probably vary, some to extremes. The writer, the librarian, the editor, the book-seller, the publisher, the teacher, the mother of a fourteen-year-old boy, and the fourteen-year-old boy — all would find what is most meaningful to him in different books. For example, among those concerned with bringing together this one volume, there are sharply diverging opinions on the 1965 winner *Shadow of a Bull*. One found it a book of "towering" quality; another found it cold, too stylized, and was unmoved by the hero.

In her article, Elizabeth Gross discusses both the meaning and values in the books, and the usefulness and acceptance of the book once it is in the hands of the reader. Carolyn Horovitz concerns herself with the creation of the book, the writer's purpose and success in achieving it, and thus whether the accolade of "the most distinguished" is truly fitting or not. Norma Fryatt, in discussing the Caldecott books, is concerned with the problems inherent in picture books, the techniques which necessarily limit artists, how they find the medium which best expresses the story, and how successful they may be. A valuable contribution to the usefulness of the book is the definitive list of runners-up for the 1922-1965 Newbery awards, and runners-up for the 1938-1965 Caldecott awards. This has been prepared after considerable research by Mrs. Bonita E. Stecher of the Cooperative Children's Book Center at the State Capitol in Madison, Wisconsin.

We do not ask that one book be all things to all men. But our ideal would be for each " distinguished " book to be true unto itself, the sincere, effective, convincing creation of its author — truly the best recommendation for the final tests: that it endure and be remembered with affection, admiration and enthusiasm by generations of readers.

— Lee Kingman

The Origin of the Newbery and Caldecott Medals

by Frederic G. Melcher

THE MEDALS of the children's librarians, which have grown so in significance in these forty years, had their start at a convention of the American Library Association held in 1921 at Swampscott on the New England coast.

An upsurge of attention to children's books and reading had been developing in various directions: — public libraries expanding their services to children; schools encouraging " free reading "; children's work had achieved notable leadership, while at the same time publishers had begun to staff separate departments for children's books; and Bertha Mahony had established the Book Shop for Boys and Girls in Boston.

The Swampscott program was called " Children's Book Week — a National Movement." Franklin Mathiews of the Boy Scouts, patron saint of book weeks, led off the discussion; Clara W. Hunt, of the Brooklyn Library, spoke of the libraries' interest in the success of the movement. I spoke as organizer and chairman of the two national observances which had been held so far.

As I watched from the platform the rising enthusiasm of this audience I could not but speculate as to how the organized support for children's books might be given fresh impetus from such a start. I asked Alice Hazeltime, of St. Louis, chairman of the Section, for permission to present a new idea to their afternoon business session. This idea was for the award of an annual medal for a distinguished children's book. I was to supply the medal and I had a name for it ready — that of John Newbery of London, the bookseller who in the Eighteenth Century had first published books specifically for children.

The group was delighted with the plan and later the project was approved by the directors of the American Library Association. Fifteen years later my proposal for the Caldecott Medal for a distinguished picture book received the same enthusiastic approval.

To me it seemed that the conducting of such awards might bring many benefits to books. I could see the children's librarians taking greater interest than they had in each new season's books and their encouragement would be very important. I remembered that the Pulitzer Awards had passed by children's books and that omission should be corrected. I could see the children's librarians increasing their status in the profession as a whole. I could think of more writers turning their talents to books for children and in doing so they would notice the long life which the children give to books they like. I could foresee the children's librarians being led to take broader interest in all the processes that bring about good books for children, their writing, their production, their reviewing, their distribution to library, school and home.

The machinery for making the awards, the methods of announcing them and of honoring the winners was to be wholly in the hands of the children's section of the A.L.A. Librarians are particularly competent to choose the winners as they know readers at all age levels and they also get the children's own comments as no one else does. The growing value of the medals — to writers, artists, publishers and public — has been due to the strict devotion to the standards the medals represent. Writers, artists, publishers and librarians can point out books of distinction, considered as they must be year by year, but only readers in succeeding generations can make them " classics."

Twenty Medal Books: In Perspective

by Elizabeth H. Gross

IT HAS BEEN SAID by countless people and in many different ways
that literature reflects the philosophy, the mores, the aspirations,
and the despair of the age in which it is written. The books which
have received the Newbery and Caldecott Awards since 1956
give evidence that the authors and the artists, consciously or un-
consciously, are well aware of the undercurrents of this era and
of the needs of boys and girls in these times of change, danger
and uncertainty. Taken as a whole, this group of books provides
for children the knowledge that unselfish love, spiritual as well as
physical courage, fortitude, generosity of spirit and action, and
empathy with one's fellow man, are still those qualities which will
keep the world upon its course, despite its preoccupation with
violence and the awful power of science. Elizabeth Speare in her
second acceptance speech, printed in this volume, has expressed
the needs of youth:

> Young people do not want to accept meaninglessness. They
> look urgently to the adult world for evidence that we have
> proved our values to be enduring. Yet perhaps never before
> have they looked so clearly, so despairingly at the evidence
> we offer. They demand an honest answer. Those of us who
> have found Love and Honor and Duty to be a sure founda-
> tion must somehow find words which have a ring of truth.

The problems which have led to this call for a determination
of our values are basically those with which man has struggled
for centuries. The use of gunpowder must have appeared to
men in the fourteenth century as shattering an event as the
detonation of the hydrogen bomb to us. The industrial revolution and the emergence of new and unified nations challenging
the power of the established order called forth in the nineteenth

century a like desire to rededicate and to re-affirm the fundamental goodness of the human race and man's interdependence upon his brothers.

These threads of history appear in five of the Newbery awards which have their action laid in the past ranging from Biblical times to the Civil War, with an intermingling of characters of fiction and those who actually lived.

The glorious era of the sailing vessel is reconstructed through the sometimes tragic life of Nathaniel Bowditch, who believed that all men, even the lowliest seamen, could learn the rudiments of navigation, if the material was explained simply enough. *The American Practical Navigator* is still a guide today, even to captains of great liners, and many a youngster may still learn what it means to sail by an " ash breeze " as did Bowditch, who wrote this book before he was thirty. The educational world could learn much from a man who not only taught himself, but respected the potential capacity of all his fellow men.

Young boys especially seem attracted to war stories, and despite the age of violence in which they live, the battlegrounds on land, sea, and air continue to possess an element of glamour. Conflict over the centuries has changed not only the history but the contours of the earth, and, moreover, provided youth with the opportunity to perform, vicariously, deeds of heroism and of sacrifice. Jeff Bussey in *Rifles for Watie* learned, as in the old sagas, that in war the cruelty and evil that lies buried in some people is as evident as the courage and tenderness that is called forth in others. Older children and young people have recommended this book to each other, for as one boy expressed it, " it comes to grips with life." Jeff grows up rapidly from a boy who sought the glory of war to one who after his first battle " raised an ashen face " to his buddy and declared, " Noah, anybody that ever joins anything is crazy. I'll lay in the woods until the moss grows on my back a foot long before I'll ever join anything again." Too few books on this period have presented with understanding the Southern as well as the Northern cause, and children have been quick to appreciate the author's fairness in revealing the fervor and the emotion by which each protagonist viewed his fight.

Like Jeff, Daniel in *The Bronze Bow* grew from boy to man forged and tempered by horror, tragedy, and a growing awareness that the commandment "Love thy neighbor" is more powerful than the belief, "An eye for an eye and a tooth for a tooth," and that hatred not only destroys the individual who harbors it but also those about him whom he loves. Elizabeth Speare in this book and in *The Witch of Blackbird Pond* has written compellingly of a boy, Daniel, and a girl, Kit, who change and mature through circumstances and the influence of the goodness and evil of people. Daniel, brooding and taciturn, consumed with hatred for the Romans who have killed his parents, injured his sister, and enslaved his nation; and Kit, lively and thoughtless, raised to luxury and beauty but cast into Puritan Connecticut where even the simplest pleasure is frowned upon and life is as harsh, barren and cold as the New England winter, – both learn that love, justice, freedom and dignity are forces as powerful in Biblical Palestine as in Puritan New England. Although in both books the adult characters exert considerable influence on the outcome of the story, it is the young friends of Kit and Daniel who, by their faith, courage and steadfast loyalty, enable them to work out their problems to a satisfying conclusion.

This element of friendship looms strong in these award-winning books. Karana of the *Island of the Blue Dolphins*, despite her fear and dislike of the young girl who represents the tragedy of Karana's past, is drawn by utter loneliness, the desire to hear the sound of a human voice, and the innate need for companionship to accept smiles, gestures, and a present from Tutok. The dependence of one human being on another cannot be emphasized too strongly today. Scott O'Dell has shown this most convincingly, in Karana's friendship for the leader of the dog pack that killed her brother, her care of the wounded otter, her response to Tutok's overtures and in her feeling toward the other living creatures who inhabited her lonely domain.

Friendship and the healing powers of nature bring Marly's father back to health in the *Miracles on Maple Hill*, and jolly understanding Mr. Chris exemplifies these qualities in abundance.

The authors have not flinched from bringing before their readers many of the bitter realities of life. Marly faces the harsh law of the balance of nature; Kit learns that faith and integrity can walk beside righteousness and prejudice; and Andy in *Onion John* discovers belatedly that in trying to satisfy our own needs and solve our own problems we often drive away those for whom we feel deeply. Because the emotions are touched, because the authors have felt deeply about the books they have written, and because frequently there is a level of truth more profound than the plot of the book reveals, these books are read not only by children but by adults as well. The values of Love, Honor, and Duty of which Mrs. Speare speaks are the basic themes of each of these Newbery winners, and it bodes well for our country that this is so, for Paul Hazard reminds us that:

> We can disregard the literature for childhood only if we consider unimportant the way in which a national soul is formed and sustained.*

Possibly the recent Newbery awards illustrate more than some of their predecessors the authors' abilities to come to grips with the almost overwhelming problems of a civilization moving too fast toward the solution of problems, without really recognizing their true basis.

Madeleine L'Engle presents a terrifying space world in *A Wrinkle in Time*, but her sure hand portrays with insight the children's understanding of imaginative worlds and combines this understanding with deep religious philosophy. Although the children in this book are young in years, it has found popularity with all ages of children, especially the young teen-ager. It has been universally accepted by the children even though many adults have been disturbed by some aspects of the plot, perhaps too closely associating a few of its implications with Orwell's *1984*.

One large problem facing today's world is that of urbanization. *It's Like This, Cat* by Emily Neville presents the rough, tough,

*Paul Hazard, *Books, Children and Men*, p. iii, The Horn Book, Inc., 1944.

sometimes sordid scene of the city streets against the difficult adjustment of a father and son to an understanding of each other. This Newbery book comes close to reality as portrayed in some adult fiction today. Its acceptance by the children has been gratifying, but again some adults find its realism hard to accept.

The winner for 1965, *Shadow of a Bull*, by Maia Wojciechowska, again encompasses the theme of the true meaning of courage. "Real courage, true bravery is doing things in spite of fear, knowing fear," and the locale and vehicle through which this is developed is the bull ring. The author writes with a sure and knowledgeable hand, and Manolo's decision is as courageous as any made by a matador within the bull ring; and more important, his decision is to preserve life rather than to destroy it. Many a child forced into a role he does not wish to play will, as in *Onion John*, take courage to be himself.

Two dominant themes are prominent among the Caldecott winners of this period. The traditional tale, ranging from the Indian fable, the legend of Baboushka and a Chaucerian bestiary, to the rollicking folk song *Frog Went A-Courtin'*; and the beauty, power, and influence of nature.

Since man has devised the capability for the total destruction of his world, it is well to put into the hands of children books which reveal the wonder, beauty and design inherent in the natural world to which they are rightful heirs.

In this day of bulldozers, trees have been ruthlessly demolished to make way for housing developments, shopping plazas, and express highways, but Janice Udry and Marc Simont in *A Tree Is Nice* have preserved for generations of children their importance to all aspects of living.

Robert McCloskey in *Time of Wonder* has given to children living in the interior of this country, as well as to those living on the coasts, startlingly beautiful pictures of the "time of the world" passing by "from minute to minute, hour to hour, from day to day, season to season." The moods, the awesome beauty of the sea, and the fun to be had enjoying it, are enwrapped in the embrace of family life. Mr. McCloskey in his acceptance speech, printed in this volume, speaks with conviction of his be-lief that drawing and design should have their place in the educa-tion of the child side by side with science and the machine. Only then will children be able not only to appreciate, but to create beauty in all forms.

Again, as in the Newbery winners, the integrity of the artist in his fidelity to the spirit of the text, is self-evident. Barbara Cooney's authenticity and beauty of design combined with colors which possess the brilliance of jewels, Rojankovsky's joviality and faithfulness to the folk song and to animal and insect nature, and the strong yet serene block prints of Marcia Brown's *Once a Mouse,* so in keeping with Indian philosophy and the justice of the tale, are examples.

From the artistry of Marie Hall Ets in *Nine Days to Christmas* and Nicolas Sidjakov in *Baboushka and the Three Kings* children have opened to them a view of Russia and Mexico which is some-what unusual today. The spiritual poignancy of the old folk tale takes on new meaning through the simplicity and richness of Sidjakov's illustrations. Few children's books can boast a more beautiful title page and a more complete unity of design, illus-tration and format. Ceci's joy in her first *piñata* is that of any little girl experiencing her own festive occasion for the first time. The well-worn theme of the Mexican peasant and his donkey has given way to a happy intermingling of the city locale with its modern homes and parks and the markets and customs of old Mexico.

The Caldecott winners of the most recent years also seem to have faced the problems of the world and through text, brush and paint made such problems seem solvable. *The Snowy Day* by Ezra Jack Keats shows in warm bright colors and simple but beautiful text the fun and excitement a little colored boy en-joyed, living the experiences any young child would on a snowy day. The fact that the child is of a different race is sublimated to the oneness of the human race. The theme and content is of any child's joyful experiences, and the belief that children look beyond skin-tone is emphasized and strengthened here, showing a way to solve the important issue of racism in the world.

In *Where the Wild Things Are* Maurice Sendak has caught for adults a frightening and disturbing world, but for children a delightful world of monsters. Many an adult reader viewing this book for the first time has questioned its acceptance or use by the young child. Here again, however, a child can see past the surface to what is more important — not entirely a frightening world, but one touched with humor and one in which a young boy emerges triumphant.

May I Bring a Friend? by Beatrice de Regniers and illustrated by Beni Montresor has all the tongue-in-cheek rollicking humor that both children and adults enjoy to the fullest. The illustrations complement the text matching in bold and riotous colors the ridiculous, yet plausible, childish episodes of animals and royalty participating in delightful and unconventional meal times.

Significant as the winning of either the Newbery or the Caldecott award is to the author, the artist, the editor and the publisher, Joseph Krumgold, in his speech printed in this volume, has placed before the librarians the challenge of their acceptance by the children.

> You give yourself a hard job. Surely, there must be a great variety of publications that would be simpler to get into a child's hands than the books you honor here. But I think that if this simpler way were taken, a very great deal would be lost. A long line of the oldest kind of books, I'm afraid, would come to an end.

As generations pass it will be the children who will make the final decision upon the ultimate life of any book written for them, as it will be the enthusiasm of librarians and a belief in their worth that will give children the right to consider whether to accept or reject each title.

Although the longest period of time for an award in this volume has been only ten years, it seemed valid to try and determine how the children had received their winners. Two years ago over forty librarians cooperated in giving their observations of the children's opinion on each title.* *Frog Went A-Courtin'*,

---

*1964 and 1965 winners were not included in this survey.

Rifles for Watie, The Witch of Blackbird Pond, Island of the Blue Dolphins, The Bronze Bow, Chanticleer and the Fox, and *A Wrinkle in Time* were universally accepted by the children. With these titles, child recommended to child; parents, too, were often numbered among the readers.

Carry on, Mr. Bowditch found its place among better readers and boys who are interested in sailing and navigation. *Miracles on Maple Hill* is enjoyed as early as the fourth grade, and several librarians commented that it seemed to appeal to " lonely little girls " seeking the security and warmth of a happy family life. Children are drawn to *A Tree Is Nice* because of the simplicity of theme and text and the brilliant colors of the illustrations; *Time of Wonder* seems to have found its place as a family book, borrowed more than once by the same parent, and among children of the third and fourth grades who can appreciate not only the beauty of the illustrations but also the rhythmical prose.

It is the exceptional reader, able to penetrate beneath the surface of a story, who understands *Andy and Onion John,* and *It's Like This, Cat,* but they appeal as well to girls as to boys. These are books, too, which are finding a place in the reading of parents, for they have as much to say to them as they do to the child.

Nine Days to Christmas and *Baboushka and the Three Kings* are read during the Christmas season by those who like to read about children in other lands, and by parents who appreciate new art forms. *Once a Mouse* has captured young readers who accept it as a tale of magic, and who may unkowningly absorb the deeper meaning of the fable; *A Snowy Day* has been enjoyed by children for its understandable experiences without being consciously aware of the racial implications.

Looking back once again over the winners of the past ten years, it becomes evident that the authors and artists have sought to convey to their young readers a deeper understanding of the currents of the past with their implications for the times in which we live, and to give to children experiences which will open up to them new emotions, ideals, and ways of thinking.

THE NEWBERY AWARDS:
1956-1965

THE NEWBERY AWARD 1956

Carry On,
Mr. Bowditch

written by JEAN LEE LATHAM
illustrated by JOHN O'HARA COSGRAVE II
published by HOUGHTON MIFFLIN 1955

BOOK NOTE

NATHANIEL BOWDITCH, indentured at twelve, educated himself,
sailed on clipper ships in privateering days, discovered a new
method of celestial navigation, and wrote *The American Practical
Navigator*, still used today. In this biographical novel, the historical
background and sad trials of Bowditch's personal life are vivid,
and the adventure of intellectual achievement is made as thrilling
as the dangerous life at sea.

EXCERPT FROM THE BOOK

One day Captain Prince called Nat to his cabin. The captain's grimness had not relaxed. " Tell me, Mr. Bowditch, just what are you trying to do with the men during the dog watch? "

" Teach them what they want to know, sir."

Captain Prince cocked an eyebrow. " And can learn? "

" They finally get it, sir," Nat told him, " if I just find the right way to explain it."

" But, Mr. Bowditch, why are you doing it? "

Nat was silent for a moment. " Maybe, sir, it's because I want to pay a debt I owe to the men who helped me; men like Sam Smith and Dr. Bentley and Dr. Prince and Nathan Read. Maybe that's why. Or maybe it's just because of the men. We have good men before the mast, Captain Prince. Every man of them could be a first mate — if he knew navigation."

Captain Prince muttered something under his breath. " An odd business! " he said. " But I've never had less trouble with a crew. Carry on, Mr. Bowditch."

" Aye, aye, sir."

Some one tapped on the door, and Monsieur Bonnefoy entered, smiling. " I have a confession to make, Captain Prince. I was eavesdropping through the skylight. Not by intention. I just happened to be there, and could not help hearing. Monsieur Bowditch — he has the magnificent spirit! It is worthy of the French Revolution! Liberty! Equality! Fraternity! "

Captain Prince roared, " What do you mean — the French Revolution? Who started this business of rebelling against kings? We did! We started it in 1775! It took you French until 1789 to get around to it! " Then, for the first time since the *Henry* had sailed, Nat saw a twinkle in Prince's eyes.

Monsieur Bonnefoy apologized. He was so embarrassed and he talked so fast that he started talking French. Without thinking, Nat answered him in French.

Bonnefoy beamed. " Monsieur! You speak French! Why didn't you tell me? "

" I - I guess I just didn't think of it."

Captain Prince roared again. " So you didn't think of it? And here I've been expecting all along I'd have to have an interpreter in Bourbon! Have you any more tricks up your sleeve, Mr. Bowditch? "

" No sir, I - I - don't think so, sir."

" No more languages? "

" Just - just - Latin, sir. I learned that to read Newton's *Principia*."

Prince mimicked him. " *Just Latin; to read* Principia. And you still think it's worth your time to teach those poor devils in the fo'c'sle? "

" Yes, sir, I do! " Nat snapped.

Captain Prince gave him a long, hard stare. " Carry on, Mr. Bowditch. That's all."

NEWBERY ACCEPTANCE SPEECH

by *Jean Lee Latham*

I REMEMBER once when a six-year-old pal of mine watched me finish typing the manuscript of a book. He said, " Now, Deanie, what'll you do? Send it away and get a cover on it?" I told him that was a consummation devoutly to be wished.

Writing is supposed to be a very solitudinous occupation. But the process of reaching your reader with your story — that's quite a cooperative enterprise. So I'd like to thank all those who had a part in the process of " getting a cover on the book " of *Carry On, Mr. Bowditch:*

Mary Silva Cosgrave for many things — but especially for the suggestion of the title — which I think was sheer inspiration; John O'Hara Cosgrave for the illustrations which do so much to bring the world of the story to life. Editor and artist — they played a vital part in " getting the cover on the book."

Then, after the cover *was* on the book, so many people have co-operated in helping *Carry On, Mr. Bowditch* to reach its reader: the publisher in his marketing of it, the reviewers in their comments. And of course no one group does more to keep a book in the hands of the readers than the librarians. So to them, and especially to the Children's Library Association of the American Library Association, and *very* especially to the committee who selected the book for the Newbery Award, my warmest thank-you's.

And now I'd like to talk for a bit about the preliminary time spent with a book, before it is ready to " send it away to get a cover on it."

Every time I read a good book on the subject of writing I remember my first target practice with a rifle. I remember that, after I had fired about ten rounds, I asked my teacher, " How many times did I hit the bull's-eye? "

He chuckled. " Bull's-eye? You only hit the backstop twice! "
Very meekly I asked, " What's my score? "

" Oh, you don't get any score for just hitting the backstop. But cheer up! If you can't hit the backstop, you'll never hit the bull's-eye."

The backstop of that target always reminds me of the background of a story. And teachers of writing say, over and over again, each in his own words: " Stay in your own back yard; write what you know about; the plot is only the skeleton; you must flesh the bones with reality."

Of course, when I began writing, it was a long time before I believed those wise words. As many young writers before me, and many who will come after me, I wrote of things I knew nothing about because I thought they were " interesting." I wrote dozens of little gems that could never hit the bull's-eye because I was missing the backstop.

Finally I learned better. I learned that I must stay in my own back yard, or, if I departed from it, I must take the trouble to become back-yard familiar with the world of my story.

For instance — the background of *Carry On, Mr. Bowditch*. It's the world of Salem in the late seventeen hundreds, the world of the sea in the days of square-riggers.

My back yard was West Virginia. My nautical experience consisted of two canoe rides and one trip on a ferryboat across the Chesapeake Bay. I've always been glad they did not build that Chesapeake Bay bridge sooner. I might not have had *any* maritime background.

A great many people have asked me why I chose to write about Nathaniel Bowditch. Sometimes they even say *why in the world* did I choose to write about him!

It seems to me a writer has a personal Geiger counter that, on occasion, says to him: *Dig here for treasure.* The most unexpected things may cause that personal Geiger counter to signal that a story lies buried. I remember what started me writing the best-known of my plays — *Old Doc.* I was reading a table of statistics on the average income and the life expectancy of the general practitioner.

Carry On, Mr. Bowditch started when I read the introduction to a book published by the United States Naval Department, Hydrographic Office. I was reading the introduction because there did not seem to be anything else in the book that I could understand. The book had been written more than one hundred and fifty years ago by a man not yet thirty. That was enough to pique my interest. I found a few more facts about Nathaniel Bowditch: that once the undersized, undernourished son in a poverty-stricken home had to leave school when he was ten; that he spent nine years in the near-slavery of an indentured apprentice. That was the boy who, before he was thirty, wrote *The American Practical Navigator*, which is still " the sailor's Bible " all over the world. There *had* to be a story there; I wanted to tell it.

I knew I was going to spend a long time on background. I did. There were some little matters such as mathematics, astronomy, and seamanship. I had to start at junior-high level, with books like *How to Have Fun With Arithmetic*, and *A Boy's First Book of the Stars*, and work up to celestial navigation.

Navigation was just one part of it; background is a way of life; I had to know how people lived, what happened to them, and, most important of all, how they felt about what happened.

But my personal Geiger counter said: *Dig here for treasure*. I dug.

Sometimes people ask, " What do you mean by fictionized biography? Is it true? " The facts of a man's life, insofar as they are known, are handled with accuracy. But the facts I had about Nathaniel Bowditch would not have filled twenty pages of typing. The manuscript ran two hundred and twenty pages. I had to flesh the bones with reality.

I invented characters, conversations, and incidents to bring those facts to life. It is a fact that Nathaniel Bowditch taught the man who sailed before the mast. I invented all the men of the crews who sailed on those five voyages with him, except Captain Prince and one cabin boy.

About Nat's sister, Lizza, I had one fact; she died when Nat was seventeen. The biographer said, " The two had been close together, so her death went hard with the boy." There are twenty-seven scenes in the book between Nat and Lizza, scenes full of what they said and did and dreamed about in those days. That is what I mean by fictionized biography.

There are about one dozen imaginary characters in the story; on the other hand, there are about four dozen historical characters who, whenever they touch the life of Nathaniel Bowditch, are handled with accuracy as to time, place, and personality.

So I did spend quite a bit of time on background. When I had finished my research, my notes would have filled ten books the size of *Carry On, Mr. Bowditch*. Speaking in terms of my target practice, I had learned to hit the backstop. But, of course, I did not have any score. I still had to tell the story.

To do that, I must forget the attitude of the researcher and become the storyteller, with my mind, like all Gaul, divided into three parts. With every sentence, every scene, and every chapter, I must be thinking of three things at the same time.

One part of me lived his days with Nathaniel Bowditch. Since it was his story, I crawled into his mind and stayed there, seeing his world through his eyes. I lived in the here-and-now with him, unable to see around the corner to the next day, even to the next hour.

Yet, the second part of me *could* see around the corner — the days and months and years ahead — to the final scene. I was as completely divided by two as that soldier I heard of who was waiting to go over the top. He looked down at his shaking knees. He muttered, " Go ahead and shake. If you knew where I'm taking you, you'd shake harder than that." Part of me was feeling nothing but the hope or fear of one moment with Nathaniel Bowditch; another part of me was thinking — sometimes happily, sometimes regretfully — "If you knew where I'm taking you . . ."

And the third part of me was thinking of my reader. For I knew my story would not happen on paper; it would happen first in my imagination and then in the imagination of my reader. All that would be on paper would be just enough to make the story live for him. So I thought of my reader.

Before I think of one reader in particular, I always remember three things I believe about readers in general:

First: Storytellers may come from every state in the Union, but my reader is from Missouri; I can't tell him anything. I must show him. If I want him to believe anything about my character, I must prove it in terms of what my character says and does and dreams about.

Second: This matter of happy endings. It's axiomatic that most readers like happy endings. But — what is much more important, I believe — is that readers like the story to end as soon as it " gets happy," as soon as all problems are solved. My reader likes suspense. If I am to hold him, I must overlap the end of one problem with the beginning of another, until the final scene of the story.

Third: Writing for my reader is rather like going on a picnic. Both operations take a bit of planning.

When a mother promises her son a picnic, she must not just hop in the car and ride off to admire the scenery. Sooner or later he says, " Where's the sandwiches?" It's hard to divert his attention.

She may try: " Isn't the lake blue today?" (Where's the sandwiches?) " Oh, look at that beautiful tree!" (Where's the sandwiches?) " Come on, dear, let's try to see pictures in the clouds! " (*Where's the sandwiches?*)

When I promise my reader a story, I must not forget what a story is; I must not plunge into the middle of my first inspiration and swim off through a sea of words. Sooner or later my reader says, " What happened?" It's hard to divert his attention, too.

I may try: " Isn't that a neat metaphor?" (What happened?) " Did you notice that simile?" (What happened?) " Let's read this paragraph aloud and notice the rhythm! " (*What happened?*)

However, my reader is not interested primarily in plot. He is interested in what happens because he is interested in the character it happens to. No incident has any place in the story unless it has an emotional impact on the character — and on the reader. He wants the sandwich of fiction — one layer of incident between two layers of emotion.

He likes to live with the character his anticipation of some impending event; to live with him through what happens; to live with him through the aftermath, as he himself up and starts on again toward the next event that promises or threatens.

When I had remembered these three things that I believe about readers in general — that they like suspense, that they want to *see* the story happen and, most important of all, they want to *feel* the story happen — then I was ready to think of my particular reader.

I knew I must think of him, so that the story that happened between us — in my imagination and his — would be like lasting friendship, based on what goes without saying. I must not bewilder him with something he could not understand; I must not bore him by explaining something that he did understand. So I must know my reader, respect him, and appreciate him.

Carry On, Mr. Bowditch was aimed at a specific reader — the adolescent boy.

I was lucky enough to have two younger brothers. I began spinning yarns long before I began writing. There was a very practical reason back of my first stories: I had to wash the dishes. I found that if I told stories my just-younger brother, George, would dry the dishes. Sometimes, if the story was interesting enough, George would wash *and* dry the dishes, too, without noticing what he was doing.

But don't think I wasn't working! You see, George was going to grow up to be an engineer. Did you ever try to keep a budding engineer interested in a story? It's excellent training. I learned very young not to get enthralled with my vocabulary. George was strictly a what-happened type of listener. I could either tell a good story or I could do my own dishes.

I learned a lot about boys that way, and I've learned a lot from them. They are excellent critics; they keep your feet on the floor.

I remember when I was in college and my younger brother, Frank, was still in grade school. There was a little group in college who took my writing very seriously. Of course I basked in their approval. I almost forgot my early training under a budding engineer. I'm afraid I even indulged in purple passages.

During vacation, one of that admiring group surprised me with a visit. She drove into town, found my neighborhood, and asked directions of a gang of boys playing sandlot baseball.

" Do you know where Jean Lee Latham lives?" She admitted later she probably said it in hushed tones.

One grubby little fellow answered, " That's Frank Latham's sister." He pointed with his thumb. " Her house is right over there, by Frank's pup tent."

As my brothers grew up, I had two nephews to keep my feet on the floor. And I've always been lucky enough to have friends with a son or two.

When I wrote my first fictionized biography, *The Story of Eli Whitney*, I had two excellent critics: Michael O'Mara, aged nine, and Connie Anderson, aged ten. They were younger than the reader the book was aimed at, but I knew they read in advance of their years.

We spent all one Saturday on the final draft of the book. That is, I had *thought* it was the final draft. I remember I fed them well, too; lunch, then homemade cookies and milkshakes.

I knew the book had possibilities when Michael started explaining things to me, as if I had had nothing whatever to do with it.

The story opens in 1775, just before the beginning of the Revolutionary War, when Eli Whitney was a boy. I was reading a passage where Eli's friend, Hiram Wedge, the peddler, is telling the boy of the threat of war. Hiram says:

> There's a silversmith in Boston I want to talk to. He knows what's coming. He tried to tell me, but I was too busy peddling my wares to listen.

Michael, aged nine, pointed his finger at me. " And do you want to know who that silversmith is, Deanie? Well, I'll tell you! That's Paul Revere! You just wait and see! "

Later I was reading the scene where young Eli gets a letter from Hiram Wedge. The letter is dated Boston, April 18, 1775.

> Dear Eli
>
> I promised to let you know what the silversmith said. He wasn't home when I got here tonight. They said he was out on an errand . . .

Michael stopped me again. " See, Deanie? I told you that was Paul Revere! And do you want to know where he is? He is riding to warn the people that the British are coming! You just wait and see! "

When we finished the book, they said they liked it fine. But I had learned long ago to get the full benefit out of a reader-critic. There is one question that is Open Sesame to his helpfulness. I plied them with more cookies and milkshakes. I said, " Now, I need your help. I have to cut this much out of the book." I held up about fifty pages. " *What can come out?* "

They sipped and munched; they pondered. Then, without looking at the manuscript, they reviewed the entire book, suggesting what could come out. What did they choose? The flashbacks, all the flashbacks, and nothing but the flashbacks!

They would say, " Remember when he was *here?* So you don't have to go back to when he was *there*, do you?" Or, " Remember when *this* was happening? So you don't have to go back to when *that* happened, do you? "

Every blessed flashback.

I thanked them. When they had departed, full of cookies, milkshakes and good works, I started rewriting the book. Ever since then I've written these biographies in chronological order.

Sometimes adults have told me that *Carry On, Mr. Bowditch* is not a juvenile book. They seem to mean it for a compliment.

One friend of mine, a writer himself, got quite wrought up about it. He pounded the table. " This is *not* a juvenile book! "

I said, " There aren't any words in it that I could not have understood at twelve."

He bristled. " Oh, I'd have understood them, too."

" There aren't any emotions I could not have sympathized with. I believe I knew more, and felt more, and understood more, than some grownups realized."

He sighed and looked soulful. " So did I! "

I grinned at him. " What makes you think *we* were so special? "

Some people who are familiar with my adult radio plays ask me if I don't find it a bore to " write for children." No. There is nothing boring about writing for the adolescent when you believe he knows more, and feels more, and understands more, than some grownups realize. And the most challenging thing about him is this: His dreams are outsized.

When I think of the juvenile reader, I always remember Salomon de la Selva's brief poem " Measure: "*

> In a tiny pool
> You could jump over,
> I saw reflected
> All of the sky.
>
> I wondered: How
> Should one rightly measure
> This lovely water,
> By the earth that holds it?
> By the heaven it holds?*

I hope I never forget the magnificent sweep of the imagination and dreams of youth; I hope I never forget that, when a boy comes only to a man's shoulder, his dreams are tall!

Tall as the dreams of Nathaniel Bowditch: even when he was a half-pint bit of humanity, his dreams reached the sky. Through all the hardship and heartbreak, he kept those dreams. When he died, they said this of him:

> As long as ships shall sail, the needle point to the north, and the stars go through their wonted courses in the heavens, his name will be revered as one who helped his fellow-men in time of need, who was and is a guide to them over the pathless ocean.

I'm glad that one day, four years ago, I picked up a book and read the introduction. I'm glad my personal Geiger counter said: *Dig here for treasure.*

* Reprinted by permission of *Harper's Magazine.*

BIOGRAPHICAL NOTE

by *Ellen Fulton*

Jean Lee Latham

To every thing there is a season,
and a time to every purpose under the heaven:

THE opening verses of the third chapter of Ecclesiastes are the
favorite Bible passage of Jean Lee Latham. The clearcut state-
ments please her, for they fit her way of life. Her days, her activities, her achievements all fall into their proper seasons. She goes
through life purposefully, with her feet on the ground, leaving the
past behind her, living intensely in the present, and feeling "at
home to the future."

a time to build up

"How about having coffee outside under the trees?" suggested
Jean.

From her trailer where we had been chatting over generous portions of scrambled eggs and bacon, it was merely two steps down
to the shadowed coolness of the lawn. Jean brought along a manuscript from the desk that filled one entire end of the trailer.

"This," she said, "is Nathaniel Bowditch at the age of six when
the story begins," and she read aloud the first dramatic chapter.

During the summer of the following year when I was in Nova
Scotia, a prepublication copy of *Carry On, Mr. Bowditch* was
delivered to our rural mailbox. I read it through that night. Appropriately enough, the sound of surf breaking on the beach below our
cottage accompanied my reading. I could not even wait until
morning to write to Jean about my enthusiasm, pride and delight
in her book.

a time to be born

My regret is that I never knew " Miss Winnie," Jean's mother. It has been said of her that she could do anything she determined to do. She grew to maturity with a heart damaged by a childhood illness. The family doctor told her she never should risk bearing a child. But Miss Winnie gave birth to four. Of the strong, energetic, talented quartet, Jean was the second, arriving April 19, 1902, in Buckhannon, West Virginia. As Jean says, " We really split into two camps: Julie and George, the mathematics teacher and the engineer; Frank and I, the writers."

Miss Winnie's understanding of children must have been unusual. She guided them with a " hands off " policy, realizing that what seemed most important to them at the moment should be considered as important to their development. Her children shared in the responsibilities of the home, each having appointed tasks and being expected to perform them. But they were never nagged or driven to do them. If Jean was preoccupied in writing a play and her dish-washing chore remained undone, there was no complaint from Miss Winnie. The dishes waited. The task was done when Jean's writing urge had been satisfied. Jean admits that she still keeps house that way.

a time to plant

Watching Jean conduct her seminars on " You as a Writer of Fiction " during the spring of 1954 at Craft Village in St. Petersburg, Florida, I was impressed by her teaching ability. With clarity she explained various phases of fiction writing; with pungent humor she emphasized many commonplace directions; with patience and understanding she dealt explicitly with countless details. She added to her teaching the dignity of the importance of being not only a good writer but a meticulously expert writer.

Her teaching experience began in 1926 after she had received her B.A. (1925) from West Virginia Wesleyan College and while she was taking a postgraduate course there. She continued teaching while a student of Drama at Ithaca Conservatory where she received the degree of Bachelor of Oral English in 1928, and while working at Cornell University for her Master of Arts, which was awarded in 1930.

From Cornell she went to Chicago as Editor-in-chief of the Dramatic Publishing Company. After six years, as she puts it, she " stopped working and started merely writing."

a time of war

In response to the nation's call for civilian workers in National Defense, Jean switched to a new field, that of electronics, taking a special training course, in 1942, at West Virginia Institute of Technology in Montgomery.

Her first assignment was to Signal Corps Inspection at the Crosley Plant, Cincinnati, where she was promptly given the job of writing inspection procedures on a new piece of equipment. By the end of the year she had been called to National Headquarters of the Signal Corps Inspection Agency, Dayton, Ohio. The following spring she was assigned to handle the training program of Signal Corps Inspectors in the Newark, New Jersey, region. In 1944 she was given the double job of continuing that assignment and writing and supervising the training course for the advanced training of women inspectors. Since Signal Corps Inspection jumped from 90 men in peacetime to 6,000 in wartime, with a continually shifting personnel, and since the courses were conducted in far-separated centers, it meant considerable commuting between Dayton, Chicago, Philadelphia, New York and Newark.

and a time of peace

She resigned in 1945 and came to St. Petersburg to reconvert to peacetime production — writing. It was " good weather and solitude " she sought in Florida and found both, although at times the solitude, essential to a writer, has to be insured by the cut-off switch on her telephone and the understanding of friends and neighbors.

A characteristic of Jean's is doing two things at a time. For a while, in 1949, she was Publicity Director for the American Red Cross Fund campaign in Pinellas County, Florida. For five years she worked as a volunteer Gray Lady in the psychiatric department of the Veterans Administration Hospital at Bay Pines, Florida. In 1951 she was substitute librarian at Warm Springs Foundation.

Since 1952 she has produced five books. *The Story of Eli Whitney* was published in 1953 and *Medals for Morse* in 1954. The latter has been translated into German. *Carry On, Mr. Bowditch* was published in 1955 and was chosen as an April 1956 selection of the Junior Literary Guild. This autumn *Trail Blazer of the Seas* will come out. *This Dear-Bought Land* is scheduled for publication in 1957.

a time to gather stones together

"Stones" in Jean's case might be symbolic of honors. During her career she has been the recipient of a number of them, including election to Phi Kappa Phi (Cornell University) and to Zeta Phi Eta (Northwestern University). She was awarded the War Department's Silver Wreath for work during the War. In May 1956 she received the honorary degree of Doctor of Letters from West Virginia Wesleyan College, and in June '56 the Newbery Medal.

a time to cast away stones

"Stones" are also symbolic of nonessentials in Jean's way of life. Once, when I asked her what she would like me to bring her from Nova Scotia, she said, "If I can't wear it out or eat it up, I don't want it." She glanced around her book-crowded trailer and I understood. Her needs were reduced to essentials there. And I began to call her Jeanie-David Thoreau. Like Thoreau she chose to be unencumbered by nonessentials, thereby gaining more freedom for her consuming passion for writing. When she moved into an apartment, the same simple standards were maintained. Although she now has more space, most of it is used for spreading out writing paraphernalia.

a time to seek

Jean says her zest for living and her delight in experiencing new things is an "inherited trait." These adventures have ranged from operating a linotype machine for the Buckhannon *Delta* during her last two years in college to her latest adventure, taking a course in Elementary Piloting and Small Boat Handling under the U. S. Power Squadron Training Program at St. Petersburg.

a time to speak

Jean says it shocked some of their neighbors in Elkins, West Virginia, when they learned that she was a drama student at Ithaca Conservatory, but she had a champion in Miss Winnie.

When one dear neighbor said, "Mrs. Latham, if Jean goes on the stage, what will God think?" Miss Winnie answered, "I don't believe God would have put the love of make-believe in people if He didn't expect part of them to act."

The neighbors never had to bear the shock of seeing Jean on the stage, but they might have read her stage plays or listened to her radio dramas. The stage plays include: *The Blue Teapot, Old Doc, Gray Bread, Señor Freedom, The Nightmare.* Among her important radio dramas was a juvenile historical serial in 140 episodes on the Lewis and Clark Expedition. There were many other half-hour shows for First Nighter, Grand Central Station, and other programs.

Jean is in demand as guest speaker for radio and other occasions. When she consents to give such programs, she puts into the preparation of script or speech the same meticulous work for effectiveness that she puts into her books. Thoroughness and perfection are her standards. These standards are hers by inheritance and by training.

In late May 1956, she received a request from the Library of Congress to record y On, Mr. Bowditch for Talking Books for the Blind. Jean e her consent and asked to try out as recorder herself. Sh bmitted a tape recording of two scenes from the book to The American Printing House for the Blind, Louisville, Kentucky, with the result that she received an invitation from them to make the recording and went to Louisville to do it.

Jean, dramatist, actor and author combined in this instance to contribute another literary item to the specialized department of the Library of Congress.

a time to keep silence

Jean's energy is tremendous; her achievements are varied and numerous; her capacity for making and keeping friends is a glowing, rich, warm attribute. To what objective will she turn her energies next? her friends ask. Jean doesn't say. Whatever it will be, it will be absorbing and friends will watch her build up more successes in creative writing. She may have even now a purpose in mind. She will find the right season for it.

THE NEWBERY AWARD 1957

Miracles on Maple Hill

written by VIRGINIA SORENSEN

illustrated by BETH AND JOE KRUSH

published by HARCOURT, BRACE 1956

BOOK NOTE

WITH simplicity this book recounts the experiences of ten-year-old Marly, twelve-year-old Joe, their mother, and ex-prisoner-of-war father, as they move to a country home, hoping to cure the father's problems. Adjustment comes as Joe learns friendship from Harry the Hermit, Marly learns from Mr. Chris to explore and delight in the countryside, and the whole family discovers new strengths and abilities as they save Mr. Chris' maple-sugar crop. The revelation of nature through all the seasons is an important element in this book.

EXCERPT FROM THE BOOK

Suddenly the sun came out. All day it had been hidden, but now it burst from the clouds. Everywhere the crusted snow began to shine like Christmas cotton. It was only a minute, and then it disappeared again beneath a cloud. And there, as if the blinding moment of brightness had created it like the wave of a wand, was the house on Maple Hill.

She thought Joe would never see it. But suddenly he said, " Is that it? That little house —"

" That's it," Mother said firmly, and turned the car off the road. "I told you it was just a small place, didn't I? "

" But it's pretty — little and pretty," Marly said quickly. And it was, in a way, though it looked awfully lonely in the vast countryside — and dilapidated too. The porch was heavy with snow and you could see where one step had fallen in. Huge snowy bushes hung over the railing. It looked as if nobody had lived there for a hundred years. The trees on the hill were huge and bare, like skeletons.

" I always loved the windows," Mother said as if she was trying to find something good to say.

They were all little squares, Marly noticed then, with tipsy shutters.

" They're so nice with ruffled white curtains," Mother said.
Everybody sat still. Nobody could think of anything else to say for a minute. Then Daddy spoke. " Fritz seems to have made a good big fire. Look at the smoke coming from the chimney."

" Me go in first! " Joe cried then. " Mother, can I unlock the door? "

" Maybe we'd better flip a nickel for a privilege like that," Daddy said, looking at Marly.

But she shook her head. She sat still while Joe got out and ran to the back door, while Daddy and Mother followed. She wanted time to say something to herself that she had planned to say.

It had to be the right place. All outdoors. With miracles. Not crowded and people being cross and mean. Daddy not tired all the time any more. Mother not worried. But it looked little and old to be all that. She was afraid, now that she was actually here, that it wasn't. She wished that they were still on the way. Sometimes even Christmas wasn't as much fun as getting ready for it. Maybe thinking about Maple Hill would turn out to be better than Maple Hill itself.

She whispered, " Please, let there be miracles."

" Marly! " Mother called. " Aren't you coming? "

Forever and forever now, on Christmas morning, Marly knew, she would stop on the stairs where she couldn't see the living room yet. Afraid maybe somebody had forgotten to light the tree. Because — that once — it really had happened. She felt afraid to go into this house now, even though she didn't know what she expected inside. She didn't even know what she'd miss if it wasn't there.

" Marly! " Daddy came out of the door again. She heard him say to Mother, " What's wrong with that child? In such a hurry to get here and then just sitting —"

She got out of the car then, saying the words once more, and ran every step of the way. Daddy laughed, and opened the door wide for her to go running in.

NEWBERY AWARD ACCEPTANCE

by *Virginia Sorensen*

SINCE the day the sky fell, the 4th of March, everybody has been asking, " How does it feel to receive the Newbery Medal? " At first I took this as rhetorically as " Hello, how are you? " — but then I saw that people were pausing to look at me, expecting an answer. Then the question began to come in the mail, which meant it was serious, and finally I was told that you would like an answer too.

Remember the girl in *Our Town* saying, " Isn't moonlight terrible? " The truth is that I've been wondering in much the same way how joy could be so solemn, how a feeling of new courage could have so much fear in it, how I could feel at the same time so exalted and so humble.

Several years ago I met two of my predecessors in this high place, Miss Yates and Mr. De Jong, and was awed by them and by their possession of what I decided must be a special Newbery vitality. Now in the first volume of *Horn Book Papers* (Newbery Medal Books: 1922-1955), I have had a privilege impossible before " my year " — meeting, through their own words, all the lively, solid thirty-four. I have never found in one volume so much pure gospel about writing and research, or more wisdom about living. Finding myself fallen by some miracle among these angels, I have been forced to tell myself sturdily, again and again, " I can still *work*, so maybe I can still come to deserve the Newbery."

One of the things I was taught at home and at church when I was growing up in Utah was the virtue of work. I recall making a Victorian-looking poster at school: Faith without Works is Dead. Even then, I'm sure, I knew that growth was a slow and painful process, and that no matter how I wished it might be so, I would never find a little biscuit labeled " Eat me " that would make me instantly big enough to face the next dilemma or to reach the next necessary height. Lately I have not only changed plural to singular in that old saying, but have turned it clear around and have found it as true one way as the other. Surely Work without Faith is Dead. Thanks to the American Library Association, to Mr. Melcher, to Margaret McElderry who seems able to make silk purses out of as odd materials as Shakespeare ever dreamed of, I shall be working with more faith for the rest of my life.

If I may, I would like to thank you not only for this moment for myself, but for the possibility of this moment for all writers for children. It is even more important than you may know for a writer to feel the existence of a great and critical and sensitive group of people whose eyes are steadily upon his work. This Medal seems to me not only a star for all of us to shoot at but a bright light for all of us to work by.

Remember Jean Christophe's thought when at last he found sympathetic listeners? "How fine it would be for an artist if he could know of the unknown friends whom his ideas find in the world — how gladdened his heart would be and how fortified he would be in his strength."*

Knowing, as every storyteller knows, that nothing is ever universal without being first intensely personal, I should not have been surprised to find an event as public as the Newbery Award posing questions that turned my eyes deeply inward. How did I happen to be a writer at all? How did it happen that I began to write for children after years of writing for adults? How did I happen, in particular, to write *Miracles on Maple Hill?*

My mother once told me that the first sentence of mine she remembers was, " Tell me a story," and that the second, hard upon, was, " *I* will tell *you* a story," which she insists I proceeded to do.

I'm sure this is as ancient as it is common, and that it was said the first time in the world because there was a mystery. The mystery is still there, and of course will always be, because it is the mystery of life itself. Storytellers are not very often people with answers, but people with questions for which they are seeking

*ROLLAND, ROMAIN. *Jean-Christophe.* Translated by Gilbert Cannan. Henry Holt and Company, Inc.

answers. I agree with Joyce Carey that every story is " an exploration and a setting forth.*

I began telling stories for and about children long before I knew there were such things as "novels." I had a Boston Friend with whom I exchanged rings and vows and with whom I made a secret alphabet. She was wonderful at sewing, but for me the needle was every bit as alive as Hans Christian Andersen said it was, forever turning on me without warning and giving me a vicious nip. Yet I had to live properly in the world, so my friend clothed my naked dolls while I earned her labor with reading and with my own tall tales.

Much later, when I was married and had a daughter and a son of my own, I began telling tales again for the simple reason that the children were there, and so was I — and so, of course, was the mystery. When the time came that I showed proudly my " first real printed book," they were fascinated, insisting at the very next bedtime reading-hour that I should read a story from it. It was my first novel, about a Mormon family, and I considered it very serious and adult and realistic. At first I felt rather at a loss, but after all there were children in the story and I recalled a scene about two little girls named Betsy and Rebecca who got into trouble going to see a neighbor's kittens while he was away. In this scene, three kittens die and Betsy learns an important lesson about cause and effect, conduct and justice. But when I had finished, my daughter Beth, then nine years old, sat up in bed with streaming eyes. " *You* made that story up!" she cried accusingly. " Why did you have to make the kittens die? "

It is hard to tell a nine-year-old that a story has its own being and that if one tells it true, and to the very end, there is always death in it. Yet I feel sure it is because of her tears (she knew that kittens die; she had lost one not long before), that I have Marly face death something short of the reality in *Miracles*, and that this seemed right for the story.

Almost every one of my novels has had children in it, for I am a family chronicler. Many times people have said to me, " I liked the

*From *Harper's Magazine*, February, 1950.

character of that boy Menzo the best . . . "; and a reviewer of *The Evening and the Morning* said, " The child Jean steals the show from her mother and grandmother, especially in the scene in the barn with the owl."

It was eleven years after that night I read about the kittens that Harcourt published my story about a little girl named Missie intended for little girls. My Betsy was by that time twenty years old, preparing to be an art teacher. I was pleased that she could at last read a book of mine with unqualified approval, and that she liked books with pictures as much as she ever did.

When people ask me, " Why didn't you begin writing for your own children?" I confess it is as much a puzzle to me as to anybody. A. A. Milne was sitting right there by the bed every night and I lived on intimate terms with a wise-looking bear my children lovingly christened Pooh. When I am asked, " Why do you write about so many places? " and look at four books and find one about Alabama, one about Utah, and two about Pennsylvania, I do wonder at my own temerity. The only excuse I have is that when I got there the stories seemed to be there waiting.

I am sure, for instance, that it was our five years in the Deep South that caused us to rediscover with such pleasure the seasons of Pennsylvania. We were people reared with seasons, from white to green, from bitter cold to a dry, bright heat. We loved much about the South, especially being able to ride our bicycles all the year around, but we missed the variations just as we missed our Utah mountains when we first moved to the Mid-West.

Being school folks, we arrived in Pennsylvania in September, and enjoyed passionately what happened almost at once to the maple trees. That breathless, unbelievable inner light! But soon they faded, the leaves fell and were burned along the village streets on smoky, chilly evenings. Then, one morning, the piles were white. Winter set in.

We had almost forgotten about winter, and Edinboro, oldtimers told us with an odd, fierce pride, had the worst winters in the world. The name the Indians had left in the valley, Conneatee, meant " Land of Lingering Snow." And it did linger, from late

October on, steady and white and deep. The village was isolated by muddy roads and dangerous pavements and sudden blizzards. Then, one unforgettable day in late February, a fine old New Englander known as Pop Bates, head of our little college Art Department, took us out to see what was going on in the sugar bush. We had seen something of this before, in Michigan, but never so intimately, so close to earth. Here spring could actually be seen and smelled and tasted, rising out of the ground.

That was only the beginning. Flowers we had never seen before burst in April magic from the dead leaves on the forest floor. Birds that Pop could talk with came flying home. Wild swans spent a day and a night on our little lake. My husband, who is an explorer by nature and instinct, played Joe to my Marly as he always has, wherever we've been, and began to show me one miracle after another. I shall always remember the time he showed me a den of little foxes playing in the dusk, and the morning he rushed me out to see the bloodroot opening in the Easter sun.

The natives of Edinboro were pleased with our excitement which seemed to regenerate their own. We became especially fond of the huge Pennsylvania Dutchman and his wife to whose ample farm Pop had first taken us. Mr. Kreitz really looks like a tree. But I couldn't forget something that happened the first day he showed us the sugar-camp and told us about "sugaring off" and did a Magic Trick to keep the boiling down. When we were leaving, enchanted with the life we had seen, I said to Mrs. Kreitz, "How you must love this season! " and she answered, "I hate it! He hasn't enough help and always works too hard. One year he had a heart attack, but he'll never stop while there's work to be done."

Here was the human dilemma laid upon nature, here were the vital relationships upon the earth, the stuff and symbols of a new tale.

The next year the story was ready to begin. I heaved buckets full of sap in the raw cold air and ate such meals in such ardent spring hunger as I shall never forget. The story grew, the people began to move about in its landscape. Some greenhorns came up from the city one day to marvel, and to them I was the knowing native. As we gathered in the bush and sat by the fire in the sugar-camp, I came to know the hired man.

Mr. Kreitz had told me what a fine and intelligent boy he was, and how much to be trusted — except, of course, with the final boiling, a touchy business. " You wouldn't believe it to meet him now, but he came to us from Reform School. He had a poor deal of it at home, and then felt low-down at school, and finally got into real bad trouble with a gang."

So the theme of renewal, of rejuvenation, began to stir in the story, though it was used in an entirely different way.

One day, as we were sitting by the fire drying our pants where the sap had spilled, the boy said to me, " I hear you're writing a story about the sugaring," and I said, " Yes." " How does it go? " he asked. So I told him the plan as I had it up to then, about a girl and boy who come to the farm and when the farmer is taken sick help to save the crop. He nodded at the end, but he was frowning too. " They school kids? " he asked. I said yes, maybe ten and twelve, and he said, from the depths of his own experience, " Sugar season, school's still on. If them kids stay out to help us, there's sure gonna be trouble, you know that? Truant officer's coming out here."

He had added a whole new chapter to the tale, a marvelous turn of the screw. " I guess that's so; I hadn't thought about it," I said. " What do you think we'd better do? " And he thought for a while and then said, grinning, " When she gets out here, we better give her some syrup."

I found out that the local truant officer was also the school nurse, a kindly woman who was not at all formidable except in devotion to duty. When I asked what she would do if two kids didn't appear at school, she replied that she'd be out directly to find out what ailed them. " Nobody gets away with anything in my school," she said. " You know what the kids around here call me? Annie Get Your Gun! "

Here fact certainly had the better of fiction, and Miss Annie told me to use it whole.

The last day of boiling, the hired man asked suddenly, " Virginia, what we gonna call our story?" I didn't know yet. Did he have any idea? And this is what he said, this boy who had had so poor a deal, so many troubles: " Well, it ought to have something about the sugar in it. And it ought to have *something about kindness.*"

The wise philosopher, Martin Buber, now writing from one of the oldest cultures in one of the newest nations on earth, has said, " The world . . . has its influence as nature and as society on the child. He is educated by the elements, by air and light and the life of plants and animals, and he is educated by relationships."* In widening and deepening what they learn of our complex world, what a vital role the books they read must play! We adults tend to skip along in books, touching what interests us or reiterates our own opinions, but I have been amazed and disconcerted by what children have *not* skipped, such small things that I am forced to conclude they miss nothing at all. Maybe they still believe there might be a secret hidden in even a very small corner of a tale. If this is so, then one has an obligation to get the secrets hidden there, as one gets the eggs hidden about the house for Easter morning and the candy and nuts into the socks on Christmas Eve.

It is hard, as they grow up, to find ourselves unable to make the world conform to some of the most natural, the most simple shapes of their hope.

In her splendid piece, " The Test of Recollection," at the end of *Horn Book Papers*, Elizabeth Nesbitt finds it significant that many authors turn to writing for children " when they feel impelled to put into expression an idea, a strong conviction, a moral and spiritual solution to the confusion and contradictions of the modern world.**

I have no solutions, certainly; when and if they come, they will be a vast, cooperative venture. Yet Miss Nesbitt describes aptly the " impelling need for expression " that came upon me when Lois

*BUBER, MARTIN. *Between Man and Man.* Translated by Ronald Gregor Smith. The Macmillan Company, 1948.
**MILLER, BERTHA MAHONY, and FIELD, ELINOR WHITNEY, editors. *Newbery Medal Books: 1922-1955. Horn Book Papers. Volume I.* The Horn Book, Inc.

Green told me about the urgent problems of librarians in Alabama. There were questions and no way to get at the answers; there were books but no way to get them to the people who needed them so much. " Don't think it's just *our* problem," Lois said. " It's everywhere." Seeing Alabama by bookmobile at her invitation, seeing the vast expanses yet to be reached, watching the old people and the young people coming faithfully for their books, rain or shine, was an experience I shall never forget. When the writing began to happen, it felt good. I liked its reality, its solid, useful feel, just as I had always liked making bread, hanging clothes on the line, putting fruit into jars against the winter. More than a story had been waiting for me in Alabama.

I knew I was writing for children. It was only long after *Curious Missie* was written and published that I happened to read again something Hans Christian Andersen said of his tales, and it occurred to me that the grownups might be listening.

The problem of being different in a world more and more determined on conformity had engaged my thoughts for a long time before I went to Pennsylvania, and I had written at least one novel about the common difficult task of reconciling old ways and new. In the West I had found my symbol in Indians and in three generations of Mormons; in Pennsylvania a teacher told me an incident about a little Plain Girl. So it happened again, the " impelling need." The machinery began running and the meaning was clear.

Then came the *Miracles*. I know the peril is, for me, that I try to put upon the shoulders of simple stories more weight than they will carry. Yet when Amy Kreitz spoke so passionately of her husband's danger, when the death of winter became the life of spring, it was all there again as certainly as falling in love. I know as well as anybody that there is nothing new or revolutionary in the little story to which you have been so sympathetic. I know in fact that it has the most ancient theme in the world, the recurrent pleasures, the rhythms of existence that we human beings are privileged to observe, if we will.

It could be that when at last it seems futile to criticise the endless ills that we are heir to, some of us turn to writing for children because the value of life becomes more and more apparent and we must turn to celebration. Do we not have every day, from light to dark to light again, in the rich variety of cold and heat, rain and snow and sun? Still nearer to life, do we not have the seasons, those large rhythmic patterns of dark and light that are gradual enough to be observed with savor and awaited with eagerness? Can there be too much celebration of these simple and profound things?

Before saying goodby, there is one more little Edinboro story I should like to tell because it seems to me it is really about you. The Erie County Bookmobile comes to Edinboro every other Tuesday at three o'clock and parks in front of the post office. I like to leave my desk for a visit with Marian Kelly, the red-headed book-lady on page 127 of *Miracles*, and with the children who come in and out. This day there was still a little snow (it could have been early May!) and a very pretty girl in a blue jacket got on the truck. Marian and I enjoyed her while she made her selections. She was about fifteen, with just that edgy touch of knowing her own value, but not quite sure. When she left, Marian watched her and said, " Isn't she beautiful? Do you know what I've seen happen, right here on this old truck? I've seen this — " and she indicated a homely, rumpled little after-school girl kneeling on the floor by the lowest shelf, " — turn into *this!* " and she nodded toward the girl disappearing down the street, touching at the same time the adult reserve shelf at her side. It happened that *A Certain Smile* was there, beside it *Gift from the Sea, War and Peace,* and — very movingly to me — a copy of one of my own books.

We laughed together. I suppose it was laughter, although it seemed much else besides.

I need very deeply, as a writer and a person and a citizen, to feel all of you there, all over the country, watching *this* happen from *this*. The wonderful, unprecedented flooding of life! And all new. Every hour, as our wise man of Tel Aviv has also said, the human race begins. How blessed we are in our responsibility for that immense potential streaming upward — the children who will be men — each unique, as yet unsquandered, in the full grace of beginning again.

BIOGRAPHICAL NOTE

by *Anna Marie Smith*

My Friend, Virginia Sorensen

I FIRST met Virginia Sorensen at a faculty wives' tea at Indiana State Teacher's College in Terre Haute one fall afternoon, in the late thirties. Out of the level of matronly conventionality represented by faculty wives en masse, she emerged emphatically, partly, of course, because she was a newcomer, but more particularly because of a kind of radiance of youthful personality. Almost at sight she stirred, out of the recesses of my subconsciousness, recollections of Willa Cather's character Lucy Gayheart. Indeed, I was impelled by meeting Virginia to go back to look in the novel for her proto-type. The townspeople of Lucy Gayheart's town, says Miss Cather, " still see her as a slight figure always in motion; dancing or skating, or walking swiftly with intense direction, like a bird flying home." Or again, "It was her gaiety and grace they loved. Life seemed to lie very near the surface in her. She had that singular brightness of young beauty: flower gardens have it for the first few hours after sunrise."* So I felt it was with Virginia, practically upon first meeting.

We fell into conversation. Virginia told me of her Utah birth and upbringing; of two children at home, Beth, four, and Freddie, two; of an English professor husband, freshly " Ph. Deified " (in his words) at Stanford University. I remember her saying she was working on a novel, and of being interested but not particularly impressed; in the English field practically everybody works on a novel at some time. That was some twenty years ago. Now there are six adult novels and four children's books on my bookshelf with Virginia's name on each title page.

* From *Lucy Gayheart* by Willa Cather (Knopf).

Other recollections of the earliest days of our acquaintance are vivid. Among them is Virginia's pleasure at being granted the privilege of using as a workshop an abandoned classroom far up under the eaves of the College's Old Main. Sitting primly straight on a rickety chair before a ramshackle desk, she would beat staccato music on her typewriter against the background of cooing pigeons under the eaves and the tremendous quarter-hour booming of the clock in the tower a few yards away. Beside her typewriter lay a mounting pile of neatly typed white copy paper. The only thing suggesting a decoration in the room was a scrap of lined, yellow tablet paper tacked over the desk. This was a " letter " delivered on her plate one morning at breakfast. In a child's first huge printing it said, " Dear Mama, I like you and I love you. I wish you rite a good book. Beth."

I remember, too, the meeting of our " Reading Group " where Virginia broke the routine of round-robin reading of selections of literature " which you have particularly liked " by reading a chapter of manuscript from her own emerging novel, and of the consensus of the word-wise literature professors on the way home: " The girl's got something; we'll hear from her."

When, one summer session, a Writers' Workshop met at the College, Dr. Burgess Johnson came to headline the program. He was burdened with interviews and manuscripts from regular members of the conference, and when Virginia said she had written a novel he asked her whether she could " give the gist of it in one sentence." She told him it was the story of the Mormon town, Nauvoo, Illinois, " the story of a city and a lady." He suggested that she write a letter to Alfred Knopf, saying, " Tell him just what you told me and he'll ask to see it." He looked at the first couple of paragraphs and, that night, told his wife about it.

Interested in the Mormons and bound for a week's holiday at McCormick's Creek Park near by, Mrs. Johnson asked whether she might take the novel along, and in a few days she telephoned and invited Virginia to come down and bring the children. She loved the book and wanted to talk about it. " But you've got to change the ending," she said. " I can't bear having that cat burn with the house." A year later, when *A Little Lower Than the Angels* was published by Knopf, a short sentence toward the end saved Mrs. Johnson's Mormon cat.

Although Virginia is often called a " Mormon writer," she has found from living in many sections of the United States, including the Deep South, and from brief residences in Mexico and Denmark on her two Guggenheim Fellowships, that regionalism, though interesting, is not of the highest significance. People, she contends, share the same sympathies and the same values, no matter where they happen to live. She tells of a college-boy poem written by her son containing the proud line, " My childhood is spread all over." The quality of universality in her projection of human nature was recently reimpressed upon me by the comment of a young Englishman from Rhodesia. After reading *Many Heavens*, Virginia's novel set in the Utah valley that I am now pleased to call home, he told me that the people and the culture described in the book bear a remarkable resemblance to the people and culture of his own home in Rhodesia.

Virginia has been equally successful in writing for all ages, the very young, teen-agers, and adults. I have found that *Curious Missie*, a story of a little Southern girl who is an inveterate asker of questions, is a favorite of third and fourth graders here in the West. *Curious Missie*, incidentally, is highly gratifying to the prejudices of librarians, since it is a telling demonstration of the influence of books, especially upon the impressionable minds of children.

The House Next Door appeals to teen-agers through its account of the conflict between " gentiles " and Mormons when Utah was struggling toward statehood. Gerry, an immigrant into Zion from the state of Virginia, with the unclouded vision of childhood, comes to recognize what her elders don't always perceive: that basically there is no difference between Mormon youngsters and those she had known in Virginia. Yet the book attests its author's real love for the distinctive qualities of her native West. "I had never particularly thought about how the red and white and blue come from sky-colors," says Gerry as she experiences her first Western nightfall. "In the West you think of such things, somehow, maybe because colors and rocks and sky and land are more important here. You notice more."*

The little girl heroine of *Plain Girl*, notably different in Amish dress and customs from her schoolmates, wins the sympathy particularly of those children in Utah who are conscious of their minority status in relationship to the predominant church group. Virginia's note to me announcing completion of the book says, " Whether it's for children I'm not sure, but it's true." The book won a Child Study Association award, with a citation which reads: " The tender and sympathetic story of a young Amish girl who, in reaching out for the different ways of her schoolmates, still holds dear her love and respect for her family and the traditions of her people." The narrative achieves a considerable measure of interest for adult readers through its sensitive treatment of the inevitable lack of understanding and the conflict in interests between generations.

The warm family relationship of *Miracles on Maple Hill* bears a strong autobiographical imprint to one who, like myself, has had the pleasure of observing Virginia in her role as mother. Delight in even the smallest manifestations of nature, such as the appearance of the first spring flowers, has always been shared by all the Sorensens. Going cycling or hiking with the family is a lesson in responsiveness to the simple and the significant, whether in Indiana's state parks, along the high line ditch outside Denver, up the steep ascent of Utah's Mt. Timpanogos, or through the maple groves around Edinboro, Pennsylvania, which most directly inspired the *Miracles*. On such Sorensen family nature jaunts the most childishly (in the Wordsworthian and best sense of the word) delighted member of the group is probably the father and professor.

The Sorensen children, from infancy, have been imaginative and creative; I recall my own particular pleasure in introducing them to books like *Mary Poppins* and *I Know a Secret*. Freddie, when taking his first piano lesson at the age of six, was told by his teacher that one must cup his hands over the keys as if he were holding a gold button or a butterfly; and it seemed as if the child in his

* From *The House Next Door* by Virginia Sorensen (Scribner).

complete abandonment to imagination was actually seeing butterflies and gold buttons. Virginia's responsiveness to this imaginative capacity of her own children early convinced me that she
could and must turn at least a portion of her writing talent to the
child reader audience.

The strong poetic quality in *Miracles of Maple Hill* — indeed
in all of Virginia's books — reflects a bent which she apparently
has had since her earliest childhood. Her mother tells me that
Virginia, as a very young child, always had pockets filled with
her own verse creations which she loved to share by reading them,
particularly at meal times, to a not always appreciative audience
of brothers and sisters. She has continued to write poems for and
about her own children. The following were enclosures with a
Christmas letter that came when the children were six and eight.

BETH AT CHRISTMAS

The baubles on our Christmas tree
Were colored mirrors filled with me,
As scarey-thin as shells of eggs.
Our kitten stood on her hind legs
And pushed a blue one. Then she caught
Her claws among the boughs. And what
Became of all that shining blue?
I told the kitten all I knew:
Like bubbles, see? or like a thought
I had this morning, and forgot.

FREDDIE AT CHRISTMAS

If you stretch your head inside
And kind of squint your eyes
You can see things twice as wide
Or high or any size.

Lots of days this year I've seen
A string turn into rope;
A bent match on my submarine
Is a periscope.

Now that the children are grown, they reflect the time Virginia and her husband spent with them in their childhood. Last Christmas when Fred (Freddie no longer) was getting his train ready to give to a child, his mother asked him if it made him sad to be repairing his train for another child after all his joy in it. He looked at her in surprise and said, " No, of course not. I had a good childhood: it's fun to remember, not sad at all." Reflected here is Virginia's own soundness — as she expresses it, " the ability to meet changes in life without regret for lost things because of their own goodness."

Of course, she always took great delight in reading as well as writing. A family anecdote concerns the fact that as a child she read with such concentration that she wouldn't hear anything that went on around her. This so concerned her father that he took her to the doctor for a hearing test and was mightily relieved to learn that her hearing was perfect.

This ability to concentrate has proved a most valuable asset to Virginia in her dual role as writer and housewife. Much of her writing has been done on the dining-room table with the family dog underneath and once, when I visited her in Denver, with a family of kittens on the table. It is characteristic of her to have felt sorry for Pal, when a lovely maple drop-leaf table was substituted for the old one and the dog could no longer lie at her feet with any comfort. When she first began to write in the quiet at MacDowell Colony, Virginia says, she had a hard time doing so in the isolated studio and had to return to Colony Hall and do a bit of washing before her thoughts got going.

In talking of an experience which she and I had in common during the lean years of helping our husbands earn their Ph.D.'s, Virginia said, " When I look back upon Stanford days I wonder why we were so anxious to be ' through.' There is no being through really, and nothing in the world is so wonderful as having something before you, looming like heaven, and struggling to it. If only one could run after a star always, sensing some distance behind." Virginia has now caught up with one star, the Newbery Award, but she will certainly go on writing. After publication of her third book, she said:

"I think I know something about writing novels now. I do it like breathing, it is a part of each day and each night for me like the other functions of my living. Because I would cease to be alive if I stopped doing it, as well as if I stopped breathing or eating, I do it over and over. I do not expect any fanfare because I go on living other ways — so why for this?"

The Newbery Award is certainly a fanfare, and is most gratifying to us who have known and loved her and followed her work through the years.

Rifles for Watie

written by HAROLD KEITH

published by THOMAS Y. CROWELL 1957

BOOK NOTE

AT sixteen, Jeff Bussey of Kansas joins the Union Army. He meets all kinds of men and boys, fighting for many different reasons. Details of his training, the long marches, the fearful battles, and his relationship with people are vivid. Assigned to scout duty, he is forced to join the Confederate Army and becomes a friend of several Confederate families. This vital story with convincing characters shows the ironies and miseries of war as unglamorized reality, and provides excellent reading for adults as well as young people. It also brings out the little known conflicts and history of the Cherokee Indian Nation and its interesting part on both sides in the Civil War.

EXCERPT FROM THE BOOK

As Jeff, John, and David turned the corner of a barracks building, they heard a thunder of hoofbeats and were almost run down by a squadron of cavalry. Spurs jingling, sabers rattling, and the oaken butts of their carbines resting against their thighs, they thundered past grandly with a drumming of horses' hoofs and a creak of leather. It was quite a sight for a boy fresh from the plow handles. Jeff could smell the horses' sweat and see the metal ring bits on their bridles flashing in the bright Kansas sunshine. He wished he were joining the cavalry instead of the infántry. But the bushwhackers had stolen his horse.

At the hospital the three boys were asked to strip to the waist while a gruff old army doctor with a fat paunch and tired eyes examined them. Jeff lined up with the scores of other men and boys awaiting their turns.

" Come on, kid," the old doctor said, finally beckoning to Jeff, " you shall have all the war you want."

" Yes, sir! " said Jeff. His father had carefully coached him never to forget that " sir " as long as he was in the army.

" Humph! " grunted the old doctor as he worked. " Lots of fellers nowdays can't wait to put on some blue clothes and go out and shoot at perfect strangers." Noisily he spat a stream of brown tobacco juice all over a brass spittoon on the floor behind him and looked suddenly at Jeff. " Are you one of 'em? "

" Yes, sir," said Jeff, promptly. "I want to shoot at them before they shoot at me."

The doctor tapped Jeff's chest roughly with his dirty, horny knuckles and grunted again. " Humph! That's a pretty good chest."

Jeff beamed modestly.

" Jest right for the rebels to shoot Minie balls through," the old doctor added. Jeff stared at him, feeling strangely depressed.

Later, when they put their blouses back on, Jeff told John and David, " Far as I'm concerned, he could have left out that last remark."

They were surprised still more when they reported to the enlistment officer and one of the first questions he asked was, " Where do you want your pay sent if you are captured? "

Pondering the question, Jeff felt better. He had been afraid the rebels would surrender and the war end before he could get into the fighting. And here was this fellow, suggesting he might be captured. Maybe he was going to see some action after all.

As they stood in line before the quartermaster, Jeff strained his neck trying to get a look at the new Federal uniforms he was sure would be issued to them, like the handsome blue outfit he had seen on the sentry at the fort's gate. But all they got was one light blue blouse, one pair of cotton socks, and one pair of drawers each.

The new recruits fell to talking about why they had enlisted.

" I came all the way from Seward County, down near Injun Territory," said one. " My family's Union. Mammy didn't want me to go to no war. But we knowed the bushwhackers was hid out in the brush, stealin' money and hosses and chokin' boys my age when they found 'em. I didn't wanta git choked. So I runned away. I wanted to run away sooner."

" I jined up fer a frolic," laughed a tall fellow from Republic County with warts on his face. He turned to his messmate, a blond boy from Fort Scott. " Why did you come in? "

" Wal, by Jack, because I thought the rebels was gonna take over the whole country."

" I joined up because they told me the rebels was cuttin' out Union folks' tongues and killin' their babies. After I got here, I found out all it was over was wantin' to free the niggers," complained another, disgustedly.

" I decided I'd jest as well be in the army as out in the bresh. Now I'm about to decide I'd druther be in the bresh," snorted another. They were nearly all frowsy-headed, boot-shod, and lonely-looking, fresh from the new state's farms, ranches, and raw young prairie towns. Before the war ended, Kansas furnished more men and boys to the Union forces in proportion to its population than any other state. And all of them were volunteers.

NEWBERY AWARD ACCEPTANCE

by *Harold Keith*

WHEN I was a boy in northwestern Oklahoma, our family visited Uncle Bob King in the little town of Quinlan. Having nothing much to do, I ransacked the house early one afternoon for something to read. In those days I read only boys' books, titles like *The Motor Boys, Dick Prescott,* the *Boy Scouts* series, and Horatio Alger that I checked out from the city library in the basement of the courthouse at my home town of Watonga. I devoured these like an Arkansas boy eating watermelon, whizzing through one in a day and a half as I sat on my backbone in the living room.

I found nothing like that in my Aunt Belle's bookcase at Quinlan but I came upon a tallish volume bound in red cloth that was written by someone named Doyle. It was an English book and so obviously for adults that I hesitated to open it. Not turning up anything else of interest, I did open it eventually. Quickly, I discovered *The Hound of the Baskervilles* the most exciting thing I had ever read. Doyle wrote so skillfully that he could make you feel the dreary bleakness of the Devonshire country, the hint of the supernatural in the mysterious deaths of the baronets of Baskerville, and the emotion of pure terror in the weird, nocturnal howling of the gigantic hound as it called for its prey from the depths of the melancholy moor.

As I sat alone reading into the night, I kept hearing noises in the darkness outside the open windows. I looked behind me, and felt goose pimples of fear rise on my arms. My heart thumped like a triphammer. The story had me by the throat and I couldn't put it down until I finished.

I never forgot the experience and as I grew older, I thought how fine it would be if some day I could write a book for boys and girls that would have all the elements of an adult novel with nothing diluted or left out.

Twenty years passed. In August, 1935, Will Rogers, the beloved Oklahoma humorist and philanthropist, was killed in an airplane wreck near Point Barrow, Alaska. A New York publishing firm, The Thomas Y. Crowell Company, decided to bring out a boys' life of Rogers and began looking for an author, preferably an Oklahoman. Robert L. Crowell, then the vice-president, appealed to his friend, Franklin M. Reck, managing editor of *American Boy*. Reck was desperate. The only Oklahoman he knew was one of his own authors who wrote sports fiction that always had to be heavily edited and revised.

My first inclination was to decline the opportunity. Researching and writing a three-hundred-page book seemed an enormous task. Besides, I thought I was doing reasonably well making ninety dollars every time I could persuade Mr. Reck to buy one of my short stories. But Joseph Brandt, director of the University of Oklahoma Press, talked me into accepting the assignment. At his suggestion, I began traveling in eastern Oklahoma, where Rogers was born, calling upon the cowpunchers and show people and schoolmates with whom he had been associated and writing down their stories. I finished *Boys' Life of Will Rogers* on schedule although I wrote it so poorly that portions of it had to be rewritten by an editor.

But the research had been enchanting. The person I most enjoyed doing research about wasn't kindly, generous, wise-cracking Will but his father Clem, a wealthy part-Cherokee soldier and politician who lived a far more exciting life than his son. During the Civil War in the Cherokee country, Clem Rogers rose to a captaincy in the rebel Cherokee force commanded by General Stand Watie. After the war, he became a politician who was active in nearly all the Cherokee Indian Nation's affairs, from the tribe's reconstruction era through the hectic period of its final dissolution and absorption by the United States government. Clem Rogers was all kinds of a man. Often he was gruff, hot-headed and sharp-spoken, lacking patience and diplomacy. On the other hand, he was shrewd, patriotic, industrious, and extremely kind to his family and friends. He loved to handle horses. He always drove at a brisk gait and when he sped past in a buggy his neighbors would say, " There goes Clem Rogers. Somebody's going to get elected and somebody's going to get beat."

So it was natural that when I wrote my master's thesis in history three years later, I chose the subject of " Clem Rogers and His Influence on Oklahoma History." Again I headed the family Ford towards eastern Oklahoma in quest of information and again I was distracted by research in another field.

Most of my personal sources this time were older people. Two of them were Clu Gulager of Muskogee and Johnny Adair of near Tahlequah who as children had refugeed south during the Civil War with Will Rogers' mother, Mary, and the women of her family, a covered wagon trip of pathos and tragedy that I partly reproduced in a chapter of *Rifles for Watie* titled " The Jack-mans." Many of the other older people I talked to about Clem had lived in Oklahoma during the Civil War.

" Sure, I'll tell you what I remember about Clem Rogers in the Civil War. But first let me tell you about my own daddy's part in it . . ." they'd say. Charmed by their accounts of the war in the Indian nations, I determined some day to do a novel about it, a full-bodied novel for teen-agers like the one I had visualized as a boy.

I finished my history thesis on Clem Rogers, rewriting it twice before I seined out most of the colloquialisms the faculty advisor objected to. I typed it, submitted it, and forgot it. But I couldn't forget all the fresh, intriguing things people had told me about the Civil War in Oklahoma where the Ross and Watie factions of the slave-owning Cherokees fought with a ferocity that exceeded that of the Southeastern theater where Grant and Lee played their famous roles. Bewitched by the subject, I decided to gather the research while participants of the war were still living. The author of a historical novel is like a college football coach. Just as a coach needs lots of good high school players from which to build a strong college team, a writer needs a world of good, fresh background material from which to organize and write his novel. I've always enjoyed interviewing people who are well informed.

I secured from the state capitol a list of all the Confederate veterans still living in Oklahoma and spent the summers of 1940 and 1941 traveling about the state and western Arkansas calling on them and writing down their stories. Although I was sports publicity director at the University of Oklahoma, the school's football team in those days had made only a small ripple on the national pond and I had more time. I found twenty-two of these old soldiers and filled three notebooks with their reminiscences.

Although most of them were nearly one hundred years old, I was surprised how vigorous some were. I remember particularly John W. Harvey of Okmulgee. He was the healthiest oldster I ever saw. Although he was then ninety-six years old, he had all his own teeth, could read without glasses, could hear well, and eleven years earlier, at the age of eighty-five, had survived an automobile wreck during which he was hit and dragged half a block. He was the one who told me how a small pot of rice he was boiling after the Battle of Pea Ridge increased itself so alarmingly that it flowed over the sides of the pot into the fire and I changed this slightly and used it in *Rifles for Watie*.

I remember James R. Arnn of Rush Springs, a wizened little cavalryman with " Pap " Price's Missouri rebel outfit, chuckling as he told about Price's raid of 1864 into Kansas and Missouri. " We chased them the first four hundred miles, then we got in front and they chased us," he described it. I spent so much summer time at the Confederate Home in Ardmore that whenever one of our athletic teams passed the home by railroad or bus on their way to a sports event in Texas, the athletes would all take off their big hats and solemnly hold them over their hearts out of deference to my interest in the Civil War.

In 1947 Bud Wilkinson became Oklahoma's football coach. He believed in taking the sports publicity man along on the plane with the team. This was a fine break for my project. During our road games against Big Seven conference schools, we stayed the night before the game at the state capitals of Kansas, Nebraska, Colorado and Missouri. I always managed to find a little time to haunt the state historical collections in each, reading the diaries and journals, many of them pencil written, of Union veterans from those states. Thus football helped greatly in the research.

Oklahoma football teams speedily became a national power and I had no more time for research and very little for writing. But I wasn't ready to start writing the book anyway. I knew I didn't write well and I wanted to do what I could about it. The University of Oklahoma has one of the finest professional writing schools in the country. For two decades I had lived within three blocks of it and had totally ignored it. The university is also host each June at a three-day writers' conference held on the campus in the Union building, just one block from where I worked. I had always left it to its ways and means, too.

One morning Kenneth Kaufman, the university's beloved modern languages professor and himself a writer, stopped me in front of the Administration building.

"Why don't you ever go to the writers' conference and learn something about writing?" he challenged. "It's a wonderful opportunity and you're not doing anything about it." Although he was usually the kindest person on the campus, he looked at me so crossly that I decided it was barely possible the writing school might be able to teach me a little something that I didn't already know. I enrolled that summer.

After the first five minutes of the first day, I realized I didn't know anything about professional writing. I had flat wasted twenty years. Like a pianist who plays by ear, I had acquired by instinct a few skills, but only a few.

I went to the writing school three different summers and took one second semester course, specializing in the short story. I wanted very much to take the novel course but it was offered only during the football season. I decided to multiply the short story formula by twenty-five and go to work. I'll probably never get to take the novel course.

I began writing *Rifles*, working mostly at night and on Sundays. Remembering my own terrific emotional experience while reading Doyle's story of the fiend-hound, I still believed teenagers would like and could assimilate a major novel written along adult specifications. I decided to use every device the writing school taught.

I learned that conflict and emotion are the backbone of any

story and the more conflict you can involve your hero in the better, particularly conflict that makes him fight with somebody near and dear to him. So Jeff Bussey, the hero of *Rifles*, fights not only with the Confederates and with his own Union commander, Captain Clardy, but also with Lucy Washbourne, his girl. I learned that conflict is best displayed in a unit of the story called the scene and the best way to put the story down on paper is by a succession of dramatic scenes. As people are the most interesting thing in the world, it naturally follows that the most important element in fiction is characterization. So when it came time to sort and classify the great mass of material I had collected from my reading and my interviews with the old soldiers, I kept only that out of which I figured I might build believable characters and dramatic scenes. I tried to follow the writing school's advice and reject any scene that didn't have an emotional impact.

Readers probably don't know it, but the reason they read a story is to be moved emotionally. Even though they have to turn to fiction to experience vicariously such emotions as love, hate, sorrow, hope, anger, fear and revenge, it makes them feel alive. So I tried to use only emotional scenes, and while some of them may appear pretty rugged for teen-agers, they have emotions that need to be satisfied, just like adults.

If you don't believe this, think back upon the many times you've seen children openly seek emotional expression by playing various games of make-believe — little girls hobbling along in their mothers' high heels and wearing big sister's dress so awkwardly that it almost trips them; little boys clad in chaps and Western hats, clutching toy pistols as they dash about the premises taking imaginary shots at each other. Later, they also learn to release their emotions by reading books and if we don't give them the kind they enjoy, the kind that entertains them and makes them feel something strongly, they are often ingenious enough to find this type of reading themselves. Children are sharper than we realize. I remember seeing several years ago on Norman's main street a little girl leading her small brother by the hand to the movie theater. The boy had to be guided because he was walking along in the bright sunlight with his eyes shut tightly. I asked the girl, " Why are his eyes shut like that? " She said, " So that when we get inside the show, he can open his eyes and find us a seat." We can learn from children.

I found the writing school's pattern dependable. For example, it stresses that your hero will be more real if he has some warmly human weakness that leads him from the path of safety. Jeff Bussey's was his habit of speaking up too boldly to the officers, taking issue with them. It teaches that the hero, and also most of the major characters, must undergo some pronounced change, either growth or deterioration, during the telling of the story. I tried to change Jeff from a carefree country boy who saw only the Union side and was anxious to get into battle, into a mature young man who was capable of understanding the enemy even if he didn't agree with what they were fighting for.

Contrast is another useful device. In *Rifles,* one contrast is between Jeff, the hero, and Lucy, the heroine. They are wide apart as the poles in politics, environment, race, and worldly possessions. We are also taught that in a novel there should be several small complications mounting to a major one in the middle. In *Rifles* the major complication comes when Jeff, a Union scout, is captured by the rebels behind their lines and is forced to join them to save his own life. Thus he begins to see the war from the enemy's viewpoint and it changes and broadens him.

Some of you may have noticed that nearly every chapter of *Rifles* happens in a different locale, introduces different characters, and presents a different phase of the war. This was done to keep the book's background fresh and ever changing.

In most good stories there must be an agonizing decision and a sacrifice by the hero. He must choose between two courses of action, his own personal desires, or the requirements of others about him. Boy heroes have to make poignant decisions, just as anyone else does. Many of you will remember Huckleberry Finn's decision. It almost drives him crazy. He is on the raft with Jim, the Negro runaway slave. Shall he turn Jim in to the authorities, as the village code and Sunday school code demand? Or shall he risk eternal damnation by treating Jim as the kindly human being he is, helping him gain his freedom? Jody Baxter in *The Yearling* is tortured between two courses of action, whether or not to kill with his own hands his beloved pet deer to keep it from eating the growing corn his family needs for winter food. Jeff Bussey's decision is whether to join his newfound comrades and jump to the rebel side in the Civil War, as his sweetheart wishes him to, or do the thing he isn't very keen about doing, obey his conscience and stay with his state and his nation to expose the source that is secretly selling repeating rifles to the rebel leader, Stand Watie.

Most important of all is characterization. There are only a few plots and only a few settings but there are millions of human beings, no two precisely alike. Thus we learned that character in fiction is interesting because it is so endlessly surprising. In my research, I never was lucky enough to find a character in complete form. There's a reason for that, too. Fictional characters are far more appealing because a writer permits the reader to enter into their hearts and minds, whereas the thoughts and motives of living people are concealed. One trick is to blend vivid traits of several people to get the one character you want. I would take two parts of some Civil War character of ninety-five years ago and mix with an individual trait of some athlete, cowpuncher, or newspaperman I know today, seasoning strongly with imagination. The plot was much easier to construct. Characters and scenes are far more important and harder to come by, too.

There are no new plots in fiction. The plot of *Rifles for Watie* is based on a very common gun gimmick. Each of you can think of several plots involving guns. There was even a popular movie awhile back built upon the theme of a heavy cannon transported an incredible distance overland by human hands. A Newbery Award book of several years ago was called *The Matchlock Gun*. It's almost impossible to find novelty in a plot. Shakespeare never invented new plots. He preferred to devise new scenes and new characters to act out some old story. Reb Russell, the former Nebraska football player who later became a cowboy actor in Western movies, once put this very well. Russell came through Norman several years ago and stopped at our stadium to say hello.

Somebody asked him why the plot in Western movies never changed.

" Shucks!" Russell replied. "All we ever change are the horses." And he's essentially correct.

Most plots have a certain formula. It consists mainly of keeping the hero in constant trouble with a series of complications that hit him one at a time. As fast as he extricates himself from one complication, another floors him. The crisis is the final knockdown punch. Just as the hero thinks he's doing fine, the author belts him over the head with the crisis. Just as Jeff Bussey thinks he's going to reach the fort, he hears behind him the baying of the Texas bloodhound. He's finished and he knows it. The reader knows it, too.

The only fellow who doesn't despair is the author. I'd known for years what I was going to have Jeff do when the hound finally ran him down. Our writing school emphasizes that you should choose a crisis to which you also see a hidden solution. That's one of the first things you should look for in any story, or even before you write a single sentence of a story. Several years ago, I had clipped and saved a true newspaper account of an Arkansas bloodhound that had been put on the scent of some boys who had escaped from a reformatory. Unknown to most people, bloodhounds are notoriously gentle creatures. When this hound found the boys, it forgot duty and joined them for a romp in the woods. That newspaper clipping came in handy. I've always been glad I saved it.

But enough of writing mechanics. It's time to make some very important acknowledgments and then get off the stage. First I want to go on record and assure you that I'm not posing as an expert in the field of professional writing techniques. I've just begun to plow. I need polish and know it. I've been so delighted with how much a good writing school can help those of us who need a lot of help that I wanted to share it with you here tonight. If each of you will look back on your own past reading and apply these patterns to any novel you've liked, I think you'll find they pretty well fit your favorite story, too.

In conclusion, I want to thank the American Library Association, and the Children's Library Division for asking Mrs. Keith and me to this wonderfully friendly affair. We're indebted, also, to Mr. and Mrs. Melcher for being such gracious hosts at the announcement party last March in New York. It was while we were in New York that we got to see Robert McCloskey's paintings in *A Time of Wonder*. They're very beautiful and we congratulate him. I've already tried to thank individually all the members of the Newbery Committee and their chairman, Elizabeth Nesbitt.

I cannot adequately express my gratitude to Elizabeth Riley of the Thomas Y. Crowell Company for her enthusiastic mothering of this book from the time she first saw it in manuscript. She and Susan Bartlett helped get *Rifles* ready to shoot. I especially appreciate their suggestions for trimming the manuscript. The whole Crowell team, I've discovered, is a very fine one. Peter Burchard's jacket is not only striking, the boy soldier on it looks exactly as I imagine Jeff Bussey looked.

The Civil War continues to be a prolific background for historical novels. In closing, I should like to tell you something that illustrates how reluctant we writers are ever to let the Civil War die. Down in Mississippi about thirty years ago there lived a fiery old veteran who had fought on the side of the South in the war. I guess he was what you would call an unreconstructed rebel. Although it was then 1928 and he was nearly ninety years old, he had never surrendered. This old gentleman worshipped his great-grandson, a handsome Mississippi boy. They were very close. One day this lad received an appointment to West Point. Knowing how sensitive the old gentleman was about the Civil War, the family hesitated to tell him that his beloved great-grandson was going north to school at the Yankee military academy. Finally they did tell him. The old fellow took it pretty well. However, he soon maneuvered the boy off into a corner where they wouldn't be overheard and told him, " Go on up there, Sonny, if yuh have to. Learn about war and tactics, son. Learn about transpote. Learn about weepons. Find out all yuh can. This thing ain't over with yet."

BIOGRAPHICAL NOTE

by *Fayette Copeland*

Harold Keith

MOST nights, after his family is tucked in bed and his neighbors have settled down to a late TV program, if you could look in on Harold Keith you'd likely find him hard at work.

His full-time job as sports publicity director at the University of Oklahoma requires seven days and three nights through most of the year. Despite this, he has managed to write six books in addition to fiction and articles in *American Boy, Esquire* and *Saturday Evening Post.* He follows the frontier philosophy: "The most important things you accomplish are done on time which you don't have."

Friends who have known Keith since his undergraduate days can't remember when he wasn't doing extra things in the extra hours he managed to find when the days had ended for others. It took stamina to meet the day-and-night demands on his energies — stamina and a dedication to the job on hand, and then a lot of added courage and enthusiasm for his own creative work at the end of days that seemed never to end.

This stamina may be explained, for Keith was one of Oklahoma's famous athletes. As a long-distance runner, he won the Missouri Valley Conference indoor mile and two-mile events in 1928, and the mile at the Kansas City Athletic Club indoor meet. He ran the anchor mile on the Oklahoma distance medley relay team that won championships in 1928 at the Texas, Rice and Kansas Relays carnivals. That year his team was chosen as the All-America collegiate medley team.

One story showing his resourcefulness and determination is told over and over. The Athletic Council sent his medley relay team to the Penn Relays at Philadelphia. The day of the meet the rain came down in sheets and the program ran thirty minutes behind schedule. The Sooners, sent to shelter beneath the stadium, were not called until the event was almost over.

Just coming up was the first 3,000 meter steeplechase ever held at the Penn Relays. Although the Sooners were not entered, Keith persuaded the meet director to let the team participate. He had never seen a steeplechase course before but he won the race over a muddy course, his greatest track triumph of 1928.

In December, 1945, at the age of forty-two, he entered the Oklahoma AAU 3¼-mile cross-country race at Norman. His friends presented him with a jersey that had lettered " Confederate Home, Ardmore, Okla.," on the front and a Confederate flag sewn on the back. He wore it gleefully, and won his first competitive race in thirteen years.

Neighbors are not surprised, any day, to see him in track suit, jogging around the old golf course near his home, and none wonders that at fifty-five he is as lithe and lean as many of the young athletes he writes about.

Writing, like athletics, came early. In the days before athletic scholarships he earned his way through school with his typewriter. Born in the little town of Lambert in old Oklahoma Territory, he was a competent young newspaperman when he came to the OU campus after three years at Northwestern State Teacher's College at Alva. He had worked on daily and weekly Oklahoma papers at Watonga, Alva, Cherokee, and Enid. As a member of the Sooner track squad, it was logical that he was chosen as sports editor of the student newspaper.

Frank Dennis, head of the press and publications division of USIA, was editor of the *Oklahoma Daily* in those days. " Keith used to dig up reams of copy on records of old-time Sooner athletes and famous teams and spectacular records and individual performances," Dennis related during a recent visit to the campus. " It was interesting, and I liked it, and we ran yards and yards of it."

Like many another territorial youngster, Keith developed an early passion for history and it was logical that he chose a hero of early Oklahoma as the subject of his first book, *Boys' Life of Will Rogers*, in 1936. Friends wondered when he had time to write it, for he had been called back to the university from a newspaper job in Hutchinson, Kansas in 1930 to begin his round-the-clock chores as sports publicity director. And he had married Virginia Livingston of Hutchinson in 1931 and their son, Johnny, now was three years old. Keith was also working, a little at a time, toward a Master's degree in history which was conferred two years later. He managed, however, to comb the old Cherokee Nation for interviews with friends and relatives of Will Rogers and write a whale of a story for young readers.

While he was doing research for his thesis, he came across fresh material about the Civil War in the Indian Nations. He finished his thesis the summer after his daughter, Kathleen, was born. Then Keith turned his extra hours to compilation of his second book, *Sports and Games*, which in 1940 was a Junior Literary Guild choice.

His book, *Oklahoma Kickoff*, published in 1948, records the history of football at the University of Oklahoma from its beginnings in 1895 to 1920, when Oklahoma was admitted to the Missouri Valley Conference. The book stamped Keith as a historian of stature, for it was more than a record of football at his alma mater. It was crammed with interviews of old-timers, anecdotes and incidents which revealed clearly a way of life which had passed with the coming of statehood, and it has been hailed as a splendid contribution to the social history of Oklahoma. Not only that, but it brought enthusiastic comments from reviewers.

Other sports books followed, and all this time Keith was building a national reputation in his professional work. His predecessor often said, "I believe the greatest contribution I made to the University of Oklahoma was in persuading Harold to come back to the campus and take over the job of sports publicity director."

Through the long, lean years Keith wrote about the struggles and the unselfish efforts of youth on the athletic teams, of their great moments in defeat; with never a complaint or an unfair word about opponents who more often than not licked the daylights out of the Sooners. He wrote with an enthusiasm and a sincerity that newspapermen liked; he wrote of the winning person, rather than the winning athlete. He stressed the value of the continuing struggle of each team member to improve himself, a struggle which brought success in the classroom. He wrote programs, brochures, news letters, and home-town stories stressing the fact that more than ninety per cent of the football squad completed work toward degrees.

He has made academic prowess very, very important to the athletes by writing about it and praising those who do well. An excerpt from the sports brochure now in the hands of hundreds of high school seniors reads: " Starring in chemistry and mathematics, Oklahoma's freshman football squad made its finest scholastic showing of all time during the first semester of 1957-58. Fourteen Boomers enrolled in Chemistry 1, and twenty-two took various courses in mathematics. There wasn't a single flunk in either...."

Colleges and universities might well adopt as general promotional pieces the flood of releases that pour from Keith's office.

Thus Oklahoma's citizens woke up to the fact that the Sooner athletic program was good, regardless of the won and lost averages at the end of the season. Keith and his interpretation of Oklahoma athletics were known far beyond the state borders before the remarkable post-war decade sent the Sooners soaring into the national spotlight.

" It would be hard to break down a successful athletic program into its component parts," Bud Wilkinson explained, " but Harold Keith definitely has been a part of Oklahoma's successful program. He is dedicated to his work. He believes what he writes. I am continually amazed," he continued. " I never meet with groups of sports writers, from coast to coast, from North to South, without their asking immediately about Keith and complimenting him. I know of no other man in his profession so widely known and admired."

" My admiration for him is great," President G. L. Cross said. " I regard him as a close personal friend, and the best in his field.

I've never known a more loyal person. He has a splended ethical attitude."

With all his achievements, and the unbelievable amount of work he manages to do with the help of three student assistants and a jewel of a secretary, many of Keith's friends are impressed most of all by his unfailing good humor. He has the rare gift of laughing at himself and his troubles. His hobby is barber shop singing and he has served as president of the Norman Chapter of SPEBSQSA (national barber shop singing organization).

Years of widening recognition stretched out before him, such as 1951 when he received the Helms Foundation Award as the outstanding sports publicity director in the nation, based on a poll of 3,500 sports writers and sportscasters over the country. Or the previous year when the press box he designed for the stadium at OU was voted best in the nation by the Football Writers Association. Or the succeeding years when his chronicles of the dramatic decade of Oklahoma sports informed the world of the record-smashing achievements of Bud Wilkinson's teams.

Because of Keith's great love and admiration for the boy who is striving to improve himself and to help his team, it is significant that all of his creative work has been written for or about young people.

Dean Earl Sneed of the University of Oklahoma Law School who has served for seven years as chairman of the Athletic Council and faculty representative in the Big 8 Conference believes that a great measure of the success of the OU athletic program is due to Keith.

"Basically, it is a sound program," Dean said, "and so Harold has a good base upon which to pitch his endeavors. But even so, if he were not extremely dedicated to young people and the ideals young people should have, we would not have the public understanding and acceptance of our program. . . . He has shown the values of loyalty and service by pointing up the feats of self-sacrificing linesmen. He writes wonderful stories of youngsters who really have no business in winning in athletics, but who do so because of determination and desire. In sum — Harold observes and appreciates balance in young people.

" He truly likes young people. You can sense in a moment his real affection for those young men who represent Oklahoma. Despite all that is said elsewhere, these athletes are just boys, and Harold respects them as such and sympathizes and understands the problems of youth."

Dean Sneed asked the wife of his minister how her son, a freshman in the University, was getting along.

" Well," she replied, " he has a part-time job working for Harold Keith and that is a wonderful experience."

Keith's friends heartily agree.

THE NEWBERY AWARD 1959

The Witch of Blackbird Pond

written by ELIZABETH GEORGE SPEARE

published by HOUGHTON MIFFLIN 1958

BOOK NOTE

AT sixteen orphaned Kit Tyler from the Barbados arrives unannounced in Wethersfield, Connecticut. She finds life in 1687 in the household of a stern uncle, a timid work-worn aunt, and two girl cousins solemn and exhausting. Her refuge and cause of her ultimate crisis is the so-called witch, a Quaker woman. Strong characterization and excellent historical background add to a convincing plot which includes both realism and romance.

EXCERPT FROM THE BOOK

The sight of Mercy's tears was more than Kit could endure. If she looked at them for another instant she would fly into a thousand pieces. In a panic she fled, out the door and down the roadway, running, blind to reason or decorum, past the Meeting House, past the loiterers near the town pump, past the houses where her pupils lived. She scarcely knew where her feet were taking her, but something deep within her had chosen a destination. She did not stop until she reached the Great Meadow. There, without thinking, she left the pathway, plunged into a field, and fell face down in the grass, her whole body wrenched with sobs. The tall grass rustled over her head and hid her from sight, and the Meadows closed silently around her and took her in.

When Kit had sobbed herself out, she lay for a long time too exhausted to move or think. Perhaps she slept a little, but presently she opened her eyes and became aware of the smell of the warm earth and the rough grass against her face. She rolled over and stretched, blinking up at the blue sky. The tips of the long grasses swished gently in the breeze. The hot sun pressed down on her so that her body felt light and empty. Slowly, the meadow began to fulfill its promise.

All at once, with an instinctive quickening of her senses, Kit knew that she was not alone, that someone was very close. She started up. Only a few feet away a woman was sitting watching her, a very old woman with short-cropped white hair and faded, almost colorless eyes set deep in an incredibly wrinkled face. As Kit stared at her she spoke in a rusty murmuring voice.

"Thee did well, child, to come to the Meadow. There is always a cure here when the heart is troubled."

For a moment Kit was too dumbfounded to move.

"I know," the murmuring voice went on. "Many's the time I've found it here myself. That is why I live here."

Kit stiffened with a cold prickle against her spine. Those thin stooped shoulders, that tattered gray shawl — this was the queer woman from Blackbird Pond — Hannah Tupper, the witch! The girl stared, horror-struck, at the odd-shaped scar on the woman's forehead. Was it the devil's mark?

"Folks wonder why I want to live here so close to the swamp," the soft husky voice continued. "But I think thee knows why. I could see it in thy face a moment back. The Meadow has spoken to thee, too, hasn't it?"

The cold feeling began to pass away. In some unexplainable way this strange little creature seemed to belong here, so much a part of this quiet lonely place that her voice might have been the voice of the Meadow itself.

NEWBERY AWARD ACCEPTANCE

by *Elizabeth George Speare*

THEY say writing is a lonely profession, and so to some extent it must be. But I wonder how many men and women must have made the discovery that when they have set their feet on this solitary path, they have come unexpectedly, around a sudden turning, upon a world of rich new friendship. This discovery has been one of the deeply rewarding experiences of my life. Of the new friendships which this lonely profession has brought me I can mention only a few — first and foremost my wonderful editor, Mary Silva Cosgrave, and second, the many members of your Library Association. I have always been acquainted with librarians, of course. But in the past few years, in unexpected places, the little gate marked "For Employees Only" has sometimes swung open, and I have found that behind that gate there exists an exceptionally warm fellowship. Ever since the announcement of the Newbery Award in March you have made me feel that I have come around another turn in that road, and that the richest part of this award, which I am so very proud and happy to accept from you, is something which I cannot hold in my hand — the friendship you have offered me.

In another sense, too, the occupation of writing can never be lonely because the solitude is so richly peopled. All writers must feel, like Tennyson's Ulysses, that "life piled on life were all too little," and in a very real way the hours spent in creating a book are hours crowded with encounters. It has been noted that all our conscious impressions, even the vicarious adventures of reading or the unsubstantial but vivid excursions of our dreams — even of our daydreams — pass into our memory and become one with our experience. I am sure it must be true of all writers, that in the months in which they live closely with the people they have created, these fictitious lives become entangled with their own, and on looking back they find that the imagined experiences have merged with the actual past and that the past is infinitely richer because of them.

Where these imaginary people come from is one of the intriguing mysteries of this solitary profession, just as I presume the gift of a lovely melody can never be explained. One of the most common questions asked any writer is, " How do you begin your stories? Do they start with an idea, or an incident, or a character?" Looking back, I can answer that for me they begin with people.

The main characters in the first book which I wrote, *Calico Captive*, came to me full-grown from the pages of an actual narrative published in 1807. As I thought about Susanna Johnson and her husband and children and her younger sister Miriam, and as I followed their adventures, filling in from my own imaginings the events about which the narrative itself is silent, other people emerged from nowhere to join them, and in the end these people of my own creating were no less real than the characters I had adopted.

When I began to think about a second novel, I had every intention of following the same pattern. I turned this time to Connecticut, my adopted state, and I found its history both dramatic and inspiring. But after months of reading I had not found a single incident that seemed to spark a story or a plot of ground on which I could stake a claim. Then gradually I became aware that some people were waiting, not in the pages of history but in my own mind. There was a girl, lonely and insecure, a child who needed friendship, a gentle and wise old woman, and two young men, one shy and uncertain, the other self-confident and merry. Behind them, shadowy, indistinct, other people waited. Each of these people began to take on sharper outlines, individual dimensions, and they were already moving and talking and reaching out in relationship to each other, long before I had found a place for them to live or a time in which they could be born. Finally I was compelled to find a home for them.

I chose Wethersfield, the town in which my husband and I have lived for twenty years, because it is one of the oldest towns in New England, one of the first of the Connecticut settlements;

because it was once a bustling river port with all the romance and color of the old sailing ships; and because the girl I could now see quite clearly seemed in some way not yet known to me to be at home in the quiet and lovely Wethersfield meadows that still lie for undisturbed stretches along the Connecticut River. I chose the year 1687 arbitrarily because the story of the Connecticut Charter was irresistible, a perfect little vignette, revealing in miniature all of the powerful forces which, nearly one hundred years before the Revolution, were moving America irrevocably toward independence.

Once time and place had been established, the most delightful part of the work began. The usual term for this procedure is historical research, but I should hesitate to dignify by such a scholarly term the haphazard, indiscriminate, greedy forage in which I indulged. History, geography, town records, genealogies, novels set in the same period — I gulped all these down with, at first, little thought of anything but my own enjoyment. There were fascinating bypaths from which I had to drag myself back — Quakerism for one, and the early development of education in New England. The astonishing thing is that I do not remember anywhere in my long-distant schooling a fondness for history. It seems that only now that my imaginary people have lured me back into the past it has become absorbing, and it has taken me more than half a lifetime to discover for myself what Elizabeth Gray Vining said in her Newbery acceptance speech, that "History is people."

Gradually, as I steeped myself in the past, the terrain began to appear familiar and natural. It is a very exciting thing to use the magical magnifying glass that is called historical research — a glass with the added perspective of Time. I can move this glass over a map of the world and focus it on a chosen spot — Wethersfield, for example, in 1687 — and what was only a black dot on the map leaps into focus and becomes a town, with grassy lanes shaded by ancient elms, with square rough-timbered houses, a spacious green and a small, turreted church. As the glass moves closer I can see the new bell in the turret, and the bloody head of a wolf nailed to the church door. I can peer inside the houses and see the wooden and pewter dishes on the long board, and the Indian corn pudding on the dishes, and the rough flax waiting to be spun, even the words in the letters hidden in an old chest. Just beyond the town the shining ribbon of the Connecticut River is alive with sailing ships, and the glass moves closer to reveal the rigging on the ships and the cargo they carry. Most exciting of all, the people who move in and out of those houses and ships are exactly the same as the people I know there today — people who are kind and quarrelsome, ambitious and anxious, well-intentioned and blundering, fighting and loving each other, like the people in my own family and on my own street.

Within the framework of the magnifying glass these people begin to act out their story. Part of this is involuntary on the part of the author. I had always been skeptical of writers who claimed that a story wrote itself, but I understand now exactly what they meant. However, there are deliberate elements as well. Much as one hopes to conceal the machinery, no story can be constructed without it. One can only hope to camouflage the engines and to muffle their chugging.

Once the focus is established, the rim of the magnifying glass becomes a fixed frame, beyond which one cannot move. Now, to switch similes in midstream, constructing the historical story becomes much like putting together a Chinese puzzle, in which there are a number of brightly colored and oddly shaped fragments which may be fitted into an infinite number of designs, all within the one determined frame.

In the forming of this design there are certain rules. I did not discover these rules, but by trial and error proved their truth for myself. One of these rules, for example, is that, once the pattern is determined, some of the pieces, lovely and intriguing as they appear, must be discarded, and this can be just as difficult and heart-rending as having to leave one child at home from a picnic. Not only must every piece that is chosen be shaped to fit the final design, but to be most effective it must also be colored to blend with every other piece. No matter how tempting a fragment of history, a quaint local custom or a curious recipe, no matter how fascinating it is in itself, it must also have a chameleon quality. It must blend with the piece beside it. The fragment of history must take on a new color because it is seen through the eyes of a person and tinged with his emotion, or it must lend some of its own color to the character and be itself reflected in his thoughts and actions. Anyone who has ever constructed a Chinese puzzle knows how baffling and exasperating these stubborn fragments can be, but he also knows the feeling of triumphant glee when a cherished piece finally drops snugly and beautifully into a carefully prepared spot.

All this is like having my own personal Berkeley Square into which I can step every morning. For the duration of a novel I can lead two lives, the imaginary life becoming more and more engrossing and real, so that now, looking back upon those days, the life that I led in Wethersfield in 1687 is woven deeply into the fabric of my actual life, and is truly a part of my experience.

I do not want to let this occasion go by without speaking of my gratitude not as a writer but as a parent for the establishment of the Newbery Medal. It is a wonderful thing to know that such encouragment is being offered to literature for children, and it is especially reassuring in this year, when science and technology have been so much in the forefront of our thought, that recognition has been given to a book of fiction. While I share with other parents a feeling of urgency regarding our children's education, I also believe very strongly that one of the greatest gifts we can give them is the opportunity sometimes to escape from our urgency — an opportunity to be somebody altogether different from themselves, to live in another time and another place, to swing out on a vast arc of experience into a realm of pure adventure.

Children need textbooks for the heart as well as for the mind. The enduring values of life — courage, devotion, compassion, forgiveness — none of these can be absorbed entirely by the mind but must instead be received into the heart. These values are the raw material of fiction. When a story stirs us deeply, for a moment at least we realize these qualities in ourselves, we possess them in our hearts. In a very real way they become part of our experience and we can never altogether lose them. In our anxiety to prepare our children for a Space Age, we must make very sure that they do not miss those imaginary adventures which can so greatly illumine and enrich their lives.

BIOGRAPHICAL NOTE

by *Helen Reeder Cross*

Elizabeth George Speare

I REMEMBER the first time I saw her. It was from a cramped choir loft perched high above the minister, from which vantage point we looked down into the faces of the congregation. I had no idea who the lady in blue might be. But Elizabeth George Speare's serene and sensitive face was one that I, a stranger in this New England church, felt drawn to.

It was no surprise, when we met soon after, to find that her quietly glowing spirit matched that first impression sensed from the choir loft. Nor was it a surprise to discover that she was a hopeful writer. One doesn't need to scratch a former English teacher very deeply to find an incipient writer.

Soon we were meeting with a small group of women possessed by the same urge. Officially known as " The Quill Drivers," there is nothing else official or organizational about the group. No officers, no mission, no constitution; just a desire to talk the peculiar language of the working writer with others bitten by the same bug. Elizabeth Speare claims to have been inspired by the give-and-take of the group and it pleases us that the stimulus may have been reciprocal. Certainly she is our star performer. We are terribly proud of her Newbery Award. Individually we remember the deft criticism with which, as informal teacher of the craft, she has helped her fellow quill drivers.

Elizabeth Speare has stated that her writing is secondary in her scale of life values. First comes her home — the husband and two teen-aged children who fill her heart and most of her time. This is apparent to all who know the Speares. They have always done interesting things together, things that take time, such as ski trips in winter ever since Al and Mary were first able to balance on skis; hikes and picnics in summer; lazy vacation days in the Maine wilderness that surrounds Schoodic Lake; long hours spent fishing for the lake trout that might with luck sizzle in the frying pan, come supper time. And always stacks of books waiting to be read on rainy days.

Winters were spent doing her stint as Cub Scout den mother and as a teacher in the Sunday School, and included endless miles of chauffeuring, children's partying, and the careful typing of her twelve-year-old son's neighborhood newspaper for which he was reporter, editor, printer, and publisher.

Even now that Al is away at Cornell and Mary busy with her studies at Chaffee School for Girls, even now that Elizabeth George Speare has become a famous name, home still comes first, writing second. Despite the heavy correspondence and the requests to lecture, there is still time to stir up a party during school vacation or to make that lovely red dancing dress for a pretty seventeen-year-old daughter. There is still time to cook and serve a delicious company meal for friends, more than likely featuring Alden Sr.'s backyard raspberries or asparagus, the mushrooms grown in the cellar, or fresh clover honey from the hive he keeps in a suburban garden surprisingly pastoral in its beauty and its produce.

Her writing, far from becoming cramped by its secondary spot in her life, has been infinitely enriched by the activities and values of the Speare family, by her own equally happy childhood home in Melrose, Massachusetts, and by that most personal of homes — the realm of the imagination now shared so abundantly with her readers.

The influence of these homes often shows in the subject matter about which she chooses to write. Elizabeth Speare's first pieces to sell were what she called "Helpful Hannah" articles, based on child-rearing techniques. Many of these accented the value of family participation in hobbies. Later came articles of wider reader interest, still reflecting home. Her husband is an industrial engineer. It seemed a good idea to his creative wife to suggest a carry-over of the time-and-motion study from the factory to the home. Why not show the housewife how she might spare her strength and energy by a more careful expenditure of both? The idea resulted in an article for *Woman's Day*. It led also to work with the Program for Work Simplification for Handicapped Homemakers at the University of Connecticut, under the direction of Dr. Lillian M. Gilbreth.

More than in subject matter, Elizabeth Speare's homes (childhood and present) have been a rich source of inspiration. Her beautiful philosophy, shining through her countenance, her life, and her writing, undoubtedly has its roots in those homes. The invalid sister Mercy, whose undaunted and unselfish spirit illumines the lives of all the characters in *The Witch of Blackbird Pond*, was patterned after the author's own invalid aunt whom she loved though she never saw her. The first " Mercy " died before Elizabeth was born, but her gentle influence shone upon her niece second-hand through family reminiscence. The ripples of this memory, transformed and set again in motion through the artistry of a gifted pen, can now touch the lives of other impressionable young girls who read Mercy's story.

It is this magic, I am sure, which made one young woman now in her twenties say to me wistfully, " If only I might have read this book when I was fifteen!" It is this pervading spirit of undimmed faith in the essential goodness of things which gives *The Witch of Blackbird Pond* both its charm and its meaning.

There is a school of thought which calls the teen-age book an unnecessary genre. " By that age young people ought to be sinking their teeth in the tougher meat of adult books — the classics," such critics say. Elizabeth Speare has refuted the argument. Here is a book, meant for the young reader, which is far from delicate; it manages to grapple with evil while still sustaining faith in man's yearning for the stars. Under the shadow of the twentieth century's nameless fears, thank heaven for a book which encourages compassion. Set in the seventeenth century it may be, but the values of *The Witch* are timeless.

It isn't every day, of course, that a town finds itself harboring a celebrity. Wethersfield preens its feathers at the news. There has been a great rush to read the new book by Elizabeth George Speare. Not just the teen-age girls for whom it was intended, but the grocer, the baker, the candlestick-maker; housewives and town fathers — all are reading it. For two reasons: to be in the conversational swim and to find out more about early Wethersfield history, in which the townspeople have always been keenly interested. Few villages, even in New England, can boast of having been founded in 1634. Its citizens are fascinated by its old houses, older family names, steeped in tradition.

This climate of interest in that which is hallowed by age has been, of course, another influence upon Elizabeth Speare. This must have set her off on the trail of research which has resulted in an article for *American Heritage* about our sister town of Glastonbury and her two books with colonial background: *Calico Captive* and *The Witch*. Now her neighbors look to her work to find a few more of the elusive facts which surround the distant past of Connecticut's oldest town. To our astonishment and delight, we find ourselves swept into the current of a fascinating story that is of more than local interest.

Some ask Elizabeth Speare, "When are you going to write an adult book — a real book?" To which she is likely to reply that to her way of thinking this *is* a "real book," since teen-age girls deserve the best writing that she or any other author can produce. There is to her a special pleasure in writing for the young reader whose taste is still being formed, whose responses to beauty are fresh, whose dreams are high. All dedicated teachers of young people will understand this. So will other writers of children's books.

Written with a specific age group in mind it may have been but, as its Wethersfield readers have already proved, *The Witch of Blackbird Pond* is transcending its original intention. Time may decide to ignore age limits and label Elizabeth George Speare's new book an enduring part of America's artistic heritage.

THE NEWBERY AWARD **1960**

Onion John

written by JOSEPH KRUMGOLD

illustrated by SYMEON SHIMIN

published by THOMAS Y. CROWELL 1959

BOOK NOTE

ONION JOHN, with his weird language, clothing, habits, and housing, is the town character in Serenity. His only interpreter is Andy, who understands Onion John's philosophy of life more easily than that of his father, with its ambitious plans for him. Realistic human values in this story underlie an episodic but imaginative plot, built around Serenity's plan to house and cleanse Onion John and his efforts to escape conformity.

EXCERPT FROM THE BOOK

"The boy's right," said Ernie. "I think we've done enough for Onion John."

My father lifted up from leaning on the counter. He went up straight and his arms crossed. He held his elbows. The others around quieted too, looking at Ernie.

" Hasn't it become pretty obvious? " asked Ernie. " What we think is proper and what John thinks is proper, they're two different things. What are we trying to prove to him, that he's wrong? "

" Now, Ernie. We went all through this with you at the first Rotary meeting." My father waited until a couple of men nodded, " We're not going to rehash that discussion all over again. Not now."

"A lot's happened. We almost killed the man, doing him good. I think he's had it. I think we ought to forget the new house."

" That's what I think," I told my father.

" Not now, Andy. We'll go into this later." My father came out from behind the counter until I couldn't see his face anymore, the way he stood facing Mr. Miller. " This town took on an obligation, Ernie. To Onion John. And to ourselves. We've had a setback. All right. We didn't look for this to happen, but we're not going to let it stop us."

" We'd look foolish," said Mr. Ries, " backing out now."

" Onion John's our responsibility," said my father. "We decided to help him. And he needs our help more, right now, than he ever did before."

Most everybody agreed with my father. It came to sound like politics. Democracy came into it, which is what you hear about when there's going to be a vote or an election. Ernie said that no one's private rights ought to get invaded even if it's with kindness. And my father said that democracy didn't mean we ought to leave the next fellow go hang and not care how he got along. It went too fast for me to follow, and too loud. Judge Brandstetter said the question ought to be argued out in a regular way by the town council because Onion John had become a town matter by then. They all agreed, there ought to be a meeting. But it went on anyway, Ernie and my father and Ries and Brandstetter and Wolf and the crowd of them.

I left. Even though a good stiff argument with a lot of men lambasting each other can lead almost anywhere. And usually it's worthwhile staying around to watch what develops.

But this time I thought I might as well leave. My father said we'd go into it later, anyway. And now that I was going back to school, after all it was my lunch hour. And this time, besides all that, for the first time in my life I wasn't on my father's side. So there wasn't much use in sticking around.

NEWBERY AWARD ACCEPTANCE
by *Joseph Krumgold*

SURELY the most useful, the most proper way for me to accept this honor is to offer you the one report that, by your bounty, I'm uniquely qualified to make. This is the first time that you've put anyone up here who is able to bring back to you some idea of how it feels not only to accept the Newbery Medal, but to live with that distinction.

So I propose to give you a record of that extraordinary experience.

To begin with, prior to this meeting, the lucky author suffers a steady loss of virtue. The months that lead from February, when the award is a secret, until June, when it gets to be an excellent dinner, becomes for the writer a personal calendar of mortal sin.

To be sure, at the first news, there's a moment of humility — a sense of being unworthy of a reward so great as this. But that moment passes very quickly.

And pride takes its place, an overweening and continuous pride. Physically, I've found this state to be an inward pressure resembling an old-fashioned case of dyspepsia. The only way to live with it, to keep it down, is to develop an even greater vice — a smugness that covers one's swelling importance with a general air of contented superiority. And when this grand manner is challenged or, worse yet, when it's not even noticed, then the descent down the moral ladder continues, and an arrogance develops. Until I wonder how any wife or any publisher manages to live with an author during the spring that you invite him here.

It's not your fault, of course. It seems to be a fairly widespread piece of irony that good fortune, more often than not, impairs the personality, whereas disaster, any good catastrophe, calls out all the virtues. Find a decent fire or even the smallest war, and there will be self-denial, courage, and heroism in great plenty. Even martyrdom, if things only get bad enough, and sainthood.

It's ironic — is all I want to say. I'm not suggesting that you bring your authors to torture here instead of to a banquet table. The fact is that for any writer, trained to perform in solitude, this experience is rough enough — standing up to so large a room, filled with so many people. The first time I thought this was going to be the worst part, but I return to tell you that it isn't.

The worst part comes afterwards, after the sinful calendar of these springtime months is over and all the congratulations and good-byes are spoken here. It comes when the writer returns to that still and familiar room where there's a typewriter, the place where he works.

Usually there are two people present in this room. The work that's done here must interest a reader for the four or five hours it will take him to go through a book. And it must interest a writer for the four or five months, sometimes more, it will take him to write it. It's a delicate duet between these two, and frequently a very melodious one.

But when the writer returns with his Medal, he finds another presence there in the quiet. You people. The memory of this hall stays very much alive. Except that it turns into a kind of surgical operating theater, with all of you seated in narrowing circles that lead down to the spotlight under which the author sits staring at the typewriter. And to the two questions he must ask, a third is added. Not only — Is this amusing to read? Is this valid enough to work on? But a third question — all of a sudden — Is this literature?

The question can't be avoided. The one sure point of these proceedings is that the author has contributed to a literature, and though the heavens fall — as long as he's able to type, that's what he's committed to keep on doing.

Whatever literature might be — and I'm sure this assembly could spend the rest of the night defining it — it isn't achieved by finishing your last breakfast cup of coffee and going into your room to light a cigarette and rip some of the stuff off. You can't put in a day's work at it.

And if you try, you can't put in a day's work at much else. The normal dialogue between a writer and a reader is delicate enough to keep going. Once the question is asked whether all the talk has any cultural value, the whole thing stutters to a stop. The sentence gets pencilled, the paragraph shifted, and again and again — to meet this new abstract requirement of literature — the chapter gets revised. And replotted, and redrafted and rewritten. The problem can get desperate.

Until you begin to wonder about the Newbery Medal, and the worth of it, as a piece of equipment up there on the shelf in your workroom. At least, that's the way it happened to me.

And I'm glad to report that I, personally, was lucky. Simply because the book I was working on, *Onion John*, had to deal with this very problem. Curiously, I was writing about two characters who found themselves overwhelmed, as I was, by a substantial gift. We were all three of us concerned with our role as a recipient. Andy was being given an abstract future he didn't know anything about. Onion John was being dragged out of a meaningful past into a mechanical present he didn't know anything about. And I had the honor of carrying on a literature that, the more I rewrote and revised, I got to know less and less about.

We considered the matter, the three of us. And we came to a common conclusion. Each one of us rejected our gifts. Onion John ran away. Andy finally spoke his mind to his father. And I, well I took the Newbery Medal away from the quiet — now grown desperate — of the room where I work. I put it outside my working day. I got rid of it. And when this was done, I was indeed able to go to work.

Only then, did the familiar dialogue return — between me and my reader. And soon even my reader was forgotten and the only presences in that room were Andy Rusch, Jr., and Onion John and myself — the three of us working our way to an end.

And curiously, again, we came to a common end. We three discovered that whoever presents us with a gift must wholly accept in return whatever it is we have to offer. Andy gave his father — not the rational cooperation that was expected — but the only small present a child can make to a human being, his own deep love, his devotion and the admiration he feels.

It was accepted.

And once this was done, Onion John could come back. It was safe for him again. The boy had no need any longer to misuse him as a refuge. Nor had the father, to use him as a tool. And Onion John could again send back over the town of Serenity the smoke of his oak fire — and along with it the mystery and the wonder that this oversized image of a child brought to the people of the town.

I'm sure it was accepted. For what town can get along without these gifts that our children bring us?

And I — well, I did get the book done. And with the whole esoteric concern with literature placed to one side, I find that it too, to my astonishment, is accepted.

And so I thank you.

Because now I know how. I've had a new look, through the writing of this book, at the Newbery Medal. I find that the one it places under commitment is not I, but you. The writer can bring you only what he's able. You assure him that however personal is the job he does, however indifferent it is to the market and the demand, if it's truly done it will be read.

You give yourself a hard job. Surely, there must be a great variety of publications that would be simpler to get into a child's hands than the books you honor here. But I think that if this simpler way were taken, a very great deal would be lost. A long line of the oldest kind of books, I'm afraid, would come to an end.

These are family books. Starting with the Bible, they were books to be read, as they were surely written, at many levels. Our best sellers today are not that useful. *Lolita* and *Peyton Place* don't get sent up to the nursery after they've entertained in the parlor. And if the family gets together for its entertainment at all, it's not around a book, but in front of the television or at the drive-in movie.

Not that I have anything against these mass media, which happen to be my own primary professional concern. They simply cost too much, that's all, for a person to use as a personal way of talking. And it's the book that remains the one place where an author can speak and get listened to — most purely, most responsibly, without inhibition, directly.

Where we meet the most interesting people, at their most honest, is surely in the library. And, except for those who are classically established, we rarely meet them any more in each other's company, as a family. It wouldn't happen at all, unless it were for you. And the extraordinary value of an adult and a child sharing a common meeting with a book that's new to them both, a book equally rich and meaningful to them both, an adventure that might lead them both to a better understanding of each other — all that might forever be lost.

Unless it were for you.

Because the books you honor have little reference to any specialized audience or narrow popularity. They seem to have the chance of growing old as family books — stories that can be read with great reward at all the different levels on which we live. If it were not for your commitment represented here by the Newbery Medal, the hard job that you've set yourself, such new books might not get read at all — or worse yet, never get written.

And so as a writer, my most appropriate acceptance is to thank you for the opportunity to write *Onion John*. And even more important perhaps, as a human being allow me to say — God bless you!

BIOGRAPHICAL NOTE

by *Asa Bordages*

Joseph Krumgold

JOSEPH QUINCY KRUMGOLD, my friend Joe, is a short, broad, quick man, black-headed, with a lovely wife, a fine son, a rather special house, and a bee in his bonnet. He has also a yen for miniature cannon, argument as a blood sport, and the books of Gerald Heard, especially *Pain, Sex, and Time*. He makes a deceptively soothing martini, and he practices the rare art of listening as well as he talks. He is about my speed at chess, which is a slow walk, and *Onion John* made him the first writer to win the Newbery Medal twice.

About this biographical note, he wrote me from Rome: " My hope is that you'll do more on the country where we and Onion John live than on me, who has become a sort of stale subject . . . It'd be apt. A strong sense of locality is important in my own outlook; one of the reasons I enjoy Italy, Turkey and places around is that I know where I belong, sort of. And it's thematic to the book — a boy who fights against getting flung out of the place he knows."

That, I think, is the bee in the Krumgold bonnet: a sense, an almost engulfing sense, of *place*. He is filled, filled up, with this feeling of place: a man's need for the place he belongs; the place where he is himself, really, and whole. Other men feel this, of course, more or less, from time to time, but in Krumgold it is stronger, more insistent, I think, than in any man I ever knew. In him, it is a thing. It is as much, as vital, a part of him as his liver and lights. It is the heart of the best work he has done, as it was the core of what he had to say when, in 1954, . . . *and now Miguel* won his first Newbery Medal. He found himself between two worlds. He was, and is, too much the intellectual man, too much the product of our century, to find his place in the harsh simplicity of Miguel's world. Nor was his place Los Alamos. Despite his appreciation of the " prophylactic comforts " of our civilization, despite his " respect for the analytical ingenuities of my time," he did not belong among the apostles of the terrified new world. He thought the place he belonged was somewhere between those poles, and now he is sure he has found it.

He came to it the long way round, via New York, Hollywood, Paris, London, Jerusalem, and way points. His trek started in Jersey City, where he was born in 1908. When he was twelve, he decided he wanted to make movies, and he has never changed his mind. His first job after college, in 1928, was in the New York office of MGM, a job as far from movie making as Kamchatka. He got his ticket to Hollywood, finally, as a Chinese dialogue writer for a Lon Chaney picture that was never made. He parlayed that ticket into a career, as screenwriter and producer, at Paramount, Republic, RKO, and Columbia. He even wrote a book, a whodunit, as a successful status ploy in, as they call it, the industry.

After twelve years of it, he chucked his plush career in Hollywood to gamble his neck that he could make the films he wanted to make, documentaries, saying his say, as his own writer-director. He made his pictures in America, in Europe, in Israel, and Krumgold films won first prizes at the Venice, Prague, and Edinburgh festivals. There was an Academy Award nomination, too, and he found there were some books he wanted to write.

When it was he became possessed by a sense of place, when he started to hunt for his place, I don't know. He lived three or four years in Israel, lived in New York, and he saw a great gaggle of places, making his films. Somewhere along the way, he remembered this patch of northwestern New Jersey, on the edge of the Poconos, and summers spent here as a boy, and so, remembering, he came back again, searching.

It is good country: the Water Gap country, where the Delaware river divides us from Pennsylvania. Mostly, our patch is woodland and farms, a lot of dairy farms, with valleys and hills, rocky hills, and with the Paulinskill, the Pequest, and smaller streams, a sprinkle of lakes, and a scatter of small towns. The county's big towns are down south; in our part, the only big place is Belvidere, the county seat, the Serenity of *Onion John*. It has the courthouse, a couple or so small factories that disturb nobody, and maybe 2,600 people.

This is not big history country. It was the wild frontier in the French war, and even in the Revolution, and some people were killed, but all the big battles were fought somewhere else. We did send a governor to Trenton, and Dr. Jabez Gwinnup refused to receive President John Quincy Adams, and there was a Methodist minister hanged for poisoning his wife, but mostly, I suppose, our big men have been big frogs in a little puddle.

As far as I know, we have produced only one great man, and he seems to be forgotten. Or maybe he was only a great fool, as so many said at the time. He was a Quaker farm boy, Benjamin Lundy, and some of the books say he was the father of the abolitionist movement in America. At least, he started early, on his own, and spent his life, and his family, waging his itinerant war, organizing the anti-slavery movement even in the slave states. He saw the day when America had 140 anti-slavery societies — and 106 of them were in the South. He turned up in Boston in 1828, trying to rally support, but he " could hear of no Abolitionist resident in the place." He did meet William Lloyd Garrison at his boarding house, but Mr. Garrison was on his temperance kick at the time. I suppose Lundy's big mistake was being prematurely right. In any case, in 1838, still agitating, he died broke in Illinois. I don't know whether, in all the thousands of miles of his wandering crusade, he ever came home again, but the Lundys are still here.

Krumgold's quest was a long hunt, and I suspect there were times when he thought the whole idea was crazy, a city boy seeking here what he had not found in any city in the world. Then, at last, he came to the old Moravian town of Hope. Beyond the town, on a back road, almost in the shadow of Jenny Jump Mountain, he found his place, the place he belongs.

Before the French war, the big landowner in that region was Samuel Green, Jr., who called his wilderness settlement Greenland.

When the war started, Mr. Green discreetly withdrew to safety in Pennsylvania, near the Moravian town of Bethlehem. He was impressed by the Moravians, men of peace, devoted to a simple life of work and worship, " with the Holy Scriptures our only rule of faith and practice." He was so impressed that, when the war was over and the Moravians sought sites for new settlements, he suddenly became eccentric. He offered to give them his good Jersey land. The Moravians, just as eccentric, refused the gift, insisting that he accept £563 for 1,500 acres.

So, in 1767, the advance party of the Moravians came to their land and built a mill. The next year, the rest of the Brethren followed, and they created a town and called it Hope.

Close on the heels of the first Moravians came a go-getter, a real better-mousetrap character, " an ex-pirate named Sampson Howell." At the foot of Jenny Jump Mountain, he set up a sawmill to supply the Moravians with lumber for the building of their town. Of Sampson Howell, a local historian recorded, about 1880:

" He was a man of great versatility. He drove his farm and sawmill, preached when occasion required, and yet withal was a mighty hunter. He is said to have killed more bears, wolves, deer, wild turkeys and other small game than any man in all this region of country, and has a larger number of descendants in Warren county than any other pioneer."

At last count, the phone book for our corner of the county listed 29 Howells.

The Howells prospered, but the devoutly laboring Moravians were harried by hard luck, pressed by troubles. They started small industries, along with their farms, but these brought little profit to the community; they were too isolated, too far from good markets. There was sickness, too, and strangers invaded the settlement; the country was filling up with strangers. Only the mill, the beautiful mill, was a bright spot in the dark row they had to hoe.

Then, in 1787, Joseph Swayze decided there was good money to be made from a grist mill of his own. The Moravians pleaded

with him not to build the mill, since one mill was all that part of
the country needed, but Swayze was a business man. He built
his mill, and as apparently he prospered, it may be assumed that the
non-brethren took their grain to him.

At last, in the bright spring of 1808, the same year young
Benjamin Lundy left the family farm to be a saddler's apprentice
down in Wheeling, in Virginia, the Moravians gave up. They sold
their town and their farms, and most of them went back to
Bethlehem. A few of the Brethren, loving this land and their
houses, stubbornly tried to hang on, but by 1881, only one
Moravian was left in Hope, and the region belonged to the strangers.

Still, they left their mark on the land, and they left their enduring houses. They built their houses of field stones and "a
secret mixture of lime and clay," and where wood was needed,
they used the lumber from Samp Howell's sawmill, wood worn
now and warmed by almost two hundred years of human life.
They built their houses to last as long as time, and after the great
fire of 1918 wiped out a large part of the town, people found
they could often rebuild around the old Moravian walls, as good
and as strong as ever. The Brethren built dignity into their houses,
too, and I think we build nothing today that can touch them;
nothing that does not seem a little sleazy in comparison, no matter
how bright and shiny and form-following-function it may be.
(Krumgold would say I have on my Miniver Cheevy hat. He
deeply loves his Moravian house, but he also admires Miës van der
Rohe, on this side idolatry, as much as any.)

There have been a lot of changes since the Moravians left,
and some provoke a jaundiced eye. Log Gaol is now Johnsonburg,
and nobody celebrates the 20th of November, though that was the
day when, in 1753, the county's First Court of General Sessions of
the Peace and Common Pleas convened in Jonathan Pettit's log
tavern. The jurors, loyal lieges of His Majesty, promptly con-
victed Richard Duddy, a Scot, on a charge of "damning His Grace
the Duke of Cumberland." The criminal was " duly punished,"
but he couldn't be put in jail because there was no jail. So, at a

meeting at Sam Green's house, it was voted to build a jail on Sam Green's land, but at the expense of the county. It was the first civic building in the county, and the settlement proudly took the name Log Gaol. The only trouble was, the jail couldn't hold fleas. So many debtors escaped from it that, in nine years, the county was held liable for £600. That was about fourteen times what it had cost to build the jail.

You can still ride along Shades of Death Road, over in Great Meadows, but nobody can get buried now in the Dark Moon Burying Ground. And Sodom, with its gaudy past, is now Hainesburg, somnolent and respectable. There is even talk about building a subdivision back of town.

Time was when: "There were about ten taverns for every schoolhouse and a dozen distilleries (illegal) for every church in the county." This is no longer true, and the change is, I believe, generally regarded with approval.

In Hope, the Moravian church is now the bank, but the mill is still the mill. The town has grown, of course; there must be five hundred people now. Tourists come to see the Moravian houses, detouring from the main highway, even if it is only a pause on their way to Jenny Jump State Forest or The-Land-Of-Make-Believe.

Joe Krumgold's house, cupped by wooded hills, with the lake he built, is beyond the tourists' range. That is where he lives and writes and, I suspect, replenishes his soul. He has become a part of all that is around him. He was on the township school board, and people tell me he was instrumental in starting a first grade library experiment that has served as a model for other county primary schools. We were seeing a lot of each other then, but he never mentioned it. He talks less about himself, about what he is doing, about what he has done, than any writer I ever knew; less, for that matter, than any lawyer, doctor or Indian chief of my acquaintance. Yet on any subject except Krumgold, he is ready to talk, discuss, argue all night.

The Krumgold routine is simple: He writes the books he wants to write between making the films he wants to make. To make his movies, of course, he still goes jaunting about the world. At the moment, the Krumgolds are in Rome, where Adam won two prizes in school last term. While Helen and Adam hold down the apartment, Joe shuttles between Rome and Istanbul. He is making a film in Turkey. When that is in the can, he will make a film in Italy. Then he will come home, I think. There are two books which need to be written, and I think he will need to feel his land after so long a time away. He will need to be in his place.

The Moravians who cleared that land and built the house called it " Shiloh," which is to say, " peace." That is, and aptly, still its name.

THE NEWBERY AWARD 1961

Island of the Blue Dolphins

written by SCOTT O'DELL

published by HOUGHTON MIFFLIN 1960

BOOK NOTE

Karana is a courageous Indian girl who survives alone for eighteen years on the Island of the Blue Dolphins. She loses everything — her father, her people, the brother she sacrifices herself to save. Her attempt to flee by canoe is defeated. But in all she does — from daily chores to discovering nature and her ancestral history, from attacking wild dogs to taming birds and animals, the worth and wonder of life is implicit. Based on historical fact, this story is exciting reading for child, young person, and adult.

EXCERPT FROM THE BOOK

I do not remember much of this time, except that many suns rose and set. I thought about what I was going to do now that I was alone. I did not leave the village. Not until I had eaten all of the abalones did I leave and then only to gather more.

Yet I do remember the day that I decided I would never live in the village again.

It was a morning of thick fog and the sound of far-off waves breaking on the shore. I had never noticed before how silent the village was. Fog crept in and out of the empty huts. It made shapes as it drifted and they reminded me of all the people who were dead and those who were gone. The noise of the surf seemed to be their voices speaking.

I sat for a long time, seeing these shapes and hearing the voices, until the sun came out and the fog vanished. Then I made a fire against the wall of the house. When it was burned to the earth I started a fire in another house. Thus, one by one, I destroyed them all so that there were only ashes left to mark the village of Ghalas-at.

There was nothing to take away with me except a basket of food. I therefore traveled fast and before night fell I reached the place where I had decided to live until the ship returned.

This place lay on a headland a half league to the west of Coral Cove. There was a large rock on that headland and two stunted trees. Behind the rock was a clear place about ten steps across, which was sheltered from the wind, from which I could see the harbor and the ocean. A spring of water flowed from a ravine nearby.

That night I climbed onto the rock to sleep. It was flat on top and wide enough for me to stretch out. Also it was so high from the ground that I did not need to fear the wild dogs while I was sleeping. I had not seen them again since the day they had killed Ramo, but I was sure they would soon come to my new camp.

The rock was also a safe place to store the food I had brought with me and everything I should gather. Since it was still winter and any day the ship might return, there was no use to store food I would not need. This gave me time to make weapons to protect myself from the dogs, which I felt would some time attack me, to kill them all, one by one.

NEWBERY AWARD ACCEPTANCE

by *Scott O'Dell*

SAMUEL JOHNSON has said that a man may turn over half a library to make a book. It is equally true that a writer may turn over a whole lifetime to make a book. Indeed, this is what I did when I wrote *Island of the Blue Dolphins*.

Down the corridors of memory, at the far end of that labyrinth, I saw clearly a certain night.

I was four years old and I had awakened out of a long sleep. The room was dark. The sea made faint sounds among the eaves, like mice stirring. From far off came the sound of waves breaking upon the beach. Though I listened, I heard nothing else.

Lying there in my small bed, in the deep night, it suddenly came to me that the house was deserted, that I was alone. Quickly I slid to the floor and groped along the hall to my mother's room. I felt the bed. It was empty.

At that instant I heard from a distance the sound of music. By some strange alchemy of love and fear and memory, standing there in the empty room, music and my mother became one. I would find her where the music was. They would be together.

I tried to open the front door, but it was locked and the back door was locked too. Then I noticed that the window above the kitchen sink was open. I found a chair and climbed upon it and thus reached the window. (To this day I can feel the coldness of unwashed silverware on my bare feet.) I grasped the window sill, squirmed outside, hung for a moment, fell sprawling on the sand, and picked myself up.

Now the music was clear on the summer air. Against the sky I could see the glow of colored lights. I ran toward it, falling in the deep sand and getting up, running again, shirttails dragging at my ankles.

I came to a boardwalk. The walk led to a pavilion, to the source of the glowing lights, where clusters of people moved about. But the music was still farther, beyond them; and I went toward it, feeling my way through a forest of legs and a sea of dresses, to a place where couples drifted about.

There on a platform above them was the music and below the platform, the lights shining on her, was my mother. Her back was toward me but I knew well the golden hair. With my last breath I ran across the floor, unaware of the eyes that must have been turned upon me. I stretched out my arms and clutched her dress and though she was whirling, held on. As she turned and stared down at this apparition in a nightshirt, at her son, I am forced to say that she was not so glad to see me as I was to see her.

You will not find this incident in *Island of the Blue Dolphins*, but you will find its meaning. The human heart, lonely and in need of love, is a vessel which needs replenishing.

I saw a boy of eight, towheaded and restless, who with other boys of his age went out on Saturday mornings in sun or rain in search of the world.

This was a small world, but a world in microcosm. It was bounded by the deep water and wharves and mud flats of San Pedro Harbor. By the cliffs and reefs of Point Firmin and Portuguese Bend. By the hills of Palos Verdes, aflame with wild mustard in spring, lion-colored in summer.

Many summer days we left the landlocked world and went to sea. How? Each of us on a separate log. The logs had been towed into the harbor in great rafts — from Oregon. They were twelve feet long or longer, rough with splinters and covered with tar. But to each of us young Magellans, they were proud canoes, dugouts fashioned by ax and fire. Graceful, fierce-prowed, the equal of any storm.

We freed them from the deep-water slips where they waited for the saw mill. Astride, paddling with our hands, we set to sea, to the breakwater and beyond. We returned hours later, the watery world encompassed.

These memories went into *Island of the Blue Dolphins*. You will find them in the book — where Karana leaves the Island in search of the country that lies to the East.

Many mornings we went into the Palos Verdes Hills. There we turned over every likely rock, looking for small monsters. We thrust our hands down every squirrel and coyote hole in our path. Commonly we found an owl. This was the prize of all prizes. It was twice the size of your fist, soft-feathered, with great yellow eyes that blinked in the sudden sun.

What did we do with this creature of the nocturnal air? We killed it, of course. We wrung its neck. We cut off its legs. For the exposed tendons of an owl's legs, when pulled in a certain way, made the tiny claws open and retract in a ghastly simulation of life.

To this day, indeed to this very minute, I remember these depredations with horror.

This horror, muted but nonetheless real, you will find in the latter part of *Island of the Blue Dolphins*. The latter part of the book, only, because my Indian girl began where youth begins. In the closed world of selfishness and cruelty where everything, whether of fur or feather, whether it creeps or walks or flies, is an object of indifferent cruelty.

Down that dark corridor of time I also saw Jack Iman.

Freckled, with black eyes alert under a bang of black hair, a Hercules in miniature, Jack hated me the moment we met. For no other reason, I am certain, than that I was a city boy, lately come to his town. I also hated him. And for no other reason except that he hated me.

In all weather, during the school week and even on Sunday, Jack pursued me. In class with his black eyes. On the school grounds with taunts. Off the school grounds with his fists. He was my nemesis. My tormentor. The embodiment to me of all evil.

Years later I read in the newspaper that Jack had become a prize-fighter. Sometime later I saw him fight. I went to see him beaten. But the same Jack Iman I remembered, only with vaster muscles, was the victor. I went again and again to see him fight, each time hoping for his humiliation. Finally, after a year of fights, Jack Iman was knocked out and carried groggily from the ring. To my surprise, sitting there at ringside, I somehow felt diminished.

I went back, using the privilege of a press badge, to his dressing room. I went there to introduce myself, for I was sure he wouldn't remember me, and to quietly gloat.

Though he was just returning from another world, Jack Iman recognized me at once. Unsteadily he came towards me, put his arms around my shoulders and wept.

That too is in *Island of the Blue Dolphins*. It lies in the heart of the episode of Karana and her enemy, the Aleut girl. It also colors the climax of the book. For I believe and wished to say, with whatever power I might summon to the task, that we must forgive our enemies. Further, I believe that the hopes of civilization, unique and obscure as they are, really exist in the act of identification with our enemies.

Memories come from books, too, from that vital spring, the library. This is one of them, culled from many sources, that in spirit I used.

At Warner's Ranch, near my home in Julian, the Cupeño Indians revolted in 1851. Bereft of their ancestral lands by the Americans, impoverished and abused, they attacked under the leadership of Antonio Garra and burned a few buildings. The citizens of San Diego sprang to arms, rode in pursuit of Garra and his men. The men scattered into the chapparal, but Garra was captured and brought to trial in San Diego.

He was first tried for murder, but the evidence was lacking. The charge was changed to theft. This also lacked evidence.

Hard pressed, the court decided on a charge of treason, based upon the fact that Garra had not paid his county taxes, and sentenced him to death.

Garra joked with the firing squad as they marched him out of his cell. The attending priest reprimanded him for his levity and said that his last minutes might more appropriately be spent in prayer.

To which Garra replied: "What is the reason? I am nothing. You are nothing. This, too, is nothing."

And then, as the procession set off for the grave, he expressed the desire to walk in front, but was overruled by the priest, who again found his attitude undignified.

"Why is it undignified?" Garra asked.

The priest brought the procession to a halt. "I insist that you be more solemn. Kneel and listen to me while I pray."

Garra said, "I will listen, if it pleases you. But I will not kneel."

The priest got down on his knees and began to pray, but, upset by what had transpired, botched his Latin.

"Pardon me, Father," Garra said, "but these are the words you should use for what you are trying to say." And he supplied them from his brief studies at the mission, years before.

The priest drew himself up and began an argument which lasted until they reached the grave. In a final effort to establish decorum, he suggested that the Indian ask the pardon of all those present.

With the rifles pointed at his heart, Garra smiled and said, "Yes, gentlemen, I ask your pardon for all my offenses, and I pardon you in return."

The rifles put a period to his words and he fell into the open grave.

If Antonio Garra had killed fifty Americans or ten, his name like Geronimo's would be remembered, but he belonged to a peaceful tribe which lived amicably with each other and with the other tribes of Southern California, whose lives are unknown because they went in peace. Karana belonged to such a tribe.

Places I have known, creatures I have loved are in *Island of the Blue Dolphins*. The islands — San Nicolas, Santa Cruz, San Miguel, Catalina, Anacapa, Todos Santos, San Martín, the Coronados — seen at dawn and at sunset, in all weathers over many years. Dolphin and otter playing. A mother gull pushing her grown brood from the nest, watching them plummet a hundred feet into the sea, then flying down to herd them onto their new home, a rock safe from the tide.

And finally there is Carolina, the Tarascan girl of sixteen, who lived on the shores of Lake Pátzcuaro in central Mexico. She was one of nine children, the oldest daughter of Pedro Flores who took care of the small quinta my wife and I had rented for the summer.

The Tarascans are a great people. They were never conquered by the Aztecs, the only tribe, incidentally, that did not fall under the Aztec yoke. Nor did the Spaniards, led by the incredibly cruel Guzman, subdue them. When the Conquistadores took their capital city of Tzintsuntsan, The Place of the Hummingbirds, tortured their king by dragging him around the city square attached to the tail of a horse and at last tossed him into a bonfire, the Tarascans retreated into the high mountains.

Carolina was tall for a Tarascan, with small bones but broad shoulders. Her eyes were black and deep-set, slanted at the corners, and her black hair fell heavily to her waist. She stood in her bare feet squarely on the earth as if growing from it.

Carolina, when she first came to work for us, wore a long red skirt of closely woven wool. As a bride her mother had received the gift of sixty yards of this red cloth from her betrothed, a custom of the Tarascans. With it, by winding it around and around her waist, she made a skirt. At night she used it as a blanket for herself and her husband, and later for their children, against the fierce cold of the mountains. For each girl child she cut lengths of the cloth and this in turn became a skirt. The red skirt, the *falda roja* which Carolina wore, came to her in this fashion. She wore it proudly, as a shield against the world, in the way Karana wore the skirt of cormorant feathers. The two girls are much alike.

Through them I wanted to say to children and to all those who will listen that we have a chance to come into a new relationship to the things around us. Once, in Defoe's day, we were cunning manipulative children, living in a palace of nature. In her brief lifetime, Karana made the change from that world, where everything lived only to be exploited, to a new and more meaningful world. She learned first that we each must be an island secure unto ourselves. Then, that we must " transgress our limits," in reverence for all life.

BIOGRAPHICAL NOTE

by *Maud Hart Lovelace*

Scott O'Dell

SCOTT O'DELL's earliest recollections are of a house standing on stilts beside the Pacific Ocean. The tide came up beneath it. This was on what is now Terminal Island, near Los Angeles, where he was born. His father was a railroader, and the family moved frequently, keeping to the same general area. Never during Scott's boyhood was he far from the wash of the sea. This is one of several factors which explain the ring of authority in *Island of the Blue Dolphins*.

From his home in San Pedro, where he lived from ages six to nine, he could almost see San Nicolas, the island on which an Indian girl had once lived alone for eighteen years. San Pedro then was a roaring port, overrun by seamen from tramp steamers and even a few sailing vessels. The school took its temper from the town, with fights in the school yard every day. Scott's schoolmates were the sons of Portuguese and Italian fishermen, and at first did not take kindly to the blue-eyed, Scotch-Irish, too-literate O'Dell. He was the butt of jokes and the target of bullies, and school was a frightening ordeal. Fortunately, he could hold his own in the pigmy battles, and no doubt he already had some of the effortless charm which is so much a part of him now. At last he was allowed to join the crowd on a Saturday expedition to the beach.

Racing to their favorite cove, the boys stripped, climbed a steep bank, and leaped joyfully into the surf. Scott did not mention not knowing how to swim. He would have preferred drowning to confessing such damning ignorance. He leaped, along with the rest, and somehow dogpaddled to shore.

After that, such excursions filled every Saturday . . . in summer, almost every day. The boys swam. They dug cockles and steamed them in a washtub borrowed from an amiable mother. Someone always brought along a long loaf of chewy Italian bread. They gathered abalones and searched submerged rocks for little devilfish and came to know the world of beach and sea.

By the time he entered Long Beach Polytechnic High School, Scott's present easy gregariousness was established. He excelled in water polo and the 440-yard dash. With little effort he achieved fine grades, and in his sophomore year found time to make a collection of synopses of forty plays . . . not for a school project, but for fun.

He started college at California's Occidental when the emphasis was chiefly on military training and getting into World War One. But the war ended, and he had the inspired idea that attending a different college every year would be a fine way to see the world. So he moved on to the University of Wisconsin. He ended there with only a B average.

"I was chagrined. I wanted top grades but wasn't used to working for them."

At Stanford, he revolted against the curriculum, which seemed to reserve the most fascinating subjects for seniors and graduate students. He became a special student, and took twelve hours of philosophy, including the beginning course and the one most advanced, also courses in Shakespeare and Russian Literature. Then, gorged with learning, he went to Hollywood and taught a mail-order course in photoplay writing, producing a textbook on the subject.

This was the glamorous Hollywood of Greta Garbo and Rudolph Valentino, and soon Scott was working in Paramount's technical department, preparing sets. He changed to Metro-Goldwyn-Mayer and was sent to Rome for the filming of *Ben Hur*. In off hours, he studied at the University of Rome, and this ended his unorthodox college career.

When the last wheel in Ben Hur's chariot race had turned, he went to Florence and wrote a novel.

"*Pinfeathers*. It was an appropriate title," he says. For after he returned to New York, an agent advised him to write it off to experience, all 100,000 words of it.

Back in Hollywood, he kept on writing, worked on magazines and newspapers, and ranched with his father, who had bought an orange grove near Claremont. Here Scott discovered the old Spanish families of the Pomona Valley, visiting their ranchos and listening to evocative tales of the past. This led to his fine historical novel, *Hill of the Hawk*. He wrote three novels in all and *Country of the Sun*, an informal history of the nine Southern California counties.

It was in the period of the early novels that he owned Eric von Ebrochtal, the nobly handsome German shepherd, brother of Strongheart, who shared his life for seven years.

"I took him with me everywhere. I stayed only in hotels that would accept him. He never saw a kennel."

During Eric's final illness, his master nursed him with loving sorrow, played a fan upon him through long hot summer nights. When Scott tells of his death, it sounds like the death of Karana's dog, Rontu.

"Slowly, he walked to where I was standing and fell at my feet. I put my hand on his chest. I could feel his heart beating, very slowly . . . and then no more."

There are French poodles around Stoneapple Farm in Julian, California, where Scott lives now. He is married to his gay, exciting Dorsa, daughter of Mr. and Mrs. William H. Rattenbury of New Britain, Connecticut, and Claremont. She gives, he says, valuable editorial advice and even types his manuscripts. The poodles romp about the book-lined living room, snooze beside the huge fireplace, sniff appreciatively in the roomy old-fashioned kitchen, and keep quiet in their master's study.

Julian is not far from two Indian reservations, and Scott is knowledgeable about the Cupeños and the Luiseños, but he learned more about the Indian temperament, he says, from the Tarascan Indians whom he and Dorsa came to know during a summer near Lake Pátzcuaro in Mexico.

They lived in the guest cottage on an estate cared for by the Indian father of nine children. Carolina, the sixteen-year-old eldest, was the O'Dells' cook. The others hung around all day and in late afternoon came inside to chatter over chocolate and *buñuelos* with the friendly, relaxed, soft-voiced *señor* and the blonde smiling *señora*. This family sponsored the Americans at secret Tarascan *fiestas*, helped them obtain a native canoe.

"We used to take Carolina to the Friday market," Scott says. "Anything we bought as a gift for her she would take home carefully to share with her brothers and sisters."

It is not hard, when he talks of Carolina, to see Karana caring for her little brother.

Scott O'Dell's life brought him naturally a knowledge of Indians, dogs, and the ocean; and he was born with an inability to keep away from writing. So he gave us the moving legend of Karana.

The Bronze Bow

written by ELIZABETH GEORGE SPEARE

published by HOUGHTON MIFFLIN 1961

BOOK NOTE

AT eighteen fugitive Daniel bar Jamin longs for freedom from Roman rule for his people, the Jews. Rosh, leader of an outlaw band, promises one way of fighting. Simon the Zealot brings Daniel to hear Jesus, whose teachings promise that love — not hate — will conquer. Two friends, Joel and his twin sister Malthace, and Daniel's ill sister complicate the decision he must finally make as to which force to join. Full of interesting detail, this book gives an excellent picture of the conflicts and excitement of this era.

EXCERPT FROM THE BOOK

The man's figure was not in any way arresting. He was slight, with the knotted arms and shoulders of one who has done hard labor from childhood. He was not regal or commanding. He was dressed simply in a plain white tallith that reached to his feet. His white head covering, drawn closely over his forehead and hanging to his

shoulders, hid his profile. Yet when he turned and stood before
the congregation, Daniel was startled. All at once nothing in the
room was distinct to him but this man's face. A thin face, strongly
cut. A vital, radiant face, lighted from within by a burning intensity of spirit.

Yes! Daniel thought, his own spirit leaping up. This man is a
fighter! He is one of us!

Jesus received the scroll and stood unrolling it with reverence,
as though he were seeking for some passage already determined
in his own mind. Then he raised his eyes and spoke from memory.

" The Spirit of the Lord is upon me, because He has anointed me
to preach good news to the poor. He has sent me to proclaim release
to the captives, and recovering of sight to the blind, to set at liberty
those who are oppressed, to proclaim the acceptable year of the
Lord."

A shock ran through Daniel at the first words. A gentle voice,
barely raised, it carried to every corner of the room, warm, vibrant,
with a promise of unlimited power. It was as though only a frac-
tion of that voice were being used, as though if the full force of it
were unstopped it would roll like thunder.

Jesus closed the book and gave it back to the attendant. The
waiting congregation seemed to surge forward and to hold its
breath. Again that voice made the blood leap in Daniel's veins.

" I say to you, the time is fulfilled, and the kingdom of God is at
hand. Repent, and believe."

Now! Daniel leaned forward. Tell us that the moment has come!
Tell us what we are to do! Longing swelled unbearably in his
throat.

But Jesus went on speaking quietly. A rippling murmur passed
across the crowd. Others too waited for the word that was not
spoken. What had the man meant? He had said liberty for the
oppressed. Why didn't he call them to arms against the oppressor?
Repent, he said now. Repent. As though that could rid them of
the Romans. Disappointed and puzzled, Daniel leaned back. The
fire that had leaped up in him died down. The man's voice had been
like a trumpet call. Yet where did the call lead?

NEWBERY AWARD ACCEPTANCE

by *Elizabeth George Speare*

Report of a Journey

How can I thank you for your vote of confidence? For I feel
that this time you have given this honor not so much for an achievement as for an endeavor. And with special gratitude I treasure this
big, beautiful, totally unexpected " A for Effort."

Because for me *The Bronze Bow,* which was my third book, was
quite different from the first two, both in the purpose and in the
making. It was not so much an adventure as a challenge, and at the
book's completion I knew that I had recorded no more than the
first steps of a lifelong search that can never be fulfilled.

Mr. Theodore Holden, literary editor of the Hartford *Times,*
who had given me encouragement and support from the beginning, led off his review of *The Bronze Bow* with the words, " She
walks serenely where angels fear to tread." His tactful paraphrase
was flattering, but also disturbing. I was only too well aware of
my temerity. Even now I wonder how I had the rashness to venture
upon ground which is not only hallowed but salted as well with
traps for the well-meaning trespasser. For many years there had
been in my mind the urge to write something about the land of the
New Testament, and I could only have explained this compulsion in
the words of George Mallory when he was asked why he had
wanted to climb Mount Everest and he replied, " Because it's
there." True, I did not rush in, but never for one moment did I
walk serenely. I approached with uncertainty, and I was beset
every step of the way by doubt and discouragement.

When I stood in just this spot before you in June of 1959, I was
already committed to this quest. I had completed a year of research, but my characters and story existed only in the shadowy
glimpses I tried then to describe to you. One scene only was very

clear to me, and you might like to know the part the American Library Association had played in that scene.

On a Friday afternoon the preceding March, in Mr. Melcher's office in New York, the unbelievable moment had come when the Newbery medal for *The Witch of Blackbird Pond* was placed in my hand — to be held for a moment only. After the ceremony, Barbara Cooney, the Caldecott medalist, and I, with our long-suffering husbands, were feted at a party which included not only champagne, but the kind of talk about the making of books which was far more heady to a still green writer from Connecticut. On Sunday morning my husband and I ended this improbable Queen-for-a-day week end with a service at Riverside Church. In my overstimulated state the trumpeting organ prelude was a final intoxicant. I did not hear a word of the service, because, in response to the music, the climax and final chapter of my new story began to play itself out in my mind so compellingly that I was aware of nothing else. From that moment I knew where I was going, and in all the changes and about-faces that were continually to alter my course, that final chapter, though it was many times rewritten, remained essentially intact, just as I first saw it that morning.

I told you that June that my stories began with people. Yet I made the mistake of trying to begin this story with a theme. I knew what I wanted to do. I was teaching a Sunday School class at the time, and I longed to lift the personality of Jesus off the flat and lifeless pages of our textbook. I wanted to give my pupils, and others like them, a glimpse of the divided and turbulent society of Palestine, an occupied country with many parallels in our own day. And I wanted to stir in them some personal sharing of what must have been the response of boys and girls who actually saw and heard the Carpenter from Nazareth.

I think the initial theme of the book rose out of a discussion our class had one Sunday morning on the great heroes of history, and on what qualities a hero must possess. I longed to have them see that the preacher who walked the hills of Galilee was not a mythical figure, but a compelling and dynamic leader, a hero to whom a boy in any age would gladly offer all his loyalty.

I had no illusions that this would be easy. But I did not foresee the almost insurmountable difficulties that would block my way for the next three years. The research itself was never a barrier. I plunged eagerly into Jewish history, into the accounts of travelers who spread before me the land, the people, and the ways of Palestine, and into the rich and complex treasury of Bible scholarship. Finally I knew that I must pull myself from the absorbing joy of reading and begin the task of writing.

And here I came up against the truth I stated to you. There was no story to write, because there were no people. I had an outline, and some shadowy figures. But no real and living people.

There was a girl, of course. I had written two stories about girls, and I assumed that was my natural province. So I forced myself to begin Chapter One. I gave my girl a brother and sent them off on a lighthearted picnic on a mountaintop in Galilee, bright with spring flowers. In Chapter Two my heroine, hidden behind a rock, witnessed some lively action. But Chapter Three brought me to a dead end. I suddenly saw that a girl hidden behind a rock would never be a heroine. Palestine was an eastern country in which women stayed submissively at home. Even the remarkably emancipated female my heroine was going to be would need the most ridiculous contriving to be on stage at the right moments. And a girl's-eye view of Palestine would be a narrow and limited view.

Suppose I were to write from the brother's point of view instead? I rewrote the three chapters, and this time my boy and his sister met a young outlaw on the mountain. Daniel was not a new invention; he was the hero I had had in mind all along. He was to be the romantic and bold young leader of a band of Zealots. But the boy I saw on the mountain was quite different from the confident leader I had planned. This boy was unsure and defiant and bitterly unhappy. All at once he began to move and to talk and to think with a fierce urgency that left no room for doubt. I had a person at last, a real person, and to my dismay he was a wild and difficult one. But the story had to be his. As I began the first chapter for the third time, the girl and her brother leaped to life beside Daniel, and I knew that I was on the right road.

But the lightheartedness and the spring flowers were gone. This was an altogether unfamiliar path. From the first it took a direction I had never planned. Sudden turns opened up vistas I had never anticipated. There were blind alleys from which I had to patiently retrace my steps. Events I had moved toward with confidence turned out to be mirages as I approached, and worthless. Moreover, I saw that this road must lead to violence, and all my life I have been a timid mouse, shrinking from the least hint of violence.

And the most serious stumbling block of all loomed constantly ahead. I wanted my young people to meet Jesus. But how could I portray Jesus, when many years of searching to understand his life and his teachings left me still facing a mystery? I read countless versions of the life of Jesus, most of them written with reverence and deep faith, some with skepticism, a few even with venom, each one differing from the others. The personality of the Man from Nazareth has been at the mercy of hundreds of interpreters. There is no definitive biography. The quest for the historical Jesus has never yielded the surety for which the scholars hoped. The incontestable facts of history barely established his having lived at all. Yet he stands like a mountain peak, which, however high we climb, looms forever higher, rising into the mist, its full dimension hidden from our sight.

In the end I realized that in this case research was defeating my purpose and only clouding my vision. The sum of my search is contained in one line which I put into the mouth of Simon the disciple, " We are forced to choose, not knowing." In my portrait of Jesus I failed. I know that failure was intrinsic in the attempt, but I wish that I could have climbed higher. I knew before I had gone far on this road that I was not big enough to do what I had hoped. But I set myself to do, to the best of my ability, one small thing. I would show the change wrought in just one boy who came to know the teacher in Galilee. This is the story of *The Bronze Bow*.

This is also my endeavor to share in the work that you as librarians are doing. For we are all dedicated to preparing children for life. There are many needful ways of equipping young people for the future. We have chosen to place books in their hands, books that will serve not only as companions and teachers but as guardians. For the world into which our children are about to step is filled with peril. And perhaps of all the dangers that lie in wait, the most terrifying is that they may settle for a world without meaning.

The philosophy of meaninglessness and nihilism has already reached down to our children through television and movies and in more subtle ways. In the teen years it speaks to them with the persuasive voices of some of our most brilliant, writers. We should not underestimate this appeal. The man who stands erect in the face of emptiness is an heroic figure. In the words of Martin Esslin, writing of modern drama, " The dignity of man lies in his ability to face reality in all its senselessness."*

How can we give our children something more worthy of their courage? Joseph Wood Krutch, who has spent a lifetime recording his own search for meaning, recently gave to writers this commission: " If Love and Honor and Duty can be salvaged, then someone must write about them in a fashion which carries conviction. If we are to get along without them, then someone must describe a world from which they are absent in a fashion which makes that world seem worth having."**

Many of our most talented writers are trying to make a senseless world seem worth having. I believe that all of us who are concerned with children are committed to the salvaging of Love and Honor and Duty. Not only our own faith, but the children themselves compel us. Young people do not want to accept meaninglessness. They look urgently to the adult world for evidence that we have proved our values to be enduring. Yet perhaps never before have they looked so clearly, so despairingly, at the evidence we offer. They demand an honest answer. Those of us who have found Love and Honor and Duty to be a sure foundation must somehow find words which have the ring of truth.

* Martin Esslin, *The Theatre of the Absurd*. Garden City (o.p.).
** " Challenge to an Unknown Writer," *Saturday Review*, March 10, 1962.

THE NEWBERY AWARD 1963

A Wrinkle in Time

written by MADELEINE L'ENGLE

published by FARRAR, STRAUS 1962

BOOK NOTE

MEG MURRY, her small brother Charles Wallace and her friend Calvin O'Keefe search the universe for Mr. Murry, a missing scientist. They are enabled to rescue him from Camazotz and the paralyzing evils of IT through three fantastic beings — Mrs. Whatsit, Mrs. Who and Mrs. Which, and the existence of a tesseract, or a wrinkle in time. The book becomes far more than a science fiction story because of its imaginative writing and its inventive use of science and philosophy.

EXCERPT FROM THE BOOK

"Watch," Mrs. Whatsit commanded.

It was a shadow, nothing but a shadow. It was not even as tangible as a cloud. Was it cast by something? Or was it a Thing in itself?

The sky darkened. The gold left the light and they were surrounded by blue, blue deepening until where there had been nothing but the evening sky there was now a faint pulse of star, and then another and another and another. There were more stars than Meg had ever seen before.

"The atmosphere is so thin here," Mrs. Whatsit said as though in answer to her unasked question, "that it does not obscure your vision as it would at home. Now look. Look straight ahead."

Meg looked. The dark shadow was still there. It had not lessened or dispersed with the coming of night. And where the shadow was the stars were not visible.

What could there be about a shadow that was so terrible that she knew that there had never been before or ever would be again, anything that would chill her with a fear that was beyond shuddering, beyond crying or screaming, beyond the possibility of comfort?

Meg's hand holding the blossoms slowly dropped and it seemed as though a knife gashed through her lungs. She gasped, but there was no air for her to breathe. Darkness glazed her eyes and mind, but as she started to fall into unconsciousness her head dropped down into the flowers which she was still clutching; and as she inhaled the fragrance of their purity her mind and body revived, and she sat up again.

The shadow was still there, dark and dreadful.

Calvin held her hand strongly in his, but she felt neither strength nor reassurance in his touch. Beside her a tremor went through Charles Wallace, but he sat very still.

He shouldn't be seeing this, Meg thought. This is too much for so little a boy, no matter how different and extraordinary a little boy.

Calvin turned, rejecting the dark Thing that blotted out the

light of the stars. " Make it go away, Mrs. Whatsit," he whispered.
" Make it go away. It's evil."

Slowly the great creature turned around so that the shadow was
behind them, so that they saw only the stars unobscured, the soft
throb of starlight on the mountain, the descending circle of the
great moon swiftly slipping over the horizon. Then, without a
word from Mrs. Whatsit, they were traveling downward, down,
down. When they reached the corona of clouds, Mrs. Whatsit
said, " You can breathe without the flowers now, my children."

Silence again. Not a word. It was as though the shadow had
somehow reached out with its dark power and touched them so
that they were incapable of speech. When they got back to the
flowery field, bathed now in starlight, and moonlight from another,
smaller, yellower, rising moon, a little of the tenseness went out
of their bodies, and they realized that the body of the beautiful
creature on which they rode had been as rigid as theirs.

With a graceful gesture it dropped to the ground and folded
its great wings. Charles Wallace was the first to slide off. " Mrs.
Who! Mrs. Which! " he called, and there was an immediate quivering in the air. Mrs. Who's familiar glasses gleamed at them. Mrs.
Which appeared, too; but, as she had told the children, it was
difficult for her to materialize completely, and though there was
the robe and peaked hat, Meg could look through them to mountain
and stars. She slid off Mrs. Whatsit's back and walked, rather
unsteadily after the long ride, over to Mrs. Which.

" That dark Thing we saw," she said. " Is that what my father
is fighting? "

NEWBERY AWARD ACCEPTANCE

by *Madeleine L'Engle*

The Expanding Universe

FOR a writer of fiction to have to sit down and write a speech, especially a speech in which she must try to express her gratitude for one of the greatest honors of her life, is as difficult a task as she can face. She can no longer hide behind the printed page and let her characters speak for her; she must stand up in front of an illustrious group of librarians, editors, publishers, writers, feeling naked, the way one sometimes does in a dream. What, then, does she say? Should she merely tell a series of anecdotes about her life and how she happened to write this book? Or should she try to be profound and write a speech that will go down in the pages of history, comparable only to the Gettysburg Address? Should she stick to platitudes that will offend no one and say nothing? Perhaps she tries all of these several times and then tears them up, knowing that if she doesn't her husband will do it for her, and decides simply to say some of the things she feels deeply about.

I can't tell you anything about children's books that you don't already know. I'm not teaching you; you're teaching me. All I can tell you is how Ruth Gagliardo's telephone call about the Newbery Medal has affected me over the past few months.

One of my greatest treasures is the letter Mr. Melcher wrote me, one of the last letters he wrote, talking about the medal and saying he had just read *A Wrinkle in Time* and had been excited about it. This was one of the qualities that made him what he was: the ability to be excited. Bertha Mahony Miller in her article, "Frederic G. Melcher — A Twentieth Century John Newbery," says that "The bookstore's stock in trade is . . . explosive material, capable of stirring up fresh life endlessly. . . ." I like here to think of another Fred, the eminent British scientist,

Fred Hoyle, and his theory of the universe, in which matter is continuously being created, with the universe expanding but not dissipating. As island galaxies rush away from each other into eternity, new clouds of gas are condensing into new galaxies. As old stars die, new stars are being born. Mr. Melcher lived in this universe of continuous creation and expansion. It would be impossible to overestimate his influence on books, particularly children's books; impossible to overestimate his influence on the people who read books, write them, sell them, get enthusiastic about them. We are all here tonight because of his vision, and we would be less than fair to his memory if we didn't resolve to keep alive his excitement and his ability to grow, to change, to expand.

I am of the first generation to profit by Mr. Melcher's excitement, having been born shortly before he established the Newbery award, and growing up with most of these books on my shelves. I learned about mankind from Hendrik Willem van Loon; I traveled with Dr. Dolittle, created by a man I called Hug Lofting; Will James taught me about the West with Smoky; in boarding school I grabbed *Invincible Louisa* the moment it came into the library because Louisa May Alcott had the same birthday that I have, and the same ambitions. And now to be a very small link in the long chain of these writers, of the men and women who led me into the expanding universe, is both an honor and a responsibility. It is an honor for which I am deeply grateful to Mr. Melcher and to those of you who decided *A Wrinkle in Time* was worthy of it.

The responsibility has caused me to think seriously during these past months on the subject of vocation, the responsibility added to the fact that I'm working now on a movie scenario about a Portuguese nun who lived in the mid-1600's, had no vocation, was seduced and then betrayed by a French soldier of fortune, and, in the end, through suffering, came into a true vocation. I believe that every one of us here tonight has as clear and vital a vocation as anyone in a religious order. We have the vocation of keeping alive Mr. Melcher's excitement in leading young people into an expanding imagination. Because of the very nature of the world as it is today our children receive in school a heavy load of scientific and analytic subjects, so it is in their reading for fun, for pleasure, that they must be guided into creativity. There are forces working in the world as never before in the history of mankind for standardization, for the regimentation of us all, or what I like to call making muffins of us, muffins all like every other muffin in the muffin tin. This is the limited universe, the dying, dissipating universe, that we can help our children avoid by providing them with " explosive material capable of stirring up fresh life endlessly."

So how do we do it? We can't just sit down at our typewriters and turn out explosive material. I took a course in college on Chaucer, one of the most explosive, imaginative, and far-reaching in influence of all writers. And I'll never forget going to the final exam and being asked why Chaucer used certain verbal devices, certain adjectives, why he had certain characters behave in certain ways. And I wrote in a white heat of fury, " I don't think Chaucer had any idea why he did any of these things. That isn't the way people write."

I believe this as strongly now as I did then. Most of what is best in writing isn't done deliberately.

Do I mean, then, that an author should sit around like a phony Zen Buddhist in his pad, drinking endless cups of espresso coffee and waiting for inspiration to descend upon him? That isn't the way the writer works, either. I heard a famous author say once that the hardest part of writing a book was making yourself sit down at the typewriter. I know what he meant. Unless a writer works constantly to improve and refine the tools of his trade, they will be useless instruments if and when the moment of inspiration, of revelation, does come. This is the moment when a writer is spoken through, the moment that a writer must accept with gratitude and humility, and then attempt, as best he can, to communicate to others.

A writer of fantasy, fairy tale, or myth must inevitably discover that he is not writing out of his own knowledge or experience, but out of something both deeper and wider. I think that fantasy must possess the author and simply use him. I know that this is true of *A Wrinkle in Time*. I can't possibly tell you how I came to write it. It was simply a book I had to write. I had no choice. And it was only *after* it was written that I realized what some of it meant.

Very few children have any problem with the world of the imagination; it's their own world, the world of their daily life, and it's our loss that so many of us grow out of it. Probably this group here tonight is the least grown-out-of-it group that could be gathered together in one place, simply by the nature of our work. We, too, can understand how Alice could walk through the mirror into the country on the other side; how often have our children almost done this themselves? And we all understand princesses, of course. Haven't we all been badly bruised by peas? And what about the princess who spat forth toads and snakes whenever she opened her mouth to speak, and the other whose lips issued forth pieces of pure gold? We all have had days when everything we've said has seemed to turn to toads. The days of gold, alas, don't come nearly as often.

What a child doesn't realize until he is grown is that in responding to fantasy, fairy tale, and myth he is responding to what Erich Fromm calls the one universal language, the one and only language in the world that cuts across all barriers of time, place, race, and culture. Many Newbery books are from this realm, beginning with Dr. Dolittle; books on Hindu myth, Chinese folklore, the life of Buddha, tales of American Indians, books that lead our children beyond all boundaries and into the one language of all mankind.

In the beginning God created the heaven and the earth. . . . The extraordinary, the marvelous thing about Genesis is not how unscientific it is, but how amazingly accurate it is. How could the ancient Israelites have known the exact order of an evolution that wasn't to be formulated for thousands of years? Here is a truth that cuts across barriers of time and space.

But almost all of the best children's books do this, not only an *Alice in Wonderland*, a *Wind in the Willows*, a *Princess and the Goblin*. Even the most straightforward tales say far more than they seem to mean on the surface. *Little Women, The Secret Garden, Huckleberry Finn* — how much more there is in them than we realize at a first reading. They partake of the universal language, and this is why we turn to them again and again when we are children, and still again when we have grown up.

Up on the summit of Mohawk Mountain in northwest Connecticut is a large flat rock that holds the heat of the sun long after the last of the late sunset has left the sky. We take our picnics up there and then lie on the rock and watch the stars, one pulsing slowly into the deepening blue, and then another and another and another, until the sky is full of them.

A book, too, can be a star, " explosive material, capable of stirring up fresh life endlessly," a living fire to lighten the darkness, leading out into the expanding universe.

BIOGRAPHICAL NOTE

by *Hugh Franklin*

Madeleine L'Engle

AFTER reading Madeleine L'Engle's novels people may think they
see a similarity in some of her teen-age heroines — the gangling,
awkward ugly duckling trying to find her way through adoles-
cence — and may think the author has written of her own childhood. Well, if Meg Murry and Vicky Austin have bits and pieces
of the young Madeleine L'Engle, their mothers have large chunks
of the mature Madeleine Franklin, chief cook and bottle washer
for a husband, daughters, fifteen and thirteen, a son, eleven, a collie
and a cat, all living with joyful noise in a rambling old apartment
near Columbia University. The hubbub of the home, with the hi-fi
blaring out Bach, Brahms, and Bernstein, the telephone always
jangling, the doorbell clanging, the dog barking, is a much more
faithful backdrop for this tall, statuesque woman ("I have the
same dimensions as Gypsy Rose Lee — or I used to") than her
shy and sensitive heroines would have us believe.

The shy and sensitive girl, if ever she was that, has developed
into a volatile, dynamic woman. With an interest in and a curiosity about everything except newspapers ("I don't have time —
you're supposed to tell me when there's an article I should read")
she is ready every morning, as soon as she wakes up and her feet
hit the floor, to discuss anything from Aristotle to Zen Buddhism,
to the bewilderment of a cantankerous husband who can't even
comment on the weather until he has had his second cup of coffee.
She devours books ravenously, thinks it immoral to pass a bookstore without buying something, and is always eying the walls of
her home for space to build new bookshelves. Impetuous, she
believes in doing immediately whatever she thinks has to be done,

to the consternation of a procrastinating husband. And she still has enough of the child in her to relish Christmas as few people do. Starting on Thanksgiving Day, she replaces Bach with carols, and during Advent she adds decorations to the house each day, some of them out of her childhood, worn with age but rich in nostalgia.

If ever she was inhibited she has outgrown it. Trying to find a taxi, especially when traveling with the whole family at rush hour, she has been known to throw herself on her knees on the pavement of Park Avenue, with hands upraised, hoping some taxi driver with a sense of humor will stop, a practice frowned upon by her husband. Prone to exaggeration (" Of course I ex-aggerate – I'm a writer "), she can't resist making everything a little bigger than life, with hundreds becoming thousands and thousands becoming millions. She even refers to Chekhov's *Three Sisters* as *Four Sisters*, and Orwell's *1984* as *1985*. She can't help it.

She claims that her graduation from Smith *cum laude* was a mistake, that she slipped through on the gift of gab. (" I'm not intellectual – I'm instinctual.") She tells of going to an exam in Survey of the Novel and finding such questions as " What color dress was Jane Eyre wearing when she met Mr. Rochester? " at which she marched to the front desk, grabbed a handful of blue books, and scrawled, " Dear Miss C- - - -: These are silly questions and I don't know the answer to any of them. But I have read the books, loved them, and shall now proceed to tell you what I think of them." She got an A.

After Smith she decided that if she wanted to write plays the best place to learn was in the theater. She got an audition with Eva Le Gallienne and Margaret Webster and won a small part in *Uncle Harry* (" They were sick of hearing Lady Macbeths and Juliets – I used my own material, which was fresh to them "), followed by a small part in *The Cherry Orchard*. In the latter play she met an actor. A year later he got up the courage to propose and they were married in Chicago while on tour with Ethel Barrymore. (" It was so romantic – we met in *The Cherry Orchard* and were married in *The Joyous Season*.") Shortly there-after her retirement from the theater was announced to her by her husband, who felt one actor in the family was enough, wrote out her resignation from Actors' Equity, made her sign it, and told her to get back to the typewriter.

How much of her writing is autobiographical only she can say. She was born and brought up in New York City (*Camilla Dickinson*) as Madeleine L'Engle Camp, daughter of Charles Wadsworth Camp, a critic, author, and playwright (" I didn't want to trade on his name so I dropped the Camp when I was first published "), and Madeleine Barnett Camp, a southern gentlewoman who gave her the family name of L'Engle. The Swiss-French family of L'Engles had come to Charleston and northern Florida in the 1700's. As a teen-ager she went to a boarding school in Switzerland (*And Both Were Young*) and came back to New York after college to make her way in The Arts (*The Small Rain*). In 1951 the Franklins left New York, her husband having given up the theater " forever," and moved to their summer home, a 1770 farmhouse in northwestern Connecticut (*Meet the Austins*). They bought the old general store in town, built it up for six years, found the dizzy pace of life in a small town too much, and returned to the peace and quiet of New York and the theater, first taking the family on a long camping trip (*The Moon by Night*). It's difficult to say how *A Wrinkle in Time* might be autobiographical; she has never explored outer space (though her husband wouldn't put it past her) but, without a foundation of characters she " knew," such a flight of fantasy would have no basis in reality and would lack its appeal.

Most of the young people who write Miss L'Engle want to know how one becomes a writer. Her answer is a simple " By writing." She explains that she always knew she was going to be a writer from the time she was able to hold a pencil, that writing is as essential a part of her as eating and breathing, and that she still gets cross if kept away from her desk more than a few days. Being unable to get words down on paper doesn't mean that she has stopped working, however; she always is turning over in her head various plots and characters, and her family has learned that unusual silences or absent-minded replies to their questions or extra time spent at the piano playing fugues means that she is in the middle of a scene and shortly will disappear into her room to write.

She also is asked by would-be writers how to get published. Her first advice is to start with what they know, with their own experiences, rather than trying too soon to make up plots and unfamiliar characters. Then she tells them not to start at the top in submitting their manuscripts but to try the small, non-paying magazines. It was in one of these that James Henle, then owner of Vanguard, saw a story by her and wrote asking if she had anything else to show. She replied that she just happened to be working on a novel, and when she finished *The Small Rain*, written in dressing rooms during *Uncle Harry*, he published it to critical approval.

Four of her eight novels have been for adults even though adolescents figure in most of them. When *Camilla Dickinson* came out in 1951 Harrison Smith in the *Saturday Review* compared it favorably as the female counterpart of a brand-new book, *The Catcher in the Rye*. Although none of her plays has reached Broadway, a few have been tried out in summer stock and the most recent one, *Letters of a Portuguese Nun*, will be made into a movie next year with Natalie Wood, and Miss L'Engle is at work on the scenario.

Lest anyone think a writer's life consists of nothing but cashing royalty checks, she always emphasizes that she has had her fair share of rejection slips and has never developed calluses to them. Each rejection is a personal affront, a biased opinion that her baby is a moron. Her family learned early that, when a manuscript is making the rounds and, instead of a phone call of acceptance, a small, thin envelope from a publisher arrives, there will be several days before the sun can shine again. They remember not too long ago when a publisher kept a manuscript three months (always a hopeful sign) and then returned it two days before Christmas, and they remember her brave but futile attempts to keep the joyous season joyous that year. The book? *A Wrinkle in Time*.

A recent article about her ended with " In the intervals between these activities she reads and leads a quiet life." ("HA!") Her quiet life consists of teaching three classes at the school her children attend, St. Hilda's and St. Hugh's, directing their Christmas pageant at the Cathedral of St. John the Divine, working on their book bazaar, and helping on various committees. Otherwise, her time is spent answering telephone calls from friends who think books and plays spring full-blown from her forehead with no necessity for time to write. She has often threatened to rent an office, with no telephone, to which she can escape during regular office hours; but somehow the thought of being out of touch with the family, not being home when the children get out of school, not being able to do the marketing and get dinner started early, has kept this only a dream. No matter how essential writing is to her, her family always seems to come first. To the world of literature she may be a writer who happens to be a mother, but to three children she is Mother, a warm, exciting woman who happens to be a writer. And to her husband, even after seventeen years, she is still the most fascinating, most exasperating, most stimulating, most outrageous, the most understanding and the most fantastic wife he has ever had.

It's Like This, Cat

written by EMILY NEVILLE

illustrated by EMIL WEISS

published by HARPER AND ROW 1963

BOOK NOTE

DAVE MITCHELL's pleasures, problems, and adventures are all part of a huge city's daily life. His pet, Cat, leads him into friendship with a troubled older boy and with a girl his own age. As Dave sees the contrast between his family life and that of his friends, he eventually perceives his own father as a kind, wise man. This is a contemporary book, showing a delight in New York city life and giving a truthful, sympathetic picture of a very real fourteen-year-old boy.

EXCERPT FROM THE BOOK

My father is always talking about how a dog can be very educational for a boy. This is one reason I got a cat.

My father talks a lot anyway. Maybe being a lawyer he gets in the habit. Also, he's a small guy with very little gray curly hair, so maybe he thinks he's got to roar a lot to make up for not being a big hairy tough guy. Mom is thin and quiet and when anything upsets her, she gets asthma. In the apartment — we live right in the middle of New York City — we don't have any heavy drapes or rugs, and Mom never fries any food because the doctors figure dust and smoke make her asthma worse. I don't think it's dust; I think it's Pop's roaring.

The big hassle that led to me getting Cat came when I earned some extra money baby-sitting for a little boy around the corner on Gramercy Park. I spent the money on a Belafonte record. This record has one piece about a father telling his son about the birds and the bees. I think it's funny. Pop blows his stack.

" You're not going to play that stuff in this house! " he roars. " Why aren't you outdoors, anyway? Baby-sitting! Baby-talk records! When I was your age, I made money on a newspaper-delivery route, and my dog Jeff and I used to go ten miles chasing rabbits on a good Saturday."

" Pop," I say patiently, " there are no rabbits out on Third Avenue. Honest, there aren't."

"Don't get fresh! " Pop jerks the plug out of the record player so hard the needle skips, which probably wrecks my record. So I get mad and start yelling too. Between rounds we both hear Mom in the kitchen starting to wheeze.

Pop hisses, " Now, see — you've gone and upset your mother! "

I slam the record player shut, grab a stick and ball, and run down the three flights of stairs to the street.

NEWBERY AWARD ACCEPTANCE

by *Emily Neville*

Out Where the Real People Are

I could not have believed four years ago that my somewhat ridiculous efforts at a typewriter could lead to the John Newbery
Medal. I hardly believe it now, even while I stand before this
great company of readers and in the unseen presence of forty-two
great writers of previous award-winning books. Will James, Hugh
Lofting, Dhan Mukerji, and others were heroes to me almost as
much as were their characters.

I am sure that all the winners who ever addressed you felt
humble at this great honor. Anyone would, for all of us dream
during much of our lives of being judged " best " at something,
while at the same time a protective mechanism warns us that it
probably won't happen. I am sure I have more reason to feel humble than most other medal winners. Each of them, at least, was
already an author when he sat down to write his book. I was
still in the would-be stage, a fiddler with a typewriter.

It is not only out of humility that I refer to my efforts at the typewriter as somewhat ridiculous. The typewriter was broken. The
children had dropped it once too often, and the ribbon had to be
cranked by hand. I recently ran across a few pages of that first version of *It's Like This, Cat*, and it was easily recognizable because
the print went dim about every ninth word.

When I started to work that day, I did have the usual drawer-
ful of rejected pieces: short stories, essays, children's tales. I had
had hopeful moments when working on all of them, but in the
end I had known that none were quite right; and the editors had
agreed.

But a New York Sunday newspaper had written me an encouraging letter, and I was groping around for a new story idea for them,

something light, set in New York City. I thought of Third Avenue and its stores, boys, and cats. I have a habit of talking to myself anyway, and I found myself, as a boy, telling off a disapproving, dog-loving father. It was fun.

I gave the balky typewriter ribbon a good crank and rattled along with the boyish grousing. At the end of the first page or so I stopped to reread, and a tingling thrill went up my spine. I thought: It's right, it's actually right! There is no excitement quite as great to an author — after the pages of nearly right, or all wrong — as feeling you have finally *hit* it. It is even more exciting to a would-be author.

The first exhilaration tapered off into some brow-furrowing thought. The rightness of the boy's chatter was a joy, but I realized I would have to dig for ideas about how boys and cats and fathers really act and feel. The digging went on slowly for about two years, as *Cat* grew from one short story to two stories, and finally to a book.

Here is a wonderful thing about having a story " in the works ": it makes me so much more alive to everything in the world of that story. While working on the book, I noticed things I had never seen before on Third Avenue, and right in my own home, too. I don't know that I reached conclusions about how parents *should* act toward children, or children toward parents. I just saw more acutely what did happen.

When I haven't got a story perking on the back burner, I think I must walk through life half-conscious; and maybe having a focus for my thoughts is a main reason for my wanting to be a writer. A great many of the scenes and conversations in *Cat* ran through my head while I was lying in bed not asleep, or sorting the laundry, or parking the car, or burning the cookies.

This partially answers the question many people ask me: When do you find time to write? Most of the homework is done before I ever get to a typewriter. Actual writing time comes in that blissful interval after children and husband have departed for school and work. After waiting seventeen years — from the birth of my eldest child to the day in 1961 when my youngest was triumphantly installed in kindergarten — I have the house to myself for a few hours each day.

There are temptations, naturally. Now that the house is peaceful, I could pick it up, do the housework, all that. But as Huck Finn resisted the temptation to steal unripe persimmons, so I resist the temptation to sweep. Dust, stay where you are, maybe someone will pick you up on Saturday.

Of course, there are the interruptions of school holidays, children home sick, dentist appointments, and other disasters. No wonder it took me most of two years to nurture the original story into a book.

To describe what happens between the writing of the first sentence and the last, I would like to quote Michel Montaigne in his " Apology for Raimond Sebond ": " Arts and sciences are not cast in a mould, but are formed and perfected by degrees, by often handling and polishing, as bears leisurely lick their cubs into form."

I like the picture of the author as mother bear. In completing a book, there's a great deal of poking and nuzzling, licking up a hair here, smoothing one down there; and there has to be some leisurely contemplation between improvements.

A book is never a solo operation, and mine was no exception. I know that a bow to one's publisher is routine, but this is more than a bow: the idea of trying to expand the original story into a boy's novel was Ursula Nordstrom's. The manuscript went back and forth between us several times, I putting in my licks and Harper's editors making encouraging noises — come on, a little more, grow a bit bigger — until the bear cub finally emerged, licked into form.

I am often asked if I used my family as models for the people in *Cat*. The answer is: Yes, both families. My teen-age son and also my daughters are physical models and a kind of perpetual sound track in my ear. When it comes to deeper feelings, for instance how Dave feels while in a street fight, I go back to my own family, the one I grew up in, and I remember my passionate fights on the nursery floor with my sister. What really goes on inside my sons' and daughters' heads is a puzzle to me, as to every mother.

There was a photograph of me, taken at eight or nine, which I have lost but remember well because of all the puzzled adult questions it aroused. Emily, what are you doing to the dog's neck? Why must you bunch up your dress like that? And why are you scowling in your brown Sunday-school hat, no one said you had to wear it.

I never tried to explain to them. I knew better. That was a long time ago, and I guess I have finally grown up, so I will explain now. My left hand on the dog was actually reining in a galloping Western cow pony. My right hand at my side was clutching a medieval sword. At the same time — since this was actually the year of the Al Smith vs. Herbert Hoover election and my family was firmly Republican — I marched stubbornly into the future with a brown derby on my head.

It makes a good story, it happens to be true, and it is a fairly good picture of many young readers' minds. Many a story-loving child lives in a world without qualifications or contradictions. He *is* his heroes, and he shall prevail. He knows bad things will happen to the bad people.

A writer for young children offends these convictions at his own peril. I received a letter: "Dear Mrs. Neville, I am 10½ and I think you are awful! You have a nerve writing things like that kitten being killed. It ruins the whole book (which is quite boring). The page I am referring to is silly, stupid and cruel. I could say a lot more about you, but I don't think I better. An ex-reader, Barbara."

I respect Barbara's position. I killed her kitten, and she hates me.

The kitten is still to her a symbol of warmth, love — Good. Nothing bad should have been allowed to happen to it. But how about the twelve- to sixteen-year-olds? They are old enough to know that a kitten is not a symbol. It is a breathing, feeling animal, and when it is mortally injured, a courageous person dispatches it.

This small illustration indicates, I think, a difference between a children's tale and a young adult's novel. I couldn't puncture a young child's convictions if I wanted to, and he may be drawing untold strength for the future from them; but an adult needs to look at the real world and keep his feet on it.

The real world, with its shadings of light and dark, its many-toned colors, is so much more beautiful than a rigid world of good and bad. It is also more confusing. I think the teen-age reader is ready for both.

I know, someone will say, " What, no imaginative stories for the big kids and the adults? " Of course, older children like flights of fancy, but these are by no means unrealistic. *Charlotte's Web*, by E. B. White, is a fantasy containing earthily real people and animals, as in last year's Newbery Medal winner, *A Wrinkle in Time*, by Madeleine L'Engle.

These two books, like most good juveniles, are good for ages eight to eighty. To return to what I was saying about the black-and-white world of little children, I might mention that my own eight-year-old sat entranced through *Charlotte's Web*, but flatly refused to believe the ending. He will come back to it and understand its philosophic rightness later.

One of the difficulties in constructing a realistic story — where, for instance, fairly nice people do some not very nice things — is that it is hard to keep suspense strong in the plot. The reader may not realize it, but often a heavy syrup of morality is what glues the fast-paced story together and keeps the reader on the edge of his chair, waiting to gallop on to victory with his brave and true hero. I think this approach is too great a price to pay for a good story (unless it is clearly in the entertainment-only class of Westerns and detectives). We are grown up now; let's stay out where the real people are.

If I should write about a boy who maliciously allowed a smaller child to get hurt, I would want him to be a real boy — unhappy, frustrated, having to expel his hatred somewhere out of sight of righteous adults. I would want my young reader to say, " Yeah, I can see how that kid felt so mean he just had to do that."

Sometimes parents and teachers fear that young readers will imitate undesirable characters if they can sympathize with them. I doubt it: a boy is better equipped to quell meanness in himself if he has once recognized what it *really* looks like rather than if he has always pictured himself as Sir Galahad.

This, then, is what seems to me to be the job for a writer of junior novels: to shine the flashlight on good things, and on bad things. It is not our job to preach that this is right and that is wrong. It is ours to show how and when and why Wrong can be so overwhelmingly attractive at a given moment — and how Right can be found in some very unlikely corners.

BIOGRAPHICAL NOTE

by *Glenn Neville*

Emily Cheney Neville

EMILY CHENEY NEVILLE is a slender, blue-eyed blonde young woman of little more than average height. She is very pretty. Her most apparent characteristic is an imperturbability that is constantly remarkable to her family and friends.

She would object to being called serene, and she would be right. She is not placid. She is not passive. She is not meek. But her gift for rising above the little annoyances of life is unusual. She ignores them. This ability is a part of her charm as a person, and it has aided her concentration as a writer.

I am tempted to say that she is complexly simple, or simply complex.

Emily was born on December 28, 1919, in Manchester, Connecticut, the seventh and last child of Mr. and Mrs. Howell Cheney. Her father, a distinguished industrialist and educator, was for many years a member of the Yale (University) Corporation. He was a pioneer in the field of industrial schooling; the Howell Cheney High School in Manchester, one of the nation's finest vocational institutions, is among his monuments. He devoted his life to the proposition that educational opportunity should not be the sole prerogative of the well-to-do. Emily's mother was the former Anne Bunce, member of an old Connecticut family much interested in the arts. Both the Bunce and Cheney families knew Mark Twain during his residence in Hartford, Connecticut. Such a heritage surely kindled Emily's love of reading and writing. It is noteworthy that some reviewers, unaware of her background, have compared her with Mark Twain.

But past is prologue; let us be present.

Emily Neville lives with her husband, five children, two large dogs, and a cat in an apartment on Gramercy Park, Manhattan, New York City. The cat, named Cat, is successor to the late, sincerely lamented Midnight. The apartment is sprawling, inelegant, and homey. It is on the ground floor (no need to worry about who lives under so many drumming feet), book-lined, darker than one would wish, grimy with the soot that emerges endlessly from New York's chimneys. It demands cleaning as a ship demands paint: when you have finished with one end of it, you go back and start all over again at the other. In this setting, Emily maintains method and amity. Part of her success is that she is a good cook, short-order or long-range.

People frequently ask, " When does she ever find time to write? " Mostly it is during those blessed two hours of weekday mornings when the house is hers alone, except for the snoring of lazy dogs. But she is no miser of writing hours and no stickler for rules.

She is a companionable wife, always ready to drop everything, plan a trip, and go somewhere. She is an affectionate and attentive mother, who believes children should be *read to*. She is a student and constructive critic of New York's public school system. She goes to school board and parents' meetings. She is co-circulation manager of the *Parent News* of Public School 40, the alma mater of the children: Tam, nineteen; Dessie, fifteen; Marcy, eleven — the girls; Glenn, Jr., seventeen, and Alexander, eight — the boys.

Emily has always written: as a little girl in the Cheney Family School; as a student in the Oxford School, Hartford; at Bryn Mawr, where she majored in economics; in New York as a reporter and writer successively on two major newspapers. (Marriage ended her promising journalistic career, for better or for worse.) Summers, at Keene Valley in the high-peak area of the Adirondacks, she writes in a studio improvised from an attic room of the family's isolated house.

Her literary roots are varied. They entwine a good deal of English history, both factual and romantic. She is not a Mrs. Miniver Cheevy, wholly immersed in the olden days (she reads almost anything good or suppposed-to-be-good that comes along), but a tale of the knights of old can still set her dancing.

It is a happy thing that she decided to write about Kids-and-Cats-on-Third-Avenue instead of the men of the Round Table. She really knows all about the Kids-and-Cats and the other stranger-than-fiction characters that enliven the crazy-quilt Manhattan world. Her romance with old English heroes is delicious but vague. It probably stems from the days when first her mother and then her governess, a stoutly patriotic British lady, fascinated her with Arthurian stories. She read, and read, and read.

She was no bookworm, though; she was more of a tomboy. She delighted in escaping the family estate and exploring the then sparsely populated countryside on her bicycle, with her dog Jump barking alongside.

Her childhood gave her a zest for the outdoors that has never diminished. She is a fair tennis player, a golfer with a picturebook swing, an excellent swimmer with a predilection for ice-cold water, a mountain climber, and a fisherman. *Fisherman* is used deliberately. She is not a *fisherwoman*. She is one of the best fly-casters in the country.

What she can do on a trout stream! Attired in her favorite costume — sweat shirt, holey sneakers, and faded jeans — she will float out a No. 16 Royal Coachman at the end of a 5-X leader, itself attached to a tapered line and thence to a three-ounce rod, and the trout just wait on queue. Many times we have watched her, my fishing friends and I, dressed in our dear best, booted and furred by the name houses of the tackle world, as she netted the best fish of the day. We would turn to each other and exclaim, among other less printable things, " Oh, help! "

I hope that I have given at least an inkling of Emily's personality. She is indeed a " simply complex " woman.

THE NEWBERY AWARD **1965**

Shadow of a Bull

written by MAIA WOJCIECHOWSKA

illustrated by ALVIN SMITH

published by ATHENEUM 1964

BOOK NOTE

THE people of the Spanish town of Arcangel expect Manolo Olivar
to fight his first bull at twelve and like his father to become the
greatest bullfighter in all Spain. Supported and taught in lore of
the bull ring by six of his dead father's friends, Manolo is never
even asked if he wishes to fight. His moment of courage does come
in fighting the bull, in finding that he possesses the courage he
doubted, and in announcing that he does not wish to be a bullfighter. This book thoughtfully explains the Spaniard's love of the
bull ring and adoration of a matador as a national hero.

Illustrations

from the Caldecott Medal Books

1956-1965

Illustration by

FEODOR ROJANKOVSKY

From *Frog Went A-Courtin'* retold by JOHN LANGSTAFF

Published in 1955 by HARCOURT, BRACE AND COMPANY

One-fourth reduction

"Without my Uncle Rat's consent,
I would not marry the president!"

Illustration by

MARC SIMONT

From *A Tree Is Nice* by Janice May Udry

Published in 1956 by Harper & Brothers

One-half reduction

ple have picnics there too. And the baby
es his nap in his buggy in the shade.

Home on the island, you pull in
the sailboat, chain the motorboat fast
to its mooring, pull the rowboats
high off the beach.

Mr. Smith hurries by with a
boatload of lobster traps that he has
been taking up.

Over in Swain's Cove, Mr. Billings
puts extra lines on the wings of his
seaplane.

Fishermen put extra lines on
herring boats and scalloping boats.

At Franky Day's boat yard
up Benjamin River, and at Hal
Vaughn's boat yard up Horseshoe
Creek, men are working with the
tide pulling up sloops and yawls,
ketches and motorboats;
shackling chains,
tying ropes,
making things fast,
battening down,
getting ready.

Illustration by

ROBERT McCLOSKEY

From *Time of Wonder* by ROBERT McCLOSKEY

Published in 1957 by THE VIKING PRESS

One-half reduction

Once upon a time a poor widow, getting on in years, lived in a small cottage beside a grove which stood in a little valley. This widow, about whom I shall tell you my tale, had patiently led a very simple life since the day her husband died. By careful management she was able to take care of herself and her two daughters.

Illustration by

BARBARA COONEY

From *Chanticleer and the Fox*. Adapted by Barbara Cooney

from *The Canterbury Tales* by Geoffrey Chaucer

Published in 1958 by Thomas Y. Crowell Company

One-third reduction

Illustration by

MARIE HALL ETS

From *Nine Days to Christmas* by

MARIE HALL ETS and AURORA LABASTIDA

Published in 1959 by THE VIKING PRESS

One-third reduction

"This is the way we will pull your piñata up and down, to fool the children when they are blindfolded and trying to hit it."

"But I don't want them to hit it!" said Ceci.

* *

A train of travelers was approaching. Leading
the procession was a magnificent sleigh drawn
by three white horses.

Illustration by

NICOLAS SIDJAKOV

From *Baboushka and the Three Kings* by RUTH ROBBINS

Published in 1960 by Parnassus Press

One-fifth reduction

In the sleigh rode three men, splendid figures, wearing jeweled crowns and cloaks of crimson and ermine. Men on horseback followed the sleigh and behind them trudged men on foot.

Illustration by

MARCIA BROWN

From *Once a Mouse . . . a fable cut in wood* by Marcia Brown

Published in 1961 by Charles Scribner's Sons

One-third reduction

The hermit missed nothing of all this, and chided the beast. "Without me," he would say to him, "you would be a wretched little mouse, that is, if you were still alive. There is no need to give yourself such airs."

6

Illustration by

EZRA JACK KEATS

From *The Snowy Day* by EZRA JACK KEATS

Published in 1962 by THE VIKING PRESS

One-third reduction

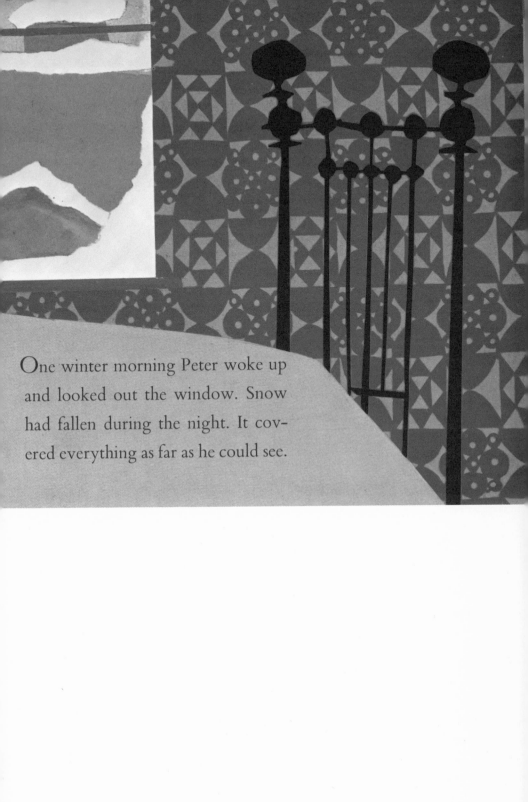

One winter morning Peter woke up
and looked out the window. Snow
had fallen during the night. It covered everything as far as he could see.

But the wild things cried, "Oh please don't go—
we'll eat you up—we love you so!"
And Max said, "No!"

Illustration by

MAURICE SENDAK

From *Where the Wild Things Are* by MAURICE SENDAK

Published in 1963 by HARPER & BROTHERS

One-third reduction

The wild things roared their terrible roars and gnashed their terrible teeth
and rolled their terrible eyes and showed their terrible claws
but Max stepped into his private boat and waved good-bye

Illustration by

BENI MONTRESOR

From *May I Bring a Friend?* by BEATRICE SCHENK DE REGNIERS

Published in 1964 by ATHENEUM

One-fifth reduction

EXCERPT FROM THE BOOK

People always talked about Manolo on the streets. They talked about him, not behind his back, but all around him, in front and alongside and behind, not caring at all if he was within earshot or even standing and listening to them. It was a habit of the people of Arcangel.

And there was a reason for it. There have always been five things that people fear: war, disease, flood, hunger, and death. And of these, death has always been feared the most.

In Spain, however, the people have found a way of cheating death. They summon it to appear in the afternoon in the bull ring, and they make it face a man. Death — a fighting bull with horns as weapons — is killed by a bullfighter. And the people are there watching death being cheated of its right.

In Arcangel the people had had their very own killer of death, Juan Olivar. He had been their own hero and their magician. Juan Olivar made their dreams come true: victory of man over death. The old saying, "Today as yesterday, tomorrow as today, and always the same," was no longer true.

But one day their killer of death met a bull that would not be deprived of his right. And the people of Arcangel, robbed of their pride, deprived of their magician, lost their hero. And when they lost him, each day became exactly like the one that preceded it and the one that would follow it.

Now the town of Arcangel was waiting, for that hero had left them a son who was growing up to once again take arms against death. They were waiting for the son to be like his father.

ACCEPTANCE PAPER

by *Maia Wojciechowska*

Shadow of a Kid

I saw her, for the first and only time, on a rainy November afternoon in 1962. We both boarded the Fifth Avenue bus, going downtown, at Forty-second Street. We both found seats at the back of the bus, and she sat across the aisle from me.

She wore glasses, had straight, long, mousey brown hair, an armful of books, an alpaca-lined raincoat, and a sad, small face. She was ugly and she knew it.

I imagined that she was the only child of an intellectual couple no longer married to each other. Her mother had a full-time job and would not be home until six. At least two evenings a week the mother took courses toward her master's; maybe once a week she went out with a man. Her father was a writer addicted to collecting, and adding to, obscure reference books. When she was little, before her parents were divorced, she was the center of their world. Now she was very much alone. Her intelligence made her a displaced person. It isolated her from other children and, even more, from adults.

All this I imagined. What I could see was that she had an old cat, or possibly dog, which shed gray hair, and that she peeled potatoes, because her fingers were stained the way they get from potatoes, unless it was some chemical from her school lab. Among her schoolbooks were two library books with their spines away from me, but with the stamp of the New York Public Library system on the accordion of pages. They were too thick to be children's books. She was the kind of child, I decided, who would get books every year for Christmas and her birthday.

I stared at the girl until she looked at me, wrinkled her nose, and turned her head away. With that visual dismissal I suddenly knew that what I really wanted to do with my life was to write the kind of books she would like. Not adult books, which she read even now, but books for her — for her age, for her needs, for her intelligence.

This special girl, unlike the others, would not grow older. For me she would always be twelve, her mind fifteen. She would never be part of my world, and I would never be part of hers. The only thing that I could hope for was to build a bridge for her, a bridge of books. Not from her world into mine, but from her childhood into her adulthood. If I could only do that, she need never jump, for the jump from one world to the other is a long and dangerous one — and I did not want this child to fall.

That evening I began to rewrite *Shadow of a Bull*. I had recently finished it as a short story, and already it had been rejected by a magazine. I decided to use the story I wrote for adults as an outline of a children's book. Not any children's book. It was to be *her* book. As I converted thirteen pages into fourteen chapters, I was worried about the unlucky publisher who might publish this book intended for an audience of one.

When the book did come out, I began to wait for a letter from the kid on the bus. I would have recognized her by the way she'd write. But she didn't write. The adults wrote, but not one child wrote me a letter until after the Newbery Award announcement.

I still have not heard from my girl. Maybe one day she will write; maybe she won't. Whether she does or doesn't, I have already written an answer to her:

You ask me why I love Spain. You can love a country as you can love a man, for all the wrong reasons or for silly ones. I love Spain because I have been more miserable there than in any other place. The first time, in 1942, I was miserable because I had seen Manolete fight two bulls, and the beauty of the man, the strangeness of his art, filled me with physical pain. I knew that the pain, surrounded by fear, curiosity, and love, could not last. With the greed of a child I wanted to make it last. And that was why I was miserable that first day in Spain.

The second time I brought my unhappiness with me and found that Spain could take it in stride, as if this country were a place for storing and keeping such things. When I left, I left it there.

The third time Spain struck back at me. By then I was divorced, and Spain seemed to know how to punish a woman for being alone. It can be utterly cruel, this country of my soul, but cruel in the way a good man can sometimes be cruel. I remember sitting in a café and hearing an elderly Spaniard at the next table address a passing woman who walked with a cane: "If it were not for your limp, I could love you," he said. I had lived in Spain long enough by then to realize that he was paying her a great compliment, and the corners of her mouth went up, ever so slightly, in a smile because she had understood.

I guess I love all of Spain the way I love all of Poland, in a vague way that has to do mostly with being proud of their past, for Spain and Poland, today's backward lands, have known the drunkenness of conquest, the glory of dominion. But I love the southern part of Spain, Andalusia, in a very personal way. Maybe one day you'll fly over it, not in a jet but in a prop plane. You'll see a desolate mosaic of aridity, with strange outposts of houses in the middle of nowhere, each one like a beggar's castle perched on the highest mountain ridge. I've often wondered who lives in those isolated places, where a trip for a loaf of bread must be like a hegira. From the air, the spires of churches will seem to reach up to you like so many accusing fingers. But it is the lacework of the olive groves and the perfect round symmetry of the bullrings that, I hope, you'll love to see the most.

It is the people, of course, that make Andalusia special. Yet the people are far from handsome; they are rather small, shabby, and look-alike, until you see their eyes and discover that each one is a Hamlet or a Lear, a Juliet or a Medea. It is because there are no ordinary people in Andalusia that I have come to love this part of Spain so much.

Yes, Manolo was a boy there once, and he lived. He had a face with a long nose and very sad eyes, and he stood in a bar behind a counter that reached to his mouth. The upper part of his face looked very much like Manolete's when he was that age. I used to go into the bar every day for two months just to look at him. And so did a lot of old men, the ones who never went to a bullfight after Manolete's death. They too looked at him, and I grew very much afraid for him because I thought those old men needed a new god, a new hero, and he, the little boy, looked so like their old one. It was through this fear that I first thought of the boy as a character for a short story. But I didn't write it then, and not for a long time.

When I did write it, it was as a book for you. *Shadow* was mostly about pride and being locked in. I say pride rather than self-respect, because in Spain the word *pride* encompasses so much — honor and dignity and self-esteem. You'll find that sort of pride in others, more often in the poor than in the rich, and you'll find it in yourself. Because you are you, you'll respect it wherever you find it in spite of what others may say about it. That sort of pride, sometimes — most of the time — makes life harder than it needs to be. But without pride, life is less.

About being locked in. Sometimes one lives in a prison without a key, without hope of a pardon. Sometimes one never gets out. And sometimes, when one gets out, it is at a cost in pride, and sometimes at a cost in success. It all depends on who built the prison. If you've built the prison yourself, you should never pay in pride. If others have built it, I hope you'll pay them in success. So, you see, *Shadow of a Bull* is not a book about bullfighting after all.

I have written another book for you, *Odyssey of Courage*, and that one is all about failure. The kind that deprives one of less than it gives. Not a personal failure. For there is so much that others have confused for you. They have put labels on things, and then they got the labels all mixed up. You'll see many doors labeled Success, but often, on going through those doors, you will have passed into Failure. So I wrote *Odyssey* not about a man called Cabeza de Vaca, but about how he discovered that one door had the wrong label on it.

I hope to live a long time, because I want to keep writing for you. You see, while waiting for your letter, and even before, I decided that you'll never grow old; but of course you will. No matter. I will still write for you as if you could not get past your thirteenth birthday. And that's an important time. It is a time of finding out about what life will be like. I want to give you a glimpse of the choices you have before you, of the price that will be asked of you. And don't fool yourself; you will be asked to pay.

When you know what life has to sell, for how much, and what it can give away free, you will not live in darkness. I hope that in books you'll find your light, and that by this light you may cross from one shore of love to another, from your childhood into your adulthood. I hope that some of the light will come from my books and that, because of this light, life will lose its power to frighten you.

by *Selden Rodman*

Maia Wojciechowska

I MET Maia Wojciechowska in 1948 or 1949. With anyone else I'd be sure about the date. But not with Maia. I had already begun to lose track of time. It's one of many things I've lost track of since. Age, locality, sequence, money, a rational explanation of politics, were other dispensable items I began to forget about.

She was nineteen then. I saw her for the first time from my window in New York, overlooking the four clay courts that then graced Prospect Hill between Forty-first Street and the East River. She was serving with grace and abandon – double-faults, one after another – and she was laughing infectiously between each out-ball. It was spring (I think) or it could have been winter, because Maia plays tennis in all seasons, and so do I. Then as now, tennis, the arts, and beautiful women were obsessions; and I could see, before the day was over, that I was going to learn a lot that I didn't know about all three. She was dressed in a blue turtle-neck jersey and a pair of the shortest white shorts imaginable. No socks or shoes – she doesn't wear either to this day, even when playing on hot cement. And her brown legs (though she is only five feet, four inches) seemed very long and shapely. "Those," said an old pro on the sidelines, who had never been known to comment on anything a woman had but her backhand and approach shots, "are the *longest* legs I have ever seen." He sighed deeply. " – And the nakedest."

Maia was writing poetry at that time, and someone had told her that I was a poet. She looked up at my window, smiled, and served an ace. In a few minutes we were playing tennis. And an hour later we were having an ice-cream soda (it *must* have been spring) in the drugstore across the street, and she was straightening me out on modern European history — from the Polish point of view.

One other thing I noted on that sunny day that was to change my life: Maia and children. Most American teen-agers are busy convincing themselves and the world that they are adults. If they are with children, they look bored — or play at being Little Mothers. Not Maia. She had taken a job as assistant to Elwood and Sarah Palfrey Cooke, both of whom were giving tennis lessons at Tudor City. They had a baby daughter, Diana, and part of Maia's job was to baby-sit. But Maia never sits. Nor does she recognize the existence of babies — as babies. There are no " inferiors " in her world: only people who are alive and people who are dead, people who are stimulating and people who bore. Babies, of course, are always alive and stimulating, before " adults " reduce them to the "normal" state of incuriosity and indifference. In Diana's company, I noticed, Maia was not only playing Diana's games, but enjoying them; not only laughing at Diana's " jokes " but inventing fantasies of her own that *Diana* laughed at. And without any self-consciousness, without any looking over her shoulder to see whether grownups might be thinking *she* was childish.

I noticed something else. With people of her own age, or ten to twenty years older, Maia spoke her mind. No matter how unfactual, irrational, or weird her opinions were — and some were weird indeed — she would hold to them with a·fanatical (albeit witty) intolerance, and go into gales of laughter over such preposterous notions as (for instance) that Churchill had saved the free world, that America was a democracy, or that Poland had been the victim of its own unprincipled power-politics, arrogance, and anti-Semitism. But in the presence of old people, to whom Americans give scant consideration or respect, Maia, I also noticed, was consistently kind, patient, and attentive, going out of her way to make them feel that their experience was something youth could profit by.

Needless to say, I fell in love with Maia Wojciechowska. We were married later on, and even had a daughter of our own, and later went our separate ways. But that is another story.

She had arrived in New York, the day before I met her, with ten cents in her pocket. She had walked out onto the Brooklyn Bridge, tossed the ten cents in the river, and then walked back to Tudor City, deciding to apply for the job with the Cookes in the morning, and if she failed to get it, to hitchhike her way back to California. She had run away from her family there, not because she was unhappy, but because their way of life put too many constraints on her carefree temperament. They wanted her to continue school at Immaculate Heart College; she wanted to write poetry, play tennis, and see the world.

I met her family in Los Angeles later: father, mother, younger and older brother, all wonderful people, and all (at that time) living in a wonderfully intense haze of unreality, fighting and re-fighting the battles of Polish nationalism, all quite convinced that some day, somehow the Poland they had known before the war would rise from its ashes.

Mme. Wojciechowska, kindly, tireless, refusing to speak a word of the hated English tongue, carried on the struggle with *food*. Cakes, pastries, stuffed red cabbage, *bigos*, Lithuanian *kalbas*, dumplings and more dumplings. Not only for the family, who were eating and drinking tea every two hours or so all day long and far into the night, but for the entire Polish colony of Los Angeles, which exploited her hospitality mercilessly.

Colonel Wojciechowski, who had been aide to Field Marshal Pilsudski, and during the war Chief of Staff of the Polish Air Force based in England, was at that time delivering telephone books from house to house. He had had a good job teaching languages at the military school at Monterey, but had quarreled with the authorities — over our failure to take a stronger stand against Russia and her satellites, I think — and his pride was much too great to permit him to trade on his illustrious past in securing a similar post. He was the most wrongheaded, intolerant, courageous, kind, and loveable man I have ever known.

The eldest son, who supported the family as a television cameraman for NBC, had all of his father's qualities, including his great sense of humor. The younger son was young enough to be on his way to being thoroughly Americanized, but without losing his devotion to the family or the Church. I used to play bridge with the three of them one winter. Between the fierce arguments generated by this game — which the Colonel played like a military campaign, snapping his tricks like whips and reaching for his imaginary dueling pistols when questioned about the bid — and the incidental political warfare, which sometimes caused exasperated would-be sleepers in the apartment above to stamp on the ceiling, I sometimes felt I was lucky to be leaving the table alive.

I think that Maia inherited her combative and restlessly adventurous spirit, as well as her courage and generosity, from her father. Before the war, when she must have been less than ten, her father took her on frequent flights in his military aircraft and once dropped her in a parachute. When they were forced to flee from Poland, finally settling in a refugee colony in southern France, she hated the waiting, the inactivity, the bickering, the sense that her father was fighting the hated conquerors while she could do no more than make faces at them or fling stones and curses from a safe distance. To come to America later and be told by Americans, whose home were intact, that *they* had " won the war " was even more galling. Poland had been " betrayed " and nobody had " won "— except possibly the Russians.

It was in the late fifties, during a lonely visit of several months to Spain, that Maia began to take writing seriously. She had always written, easily, fluently, and at considerable length, but without much discipline or direction. Her poems had been romantic outpourings, but quite formless. While our daughter was very young, Maia had started but never finished half a dozen novels. They were about herself and reflected her restlessness. As wife and mother she had felt as constrained as she had in school and with her family. Long before she went to Spain, she had " escaped " into a succession of part-time jobs — poll-taker, private detective, translator, broadcaster (for Radio Free Europe), tennis teacher, beautician, editor. During the year we spent in Mexico, she had considered becoming a bullfighter, had " trained " with young hopefuls, and had made several passes in a ring with a small but dangerously active animal. When Fidel Castro was still in the Sierra Maestra, she had flown to the Caribbean with the promise that she'd be dropped among his guerrillas, only to be dumped in the Bahamas. But it was in Spain that Maia experienced for the first time enough real hardship and heartache to want to write about other people.

She had, to be sure, written a children's book, *Market Day for Ti André*, in Haiti in 1951. It was slight, but already touched with Maia's characteristic magic — a use of English made completely fresh by the circumstance that it had been acquired after childhood and entirely by ear. Everything in the story was seen through the eyes of an unspoiled six-year-old. " Baskets so big that two little boys like Ti André could easily hide in one of them . . . ," " cabbages twice as big at Ti André's head . . . ," etc. If the book had flaws, they were my responsibility. I helped enough with the grammar and styling (Maia no longer needs this kind of help) to smooth some of the piquancy out of her way of saying things. Also, the machinery of dreams and coincidental encounters may have become overly complicated as a result of my anxiety to give the illustrator, Wilson Bigaud, every chance to score. I had been engaged in Haiti for two years directing the mural painting of the Cathedral St.-Trinité by eight self-taught artists, and Bigaud had been the star performer. He had never made drawings in ink, and I was as eager to see him win acclaim in this field as I was to see Maia's text come up to the drawings.

Maia's subsequent books, those that have won her high praise and awards, suffer from no such meddling. At least not on my part. Maia may need help with her life (who doesn't?) or with her politics, her plots, and her grammar, but in the larger questions of fictional artistry — what to write about; the ways to build character with insight and compassion; how to make people talk so that the question whether they could have been " just this way in real life " never crosses the reader's mind—Maia's intuitions never seem to fail her. *Shadow of a Bull* and *Odyssey of Courage* have been perceptively praised in public by enough people to make anything I might add superfluous.

The most essential ingredient of all consequential art, and certainly the rarest quality in modern fiction, is nobility. The capacity to seek the truth not out of egotism, or out of some pseudoscientific belief that it can be isolated from morality, but in order to console, arm, and exalt Man. . . . It is fortunate that from now on the young will be reminded of this, because they stand the best chance of profiting by it. But Maia Wojciechowska assumes the desirability of noble aims so naturally, and expresses it so well, that even adults may get the message.

Only the Best

by *Carolyn Horovitz*

In contemplating an appraisal of the Newbery Award books for
the past ten years, I have to deal first of all with a reluctance to be
frankly critical and a melancholy realization that the award is not
always given to the best book. Most distressing of all is the realization that books really worthy of that appellation " distinguished "
are rare. That a review of the past ten years should be disturbing
hardly seems consonant with the tremendous increase we have
witnessed in the field of children's publications. Yet, as William
Lipkind points out in the *Saturday Review* for May 12, 1962, we
are in danger of suffering from too much success.

> But a shadow of doubt falls on the jubilation as soon as one
> takes a critical glance at the books themselves. In all this
> plenty one thing is scarce: the book of high quality. Fairly
> good books are less rare. Their number increases as the total
> output goes up, but the proportion of them in the total out-
> put appears to be diminishing. . . . Clearly, the industrious
> pursuit of profit in a boom market leaves little time for the
> gradual maturation of creative work and the cultivation of
> budding talent. And artistic integrity seldom wins when
> pitted against mercenaries.*

It is perhaps the part of wisdom to shrug and say that the award
can only be an accolade, a recognition of what is written — it
cannot actually create the works. And this is true. However, to
review the awards of the past ten years without attempting to put
them into some sort of critical focus is to betray the true intent of
the award and to make of it an instrument which immobilizes
criticism instead of galvanizing it. If this appraisal of Newbery
Award Winners is to have any value at all, it should put forth an
invitation to dispute whether or not we are doing all that we can

*William Lipkind, " Fairy Tales," *Saturday Review*, May 12, 1962.

to see that this award gives encouragement and stimulus to what is fine and not necessarily to what is popular or what is merely competently and professionally done. In this time, when the mass of books produced for children is greater than at any other time in the history of book publishing, the problem of discernment is highly important for those adults who are responsible for what books the child will find available to him.

What is necessary, I believe, is to provoke a discussion in print among librarians and critics of literature as to some of the qualities we hope to find in a distinguished work; to engage in a discussion as to what criticism is; to determine how we are to engage in the critical art. For criticism is an art and different from the quick, reviewing appraisal of books with which we are familiar.

Criticism will vary from individual critic to individual critic, and should be responded to as coming from a certain person rather than from some abstract place on high where rigid, immutable standards have been intoned. Criticism will only grow in stature and usefulness as discussions grow, perceptions will sharpen as viewpoints are shared, and sensitivities will become more acute as areas of agreement and disagreement are carefully delineated. The field of children's literature needs this exercise desperately. There must be a firming of muscles, an aggressive, passionate approach to the selection of the award, if we are not to become passive oppressors of children in the sense that Paul Hazard used the word:

> But to misshape young souls, to profit by a certain facility that one may possess, to add to the number of indigestible and sham books, to give oneself too easily the airs of a moralist and scholar, to cheat in quality — that is what I call oppressing children.*

The problem, really, is not one of lack of concern so much as it is a matter of emphasis, of giving lip-service instead of the close scrutiny, analysis, comparison and discussion that the subject of quality demands. Exhaustive, painstaking, critical evalu-

*Paul Hazard, *Books, Children and Men*, p. 45. The Horn Book, Inc., 1944.

ation of these Newbery Award books is not going to appear in a
paper this short, nor in this setting. These books are represented
here in an appreciative sense generally. There seems to me to be
tremendous variation among them. Two, however, appear impressive in their qualities of greatness and achieve unique places for
themselves. One of these is this year's recipient, *Shadow of a
Bull;* the other is Scott O'Dell's *Island of the Blue Dolphins.*

The towering qualities of these books have to do with fineness
and depth of emotional power, of carefully controlled craftsman-
ship, of a firm welding between the writer's own emotional experiences and convictions with the fiber of the book. These are
books devoid of tricks, but rippling with power and grace, fitting
and uniting plot and language.

In *The Art of Fiction**, Henry James likens idea and form to
the needle and thread, saying that as tailors cannot achieve much
by using the needle without the thread, so the writer cannot do
much unless both idea and form work together. Each writer, in
seeking to present his own particular way of looking at his subject matter, must create his own use of language. Language affects
thought and thought affects language. Both of these books demonstrate the intrinsic relationship of form and content, a welding
which is reflected in unusual simplicity and economy of style. In
their creative use of language both writers display themselves as
artists, moving us with an indestructible combination of form and
content.

The usual phrase, the familiar technique obscures the relationship between writer and reader in most books. We read that the
hero's throat tightened, his pulse quickened, the temples throbbed,
the eyes danced — and so on. The ready made phrase is easy to
use and is the trademark of a work which is assembled instead of
being created from the inner compulsion of the writer who cannot honestly release his meaning without first struggling through
to the unique, fresh expression, the clean, uncluttered line. When
I say that the stock expression obscures, I do not mean to say

*Henry James, *The Art of Fiction*, Oxford University Press, 1948.

that the writer fails to get his point across. There is, however, a lack of fine discernment, a lack of inner clarity. In short, the author's individual power of portrayal is submerged by phrases which accomplish their work too well, obliterating in their wide swath the differentiating nuances which a simpler, more direct telling would at least leave open to the reader's participating imagination. A stock phrase is apt to elicit a stock response. It is even more possible that certain phrases and metaphors, having been seen by the reader many times, will cease to elicit any response at all. The extension of experience which is to be gained from fiction comes from the blending of the writer's and reader's imagination by the elusive quality of the written word which draws the reader into a struggle and deepens his emotional tone. A writer's style has the quality of a paradox: understanding must be created so that it is like a web spun for the emotions, strong and secure so that meaning lives — and yet of such fragile subtlety that the reader is held, enthralled unaware.

To perceive what can happen when language is renewed by the intensity of the author's vision, pick up the *Island of the Blue Dolphins*. Read it aloud. Listen to the rhythm of the words, the undertow of emotion, the sense of reality and understatement, the sustaining of character and mood. A child can read this book with emotional satisfaction — and so can an adult. For the relationship between reader and writer is tough and yet of infinite complexity, dignity and simplicity. The dynamic interplay of an heroic courage with the performance of those mundane tasks needed to sustain life is at once a reflection and an amplification of the experience of all men. According to the level of perception that a reader brings this story, so will meaning be determined. There is the successful execution of a girl Robinson Crusoe story, a story told with sustained conflict from beginning to end. On this level, the meaning is simply that she survives. There is also the philosophical level in which man's needs to kill for food are weighed against his needs for companionship. The girl, Karana, is portrayed in such intimate and close relationship with the natural elements of her background, the earth, the sea, the animals, the fish, that the reader is given both the terror and beauty of life itself. It is a book to make the reader *wonder*.

The conflict of *Shadow of a Bull* is laid on the line, so to speak, immediately at the beginning of the story. And the author, Maia Wojciechowska, deals with the necessary expository material at great length in the beginning of the book. All through the book, however, this basic expository material is interwoven because it is not only necessary to " get the story going " but is in itself an intrinsic part of the story which deals with the legacy of a hero, the expectations of a town and the development of a boy to the point where he can recognize and choose his own values. Although many will say this is a story of courage much like Armstrong Sperry's *Call It Courage*, it is more than learning to deal with fear. True, the boy has to acknowledge fear and deal with its power, but the final resolution has to do with facing the values of life. Symbolically, the boy chooses life. In many ways, this story is symbolic and proceeds with the style and rhythm of a ritual. The simplicity and dignity of the story is not only revealed in the spare, economical writing style, but the morality of this approach to writing is also part of the boy's struggle to find a way to face his problem:

> . . . He must find a way of fooling the people. He must stand away from the bull's horns, so that they would not touch him. He would have his back to the people, and they would not see.
>
> He got up and practiced the deception in front of the mirror. It seemed easy. But what of honor, he thought then. A most important thing, the *pundonor*. As a Spaniard, he could not live without it, or if he did, he would live in shame. It would be far better to be gored or even to be killed than to lose his sense of honor. No, he could not fool them because he could not fool himself. It would have to be done as was expected of him, with honor or not at all.*

The story itself is told with honor, without flinching from the

*Maia Wojciechowska, *Shadow of a Bull*, pp. 110-111, Atheneum Press, 1964.

basic ugliness and danger of bullfighting, without over-emotionalizing or making a fictional device out of the background. The author treats her subject of bullfighting with dignity, respect and authority. Her attitude toward writing, I believe, is beautifully exemplified as she relates the boy's difficulties of moving a cape in the pass known as the veronica. After he learned, with much painful practice, to do a veronica right he then tried some of the fancy passes and found that they were much easier. " He decided to practice all the passes the bullfighters do while taking the bull away from the horse. These were the passes with which they tried to outshine each other: the *chicuelinas*, the *gaoneras*, the *reboleras*, the *mariposas*."

But his happiness was short-lived when one of the *aficionadas* told him that the fancy passes were not necessary. His father used only four passes and he was the greatest of them all. The passes his father used were the simplest but the hardest of them all to perform. Perhaps this is one of the most profound comments the book has to make — and to demonstrate. For the writing is deceptively simple, the plot is straightforward in an inevitable way. There are no tricks; the book simply accumulates power as it proceeds. Here is a book, " distinguished " in its simplicity and dignity, a book concerned with beauty and terror, a book to make the reader *wonder*.

In using the word "wonder" with both these books, I am thinking of the way Herbert Read in " Surrealism and the Romantic Principle " expresses what it is that such books do for us: " Art . . . is more than description or ' reportage '; . . . it is an act of renewal. It renews vision, it renews language; but most essentially it renews life itself by enlarging the sensibility, by making men more conscious of the terror and the beauty, the wonder of the possible forms of being."*

The uncomfortable part of appraising Newbery books is that, as

---

*Herbert Read, "Surrealism and the Romantic Principle," an essay included in *The Philosophy of Modern Art*, Faber & Faber, Ltd.

Esther Averill* found in appraising Caldecott picture books over
a twenty-year period, there is no common bond. There were
other books published during the last ten years which were at
least equal, and some much better than those that received the
award. This is not to say that these books do not make a contribution to the field of children's literature. It is simply a raising
of the question: how do we apply this word " distinguished "?

A most popular and original book is *A Wrinkle in Time*.
The book sparkles with the author's vitality and imagination and
proceeds at a fast pace with recognizable character types. Her
contributions are ingenious but not deep. The climactic scene
in which Meg stands crying before Charles Wallace bothers me
for two reasons. First of all, I find it hard to understand why she
could not have done this before; secondly, if Mrs. Whatsit could
tesser her and Charles Wallace away from IT, why couldn't she
have been with them before and saved them from their father's
inept tessering? Here, it seems to me, the ground rules of the plot
have been violated. In the previous visit to IT, the children had to
go alone; now Mrs. Whatsit is there to tesser them off. This may
seem minor, but it is of a piece with the main criticism I have to
make of this book; there is a facility about it, a slickness in characterization and dialogue which makes me feel that I have been
dealt with less than directly. There is no question but that the
book is good entertainment and that the writer carries the story
along with a great deal of verve; there is some question about the
depth of its quality.

Another book which brings mixed reactions is *It's Like This,
Cat*. The author's sensitive, intuitive knowledge of a young
boy living in New York seems to be far greater than her
ability to bring this into absolutely true focus. True, she
entertains and keeps her story going at a steady pace, but her
style lacks flexibility and true plausibility. I find it hard to believe that the flip manner of a boy is a true reflection of his
thoughts. Speech and narration from the boy's point of view are

*Esther Averill, " What Is a Picture Book? ", *Caldecott Medal Books:
1938-1957*, pp. 307-314, The Horn Book, Inc., 1957.

barely differentiated from each other. Telling a story in the first person is extremely difficult and the author has to transmit certain story points as either thoughts or reported action. The total conversational style skims lightly over the surface and while, at times, the author uses this to sharpen perception, there are other times when the accumulation of this style has a constricting effect. Although the author's central attitude toward her characters is basically honest and tender, there is a blurring sentimentality as exhibited in her portrayal of the cat woman. It is significant, also, that the plot, in connection with the cat woman, becomes contrived. As William Lipkind pointed out, maturing of an artist takes time and this story represents only a beginning for a writer who may some day give us a work which is truly distinguished.

A number of winners have added historical backgrounds to our shelves: *Carry on, Mr. Bowditch, Rifles for Watie, The Witch of Blackbird Pond, The Bronze Bow.* All have value, all are told skilfully. If they lack the qualities of greatness, it is largely because their style has a commercial sameness. This comment is made not to detract from their use of history, the pattern of their plotting, but simply to point out that distinguished writing is highly individualized. Think of the great names in either the adult or children's field — Twain, Dostoievski, Stevenson, Dickens, Faulkner, Andersen, Hemingway, Carroll — and you immediately think of a way of writing as much as a particular story. Regardless of a writer's desire to achieve any gain from his writing, money or fame, the extent to which that writer attempts to bring together, in his own way, form and content, to that extent will the writer move us with the quality of his work — to that extent will his work move us, adding subtly and deeply to our understanding by the order and texture of his interpretation.

Two other books must be commented on. One, *Miracles on Maple Hill*, seems to miss its objective because of a sentimental use of language. I know this author has written better books.

Onion John does not appear to me to be a work for children but instead, a " teaching " story, a parable, aimed at parents.

Onion John, in spite of minute description, is a personification of an abstraction. Except for what he does in an accidental way, the boy who narrates the story is really not involved as an active participant; it is his father's struggle that is central and resolved at the moment of climax.

The time has come, it seems to me, to talk seriously of criticism, to take criticism seriously and to pursue it with both ardure and ardour. Humor, I hope, will not be left outside — but the polite appraisal, the " genteel " tradition, will do well to retire. We have no right to evoke the spirit of John Newbery year after year without giving due respect and acknowledgement to his pugnacious, aggressive qualities, his determination to bring out books to make children wonder in delight. We have had the medal for a long time. The field of children's literature has seldom had a sustained publication of criticism, detailed, analytical criticism devoted to works old and new, dealing with the questions of quality, depth and beauty.

For children and for adults, a work of art and especially a work of fiction can deepen our emotional capacity to live, can heal and assuage; fiction can arouse and anger, can illuminate with wit and paradox, harmonize with humor. We can see ourselves in fiction as we cannot see ourselves in life and we can explore our emotions as it would be impossible to do so in reality. Fiction, then, is a step to, into and beyond reality.

> Great fiction is the product of wise and finely adjusted minds. It is patterned: it shows us a given action in its entirety, furnishing us with all the information necessary for understanding it, excluding what is not, and tracing causal relationships. It is our experience filtered through an intelligence and made meaningful — like all art, a joy and a comfort to turn to when we are wearied by the confused face of reality. Entirely on the basis of what it has to say to the conscious intelligence, fiction is an unsurpassed medium for increasing our understanding of the human predicament and our own situation.*

*Simon Lesser, *Fiction and the Unconscious,* p. 234, Beacon Press, 1957.

To the extent that we care about the value of fiction and the significance of human experience, we will treat books written for children as the living bearers of human experience made meaningful. Criticism is not only an observation of what is being published; it is a caring, a relating of the pàst with the future, a recognition of the vital cross of the present, past and future. Fiction plays such a decisive role in our lives that the next ten years should be distinguished by a joining of dynamic criticism with the bestowing of the awards.

The real stamp of a book's living qualities comes with the increased pleasure from re-reading, a new discovery of hitherto unperceived riches. The unfolding, many-layered mysteries of a creative work of art are measured by no tape, completely explicated by no critic, congealed by no " standards," nor amply dignified by any award. To increase our pleasure in the reading of such books, to facilitate our recognition of them — such can be the true reward of criticism.

THE CALDECOTT AWARDS:
1956-1965

THE CALDECOTT AWARD **1956**

Frog Went A-Courtin'

illustrated by FEODOR ROJANKOVSKY

text retold by JOHN LANGSTAFF

published by HARCOURT, BRACE 1955

FORMAT

SIZE: 8⅜" x 10⅞", 32 pp. (unfolioed)

ARTIST'S MEDIUM: Brush, ink and crayon on acetate color separations for line reproduction

PRINTING PROCESS: Offset lithography

ILLUSTRATIONS: Front matter, full pages in alternating four-color and two-color

TYPE: Bulmer

BOOK NOTE

IN a zestful retelling of a four-hundred-year-old ballad of Scottish origin, Frog courts Miss Mousie. Their elegant wedding feast is enjoyed by all their friends, from moth to chick, until the old Tom Cat sends every one scat. Fun and frolic are the spirit of the illustrations, which are partly in four colors, partly in frog tones of green and black.

CALDECOTT AWARD ACCEPTANCE

by *Feodor Rojankovsky*

I AM deeply touched by your generous reception and by the magnificent Award that has been bestowed upon me. I wish I were eloquent enough to express adequately all my feelings and all my gratitude, but I am afraid that my words will be only a pale semblance of my actual emotion. I am really handicapped as a speaker. In the first place, as you have probably noticed, my English pronunciation is not exactly that of a Sir Laurence Olivier or even that of a New York radio announcer. And in the second place, I am a painter, not a writer nor a poet, and I am used to dealing with visual images and not with words. I am at home with lines, colors and shapes, and I am rather embarrassed when I have to make a speech. So please be indulgent to an artist who is compelled to play the part of an orator.

When I began to wonder what I was going to say tonight, I remembered all the letters I have received in this country and all the questions my readers — young and old — have asked me. Many of them wanted to know how and why I became an illustrator of children's books. Maybe you would ask me the same question. And tonight more than ever before I feel like telling you this story. I wish I could illustrate it but I am afraid I shall be able to give you only the text of the story — and no pictures.

I suppose that in my case, as in that of any artist, the roots of my vocation are to be traced back to my childhood and to my family. I must say that we were quite a family. When people ask me, " Where are you from? " I answer, " From Russia." Then I feel that I owe them an explanation. My father was a teacher and administrator of high schools and his changing jobs took him across Imperial Russia. My sister was born in Kishinev, which meant that she became Rumanian when the city was taken by the Rumanians. One of my brothers was born in Odessa and therefore became a Ukrainian or a " Little Russian "; the other brother was born near

Moscow and therefore he was a "Great Russian." My second sister was born in Estonia, and I in Mitava, Latvia. So we had five nationalities in one family. When I tried to explain that to an officer of the Immigration and Naturalization Service, he held his head with both hands and then grabbed an aspirin. I told him the story of a Jew who tried to explain that he was not a Pole. "But weren't you born in Poland?" asked the officer. "Listen," answered the poor man, "if a sparrow is born in a stable, that does not mean he is a horse."

Despite the fact that we were Rumanian, Ukrainian, Estonian and Latvian, we felt very much like Russians and there was a remarkable unity of atmosphere and spirit in our multi-national family. "I do not want you to become rich," my father used to say, "but I want you to be well educated." There was no danger of our becoming rich, with five children who were all to receive the best education on a teacher's salary which in those times was no higher than it is today. Yet we were all happy, and we were all extremely interested in the arts. Music, painting, literature were the family's daily and most beloved fare. My sister Alexandra went to St. Petersburg Conservatory. She had a lovely contralto voice. My brother Sergei studied law but he was a brilliant draughtsman and made excellent posters. The other brother, Pavel, an engineer, devoted his leisure to painting, and his water colors were so good that the Imperial Academy bought them. And my other sister Tatiana, who was a pupil in the aristocratic Catherine Institute for Noble Women, became a concert soloist and conducted church choirs.

My father did not want his children to become professional artists because at that time Russian gentlemen looked down their noses at artists, but he could not help dabbling himself in painting and drawing. I remember that he accompanied his translations of Greek and Latin poets by naive and sometimes funny illustrations or made jocular portraits of his sons — in one of his drawings he represented me as gobbling buckwheat porridge.

Two great events determined the course of my childhood. I was taken to the zoo and saw the most marvelous creatures on earth:

bears, tigers, monkeys and reindeer, and, while my admiration was running high, I was given a set of color crayons. Naturally, I began immediately to depict the animals which captured my imagination. Also when my elder brothers, who were in schools in the capital, came home for vacation, I tried to copy their drawings and to imitate their paintings.

There was another source for my artistic inspiration. After the death of my father, when I was five, the family passed through hard times but we never parted from Father's valuable library. We kept it up and stuck to it in all our wanderings and misfortunes — and it took a revolution to destroy it. There were big books in this library and I sat for hours admiring them. I remember so vividly Milton's *Paradise Lost* and *Don Quixote* with the magnificent illustrations by the great French artist Gustave Doré. And, of course, there was the Bible with the impressive drawings by the same Frenchman. One does not need to study Freudian psychology to understand the impact of these early experiences on the formation of artistic imagination and sensitivity. The whole environment in which I was brought up pushed me toward artistic expression. I was eight or nine when I started, together with my sister, to draw illustrations for Defoe's *Robinson Crusoe*, one of my favorite books. I am sorry to say that this first great work of mine was lost during the turbulent years of war and revolution.

Later when I went to school in Reval Tallinn, an ancient town on the shores of the Baltic sea, my love for art was enhanced and strengthened by a passion for nature. Tallinn was surrounded by forest. The sea presented wonderful opportunities for excursions and study of sea life. But there were also steamers, sailboats, flags, and all the excitement of a port. This was no less exciting than playing Red Indians or reading James Fenimore Cooper, the beloved author of all Russian children before, during, and after the Revolution.

What helped me enormously in my attachment to nature was an excellent teacher in the high school who initiated his students into the secrets of woods and fields and lakes, and developed in us the power of observation. While I was rather poor in classes of design because I did not relish copying clay models of a pseudo-classical kind, I put all my ardor into compositions we had to write for the class in natural history, and I accompanied my enthusiastic descriptions of plants and animals and insects with no less enthusiastic images of what I saw and loved. One such illustrated composition received the highest grade. This was my first award in art, and I was then thirteen — it has been a long way from that to the Caldecott Medal, but I was proud and happy that day, too.

I think that my training in observing nature — including such innocent things as collecting butterflies and minerals and plants and leaves, and fussing around with pet animals, and spending hours in observing wild life in forests or in Reval's 18th-century park — that all these early contacts with nature played a decisive role in my development as an artist. All my life I continued to be interested in those very things I became spellbound by as a child and as an adolescent. I believe that children who like my books feel instinctively that I see nature with the same wonder and thrill that they do.

Later other factors were added to my first initiation into the mysteries of art and nature. I worked hard to acquire skills and techniques, and this work filled me with joy. I always loved my profession and my work. I found that creativity, particularly artistic creation, is a real blessing, and nothing else gave me such pleasure and satisfaction in life, even though I like all the good things on this earth.

I was full of joy when, as a boy of 17, I was painting murals for a small theater in the Crimea, the Russian Florida, or doing some other half-professional jobs. By that time — on the eve of the First World War — everything became clear to me. I wanted to be a painter. An exhibition of paintings I saw in Moscow made me so happy and enthusiastic that I decided to present myself in the examination contest for the Moscow Fine Arts Academy. I won it, and I entered as a student in one of the best Russian institutions of higher artistic education. The course of my life was now defined. Since that time many things have happened to me: the First World War broke out, I became a combatant and an officer in the Imperial Army, I was wounded, I went through the fires of the Revolution, I lost people who were dear to me, but I continued to paint and to draw. Wherever I was I felt that my duty to my vocation as an artist compelled me to remain faithful to my artistic goal. I became an illustrator of children's books. I did it because I was an artist and loved nature and loved children.

Unfinished Portrait of an Artist

by *Esther Averill*

THE February 1932 issue of *The Horn Book Magazine* carried an article which introduced the work of a Russian illustrator whose first children's book in France had recently appeared. His name was Feodor Rojankovsky.

The current issue of *The Horn Book* publishes the speech delivered by Mr. Rojankovsky when he received the Caldecott Medal for 1955. The award, won by his illustrations for *Frog Went A-Courtin'* by John Langstaff, places Rojankovsky in the ranks of other distinguished " Caldecotters " who, after coming to live in. America, have brightened our children's books with talents stemming from cultures other than our own.

Rojankovsky, in his acceptance speech, tells us of his early happy life in Russia, his uprootings, and the forces that have shaped his art. I can merely add a few recollections and impressions.

My first glimpse of him was caught in Paris, long ago in 1929, when the modern movement in the graphic arts was in full swing. A catalogue illustrated by an unknown artist, whose signature was Rojan, had taken my eye. It was a de luxe catalogue done for the Grande Maison de Blanc, and even now I can recall its gay Russian colors, its smartness and highly decorative style. And since I worked at that time for Thérèse Bonney, the journalist-photographer whose office was a kind of clearinghouse of information on contemporary arts, we sent for Rojan, whose full name, we learned, was Rojankovsky.

The interview took place in the front office. I toiled in the wings. But presently our secretary came to me and said, " The man is nice. Oh, really nice. And you should go and see."

Instinct prompted me, and I walked softly through the rear of the front office. By doing so, I was rewarded with a view of Rojankovsky's back.

I met him face to face a few months later after I had left Miss Bonney and hung out a shingle of my own. My chief account was an American stationery manufacturer who wished to modernize his papers, boxes and Christmas cards. On this project I became associated with another American who lived in Paris, Lila Stanley. Rojankovsky was among the artists we called in to help us. He furnished us with drawings that enchanted us. They had color, gaiety and humor, and revealed how thoroughly he understood the graphic possibilities of the medium in which he worked. But his heart lay elsewhere. He wished to illustrate a children's book.

Unfortunately, French publishing for children was at a low ebb. France had had nothing to correspond with the great publishing movement begun in the field of American children's books as far back as the early 1920s. Job and André Hellé were still alive but they belonged really to a former period. It is true that lovely juveniles cropped up from time to time, but only when the spirit moved. Rojankovsky helped to change all that and tribute should be paid him for sticking to his vocation, even when the road was rough.

I know how rough it could be, for Miss Stanley and I were the publishers of his first children's book in France — his *Daniel Boone* which appeared under my imprint, Domino Press, in 1931.

This series of brilliant colored lithographs caused a stir in Europe. Its best support, however, came from the United States, where a sustained interest in children's books had been developing. Three Americans in particular helped wherever they could, and they will always be associated in my memory with *Daniel Boone*. They are Anne Carroll Moore, who was then head of children's work in the New York Public Library, Bertha Mahony Miller, whose Bookshop for Boys and Girls in Boston gave *Daniel Boone* a home, and Frederic G. Melcher of *Publishers' Weekly* fame — he whose Caldecott Medal has gone this year to Rojankovsky because of *Frog Went A-Courtin'*.

Now, back to Paris.

In retrospect I see more clearly. In working on this paper I have searched for facts and dates to place Rojankovsky properly in his period in France — the period of pre-World War II.

I find that in 1929 appeared the remarkable *Regarde*, written by Colette, illustrated by the distinguished Méheut, and published by the youthful J.-G. Deschamps who was endeavoring to do something new and truly beautiful for the children of his country. But this book was issued in a limited, de luxe edition which only bibliophiles felt they could afford to buy.

In 1930 the Nouvelle Revue Française published André Beucler's *Mon Chat*, illustrated by Nathalie Parain, a Russian with extraordinary feeling for the dynamics of a picture book. *Mon Chat* cost fifty francs, if memory serves me. (At any rate, its price was higher than the average Frenchman wished to pay for a child's book.) Our *Daniel Boone* of 1931 cost even more.

Still, Rojankovsky in believing he could make a career out of illustrating books for children had not been wrong. He had caught something in the air, as artists often do.

Over at the great publishing house of Flammarion sat Père Castor, sizing up the situation. He solved the selling problem by devising a series of simple picture books for young children which could be printed in such quantities that the retail price would suit the French. Yet one never has a feeling that Père Castor was catering to an indiscriminating public. His books were edited with artistic taste, and they offered a fine medium for Rojankovsky's talent as it burst into flower.

Rojankovsky's first work for Père Castor appeared in 1932 and his last in 1942. During that period the artist created such little masterpieces as *Panache* (the Squirrel) and *Frou* (the Rabbit), along with other memorable beasts and birds. He was doing what he likes best to do — putting down upon paper his observations of the world of nature.

I have always had the impression that he lives in close communion with the creatures he brings into being. My impression is confirmed by Margaret McElderry, children's editor at Harcourt Brace, publisher of *Frog Went A-Courtin'*. In a paper published elsewhere she speaks of the many frogs that decorated Rojankovsky's letters to her and of the feeling he gave her that frogs filled his working hours and haunted his sleep.

He himself has been likened to a happy squirrel, because in his hours of social relaxation he seems to keep in constant motion, darting here and there as lightly as a ballet dancer.* But this activity makes me think rather of a hummingbird or a bee, and the image of the bee recalls a verse which reminds me very much of Rojankovsky:

> Where the bee sucks, there suck I:
> In a cowslip's bell I lie;
> There I couch when owls do cry.
> On the bat's back I do fly
> After summer merrily.
> Merrily, merrily, shall I live now
> Under the blossom that hangs on the bough.**

Obviously Rojankovsky's habitat is not the city but the country. His present home is a white house in Bronxville, near New York. Here he lives with his Russian-born wife and their enchanting little daughter, Tania, whose drawings help decorate the rooms.

Outside on a slightly wooded incline stands Rojankovsky's studio, which is a joy for any visitor to enter. Low bookcases contain the books he constantly collects and studies. Here and there on the light spacious walls are specimens of art from various regions of the world.

Overhead there is a sloping roof in dome-shaped plastic, crystal clear, so that, when working at his drawing table, Rojankovsky may look up into the tree tops. Trees are dear to him. They remind him of the forests in his native Russia.

How did it happen that he came to live among us?

This illustrator of tremendous talent and productivity entered New York Harbor on the *S. S. Navemar* in 1941. Paris had fallen; populations once again were on the move. As I understand it, an American printing firm which eyed children's books in terms of mass production brought Rojankovsky here.

In any event, Rojankovsky for the next ten years worked ex-

---

* Early in his life Rojankovsky was strongly tempted to become a dancer.
** From Shakespeare's *The Tempest.*

clusively for the Artists and Writers Guild whose editorial office is in New York City. They were the printers of his *Tall Book of Mother Goose* which appeared in 1942 under the Harper imprint. This book, which sold for one dollar, swept the country and brought joy to innumerable children who had never encountered such gaiety as it possessed.

However, *The Tall Book of Mother Goose* marked a change in Rojankovsky's style and touched off a controversy which has not ceased to rage around him in circles steeped in the fine book traditions of the past. The change in style was probably due to his wish to give his books appeal for the mass markets of this country. (These markets would seem to have a taste quite different from that for which he worked in France under Père Castor.) This matter of popular taste is extremely complicated, and I for one am not qualified to comment, though I realize its great importance in these times in which we live.

What concerns us here is the ultimate effect upon the artist himself. I find that in the many Golden Books which the Artists and Writers Guild has produced for Simon and Schuster, Rojankovsky's work is of unequal value. This, of course, is to be expected of an illustrator whose output is so vast.

More serious, to my way of thinking, is the fact that Rojankovsky was typed, and let himself be typed, just as an actor in Hollywood often gets poured into a mold. And certainly this was at the expense of his great lyric qualities and his own brand of gentle humor which springs from nature rather than from the world of man.

Many of us felt happy when Rojankovsky finally obtained his freedom to work also for publishers who deal in smaller editions and represent a more traditional kind of bookmaking. This opportunity should permit him to develop further his unique talents. To date these publishers include Viking, Holiday House, Scribner, Harper, and Harcourt Brace where Margaret McElderry with great acumen introduced him to the manuscript of John Langstaff's *Frog Went A-Courtin'*.

A Tree Is Nice

illustrated by MARC SIMONT

written by JANICE UDRY

published by HARPER AND ROW 1956

FORMAT

SIZE: 6⅜″ x 11″, 32 pp. (unfolioed)

ARTIST'S MEDIUM: Watercolor

PRINTING PROCESS: Offset lithography

ILLUSTRATIONS: Front matter, doublespreads alternating in four colors and black-and-white

TYPE: Garamond and hand-lettering

BOOK NOTE

EVERYTHING that trees are, from landscapes of beauty to playthings for climbers, are catalogued with praise. Pages in full-color alternate with black-and-white, showing the year-round delights to be found in trees.

CALDECOTT AWARD ACCEPTANCE

by *Marc Simont*

WHEN I first received the news of the Award I was stunned. When I recovered from the shock, I did what I believe any other person would have done in my place — I celebrated. When all the legitimate reasons for celebration were exhausted, I thought up some less legitimate ones. Then, with the idea in mind that I'd have to write a speech, came the sobering up.

At first I thought of the many fine children's books that are done every year, how the choice must be nip and tuck as to which is the best and how lucky I was that mine happened to be chosen. When I began to prepare this speech, I was almost moved to tears at the sound of my own humble eloquence. Then it was as if some-one tapped me on the shoulder and said, " Simont, you are a phony — you know jolly well that the reason you're feeling so good about this is because enough members of the Children's Library Association thought you'd done the best picture book of 1956 to merit the Caldecott Medal."

It seems appropriate to me that I should have received this medal for a Harper book because Harper's, and specifically Ursula Nord-strom, constitutes my longest and most consistent association in the field of children's books.

Of course, all I've been doing during the last few months hasn't been just celebrating. For one thing, I've had to answer so many requests for my life history that my biography is beginning to sound as if it were about somebody else. Then there are all the re-quests I've received for my views and theories on art and books. It seems you have to be up against a situation like this to become aware of your deficiencies. It isn't that I haven't had plenty of theories in the past, but I have very few of them going. Theories seem to supplant one another, and I can't remember what the others were. That lapse of memory, incidentally, has the advantage of cutting down this talk by at least two hours.

Although we are forever amazed at the beautiful pictures children can make, still, their intention is not to make a beautiful picture at all, but to tell a story. You've seen them, huddled over a piece of paper with crayon in hand, muttering fantastic doings to themselves — " and the lion comes running down the hill, and the cowboy is galloping on his horse, and he's shooting at the lion, and the Indians are hiding behind rocks, and . . ." All their intent is in realistic storytelling, but the end result is closer to the abstract.

Considering the astounding results they get, it would be taking coals to Newcastle to aim solely at making beautiful pictures. What one can do, however, is offer pictorial clarification of a story. This can be done because of two things: one, because art with the illustrator is a craft, and the other because, having lived longer, we have accumulated more information about things they want to know.

After children go through a picture book, the chances are they won't remember very many facts about it. But they will retain an impression, and if the book has been presented to them with clarity and taste, it's reasonable to assume that the impression will have been a good one. That, it seems to me, is as much as an artist can hope for.

The reason a person writes a story is that he is touched by something he has experienced, and consequently, if it's a good story, those who read it will be touched in the same way. Unless the artist feels this when he reads a manuscript he shouldn't undertake to illustrate it, because in this field there's no room for cynicism or tongue-in-cheek. If it turns out to be a good story with bad pictures, or a bad story with terrible pictures, in either case the result is a bad book.

For the artist, then, the most important factor is for him to be completely sympathetic with the basic idea behind a manuscript; all the rest, by comparison, are details. Once the artist undertakes to illustrate a story, psychologically it becomes *his* story — this is a risk an author must take. When the artist makes the story " his own," so to speak, he is free to invent without getting out of character, and thus his pictures will complement — or establish harmony with — the text. Otherwise the pictures will merely supplement, which is like saying the same thing twice.

In *A Tree Is Nice*, Janice Udry had given me everything an artist could want in a picture-book manuscript. The idea of *A Tree Is Nice* is so fundamental and uncluttered that when I first read it, I said to myself, " Now, why didn't I think of that? " Well, that's what they said about Columbus' voyage to America. The trouble was it only occurred to them after he'd gotten back. *A Tree Is Nice* has a solid basic idea presented with simplicity and charm; all I had to do was keep pace with it.

Where technique is concerned, an illustrator's viewpoint is always changing. The only time it must stand still is when he's working on a specific job. But it is impossible to arrive at " the " solution for all illustration situations. Every job he starts must be approached as if it were his first.

I consider your awarding me the Caldecott Medal as your approval of this point of view and, with thanks to you and Mr. Melcher, accept it as your vote of confidence for the work that lies ahead of me.

BIOGRAPHICAL NOTE

by *Elisabeth Lansing*

Marc Simont

DURING the fall of 1940 my mother boarded her parrot with Mr. and Mrs. William Behn in Cornwall Bridge, Connecticut. Why the Behns consented to shelter this soulless bird is not now clear to me. Mr. Behn is a blacksmith, specializing in quadrupeds. Mrs. Behn is fond of animals, but even she could not love this morose misanthrope. The Behns were happier, I am sure, with a second boarder. He was Marc Simont.

I remember this in particular because the parrot escaped to a pine tree one day that fall and we went down to see whether he could be lured back to his cage. The parrot was in the pine tree all right and Marc was under the tree trying to whistle him down. He didn't succeed. That was my first introduction to Marc and the only time to my knowledge that he has failed to charm bird, beast or man. But then it must be acknowledged that this parrot was, and still is, quite without grace.

Marc had come to Cornwall to work with Francis Scott Bradford, a noted muralist, on a hurry-up commission. The work was meant to be temporary, but Cornwall is a haven for the literary and artistic and it is not strange that Marc found the atmosphere there congenial. In any case he has lived in Cornwall off and on ever since and there is no doubt at all that the inhabitants have found him a compatible spirit.

Cornwall, Connecticut, is a far reach from Paris, France, where Marc was born of Spanish parents in 1915. His father, José Simont, is a well-known illustrator who has been awarded the Spanish *Golden Pencil* and a French *Legion of Honor* for his work on the continent. In 1920 Mr. Simont came to America where he " earned lots of money " illustrating for the glossier magazines, a distribution of rewards that is highly satisfactory to him and reveals something of the differences between the European and American sense of what is due an artist. So it was by tradition as well as design that Marc became an artist.

Marc's early years were spent in Barcelona where he began what he claims to have been a " very spotty " education. " I was so bad in school," he says, " that I never thought of being anything but an artist. I was always more interested in what the teachers looked like than in what they said."

The fact that he attended six schools and crossed the Atlantic four times during his scholastic years may account for this sense of educational irregularity. In spite of this chronic state of inattention to the three Rs, Marc now speaks four languages fluently.

In 1926 the Simonts spent ten months in New Rochelle, New York, where Marc attended high school, drawing caricatures of his teachers and presumably still deaf to the flow of professorial wisdom. When he left high school he went to Paris to study at the Academie Julian, the Academie Ranson and the Lhote School, an artistic education that was far from " spotty " and where his academic vagaries found a more comfortable setting. By 1935 his formal schooling was over and Marc could settle down to being what he is — a natural-born artist.

His single-minded devotion to art was interrupted by a three-year tour of duty in the Army, but Marc was able to turn even this inartistic career to his advantage. It was during the war that he met and married Miss Sara Dalton of Reidsville, North Carolina.

" And she," says Mrs. Behn, who should know, " is just the right girl for Marc."

Thus even in the marital field Marc pursued his natural bent, for, as any man knows, finding a wife who is both pretty and intelligent is an art in itself. In 1951 they bought a house in Cornwall where Marc has a studio, carefully planned for the execution of the many illustrating commissions that come his way. The Simonts also have a nine-year-old son, Doc, whose career so far seems to involve the not-so-carefully planned exploits of a lively small boy.

In writing about Marc it is nearly impossible to separate the man from his art — they are so happy a complement to one another. If he were to be characterized by a single word, *empathy* would have to be that word. It is this quality that is strongly apparent in his illustrations for *A Tree Is Nice,* this year's winner of the Caldecott Medal.

Janice Udry's words are few and each one bears the impact of a simple truth that is beauty, too. Who can dispute her statement " Trees are very nice. They fill up the sky "? Marc's picture for this is a gay splash of wood and greenery with a small recumbent boy in the foreground to emphasize the fact that trees are worthy of a dream. When Miss Udry says that " We can climb a tree," Marc has filled a broad-limbed tree with exploring youth, each one engaged in the pursuit of an imaginative game. The pictures in every case are an extension and embroidery of the author's theme — that trees are nice. It is empathy that adds that extra twist of imagination and lends new enchantment to the text. An illustrator of children's books whose readers are sternly literal as well as highly fanciful must have this attribute in large degree.

Young readers are not the only people whom Marc has touched with this magic attribute. He has always to consider his authors, a touchy tribe with a nervous dread that people may not properly appreciate their point of view. James Thurber, an artist and writer capable of evaluating the aspects of this and most other questions, says this about Marc:

" Marc Simont not only illustrated *The Thirteen Clocks* but also my new book, *The Wonderful O,* which Simon and Schuster will publish in June. The fact that I have no other illustrator is proof of my admiration for his artistry, his humor and his perceptive grasp of the not inconsiderable problem of dealing with the people and animals of my strange world."

Humor is Mr. Thurber's province, an elevated area which he maintains as his private preserve. Humor is one of Marc's strongest characteristics and it seems quite natural to those who know him that he should be able to make a picture for *The Thirteen Clocks* of that thing that was " the only one there ever was " and the thing "that would have been purple if there had been any light to see it by."

Marc's humor and his gift for gaiety are facets of his personality that his friends find most engaging. These qualities, added to the empathy I have mentioned, make conversation with Marc something that puts the feeblest thinkers in a comfortable glow of self-appreciation. His lightning response to a word and even his eyebrows make them feel that they, too, belong to the company of wits.

For Marc himself is a wit with words and his stories are legend in Cornwall. He can turn an everyday event into a tale that literally rocks his hearers. Cornwall offers a fertile field for these talents, for the town relies heavily on amateur entertainment to maintain its civic improvements. At these events Marc is often the star performer. As an aging opera *diva* chasing a lost note, or a professor of elocution pursuing his muse, he has no rival in the opinion of a Cornwall audience. Some who have heard these rollicking absurdities feel that Marc, like Sherlock Holmes, missed his calling by not going on the stage.

But over thirty books, five of which he has written as well as illustrated, bear witness against this theory. *Good Luck Duck* by Meindert De Jong, *The Happy Day* by Ruth Krauss, and *A Tree Is Nice* are tangible evidence that Marc is first and foremost an artist.

Ruth Krauss who has worked with him on three books is a writer vehemently certain that he is dedicated to the graphic arts.

"I never knew an artist like him," she says. "He doesn't seem to care about money. All he wants is to get the pictures right and he'll spend hours and days doing it."

The Happy Day was the result of such work. The black and white drawings of bears, woodchucks and squirrels under the snow, their faces wreathed in contented smiles, are perhaps Marc's happiest contribution to art for children.

"Pictures for children have to tell something," he says. "Kids like bright colors, sure, but the most important thing to them is — what's happening?"

In my own case I have an example of how Marc was able to "tell something." He has, I am proud to say, illustrated two of my books and in one of them there is a young lady, a secondary character, named Janey. The exigencies of writing being what they are, I didn't need to describe her very fully, but I knew what she should look like. So did Marc. He drew a picture of Janey, freckled nose upturned, elbows akimbo, standing in the middle of a blackberry bush where the story had landed her. She was exactly right, a budding Lucy Stone, just as I had meant her to be and the picture told you so.

Perhaps if Marc has any hallmark in his drawings it is a character like that, be it male or female. You see him in *A Tree Is Nice*, sitting in the crotch of a tree with folded arms, obviously "in wrong" and defiant. His son, Doc, may be partly responsible for the appearance of this young sprout of Democracy in so many of his pictures. The adventures of Doc are a saga in themselves. Marc tells of the time a group of people were admiring a sunset and Doc and a water pistol appeared on the scene. But it is kinder to end this story here.

The fact that Marc writes stories for children, as well as illustrates them, is not surprising to those who have heard tales such as the unfinished epic above. *Polly's Oats, The Lovely Summer, The Plumber out of the Sea*, and *Mimi* are well written and amusing and have the added advantage of being illustrated by the author.

People who know Marc are apt to feel that he can do anything. Skating, skiing, singing, playing tennis, these are sidelines with him. But they show his most American side. He loves sports and baseball in particular. Red Smith, with whom Marc collaborated on a book called *How to Get to First Base*, reports that "when he was doing the book of baseball sketches, he'd go to Yankee Stadium and get so wrapped up in the games that he would leave the park without a line drawn in his notebook. Artists you can shake out of any tree but baseball fans like that are hard to come by."

No matter what Mr. Smith thinks of the blossoming abundance of artists, he does concede that "Marc is an extraordinarily gifted

guy, blessed with a quality of humor that few other artists have."
The two books on sports that Marc did with Red Smith and a
memorable volume called *Opera Soufflé* show a fine flair for cari-
cature, an art that requires quickness of mind and eye and the
power of making one line do the work of fifty. Red Smith was
particularly pleased with a portrait of Yogi Berra. After being
touched with the magic of Marc's pencil, " Yogi," says Mr. Smith,
" looks more like a bundle of old laundry than you would want
your old laundry to look like." Those who have seen Mr. Berra
behind home plate will readily appreciate that Marc and Red
Smith between them have done full justice to Yogi's sartorial
splendors.

From caricatures to portraits might seem a long step to some
artists, but Marc has done a great many portraits without having
his sitters complain that the result fell into the former category.
Children are a specialty with him and his success with them may
be due in large part to the fact that his young sitters have such a
good time with Marc that the finished portrait reflects that cheerful atmosphere.

Marc paints animals too. One portait of a Nubian ram was
received with such enthusiasm that Marc has been advised to
devote himself exclusively to goats. The number of Nubian goats
who wish to have their portaits painted is perhaps somewhat
limited, however, and Marc has not considered this suggestion too
seriously.

For the past two years the Simonts have lived in New York in
the winters and Cornwall in the summers. " Living in New York
hath charms," he says. " Granted, the snow isn't so white as it is
in the country, but on the other hand, you don't have to shovel it."

Whether it is this freedom from the hazards of country living
or the fact that he finds New York a stimulating place to work,
Marc has won for himself a high place in that field of art which
he most enjoys — illustrating books and especially children's books.

" Juvenile editors don't bind you to an idea," he says. " They
leave you alone."

This lack of interference is a priceless boon to a creative person.

Like every artist, Marc understands the difficulty of making that first shining idea grow and come alive in a finished picture. He once wrote an editor, " I'm never happy when I finish a job because I always feel I could have done better . . . my feeling is always, ' This should have been done completely differently.' "

But juvenile editors are wise in the ways of writers and artists; they know that they always feel this way — even a winner of the Caldecott Medal.

" That prize," says Mr. Behn, who shall have the last word, " it won't change Marc at all. He's some feller."

THE CALDECOTT AWARD 1958

Time of Wonder

illustrated by ROBERT McCLOSKEY
written by THE ILLUSTRATOR
published by THE VIKING PRESS 1957

FORMAT

SIZE: 9" x 12", 64 pp.
ARTIST'S MEDIUM: Watercolor
PRINTING PROCESS: Offset lithography
ILLUSTRATIONS: Front matter, full color doublespreads throughout
TYPE: Goudy Modern

BOOK NOTE

THROUGH rhythmic words and full color paintings the artist shares with the beholder his love of a special island off the Maine seacoast. But as he shows the changes of tide and seasons, the elemental force of a storm, and wonders where hummingbirds go in a hurricane, his book encompasses far more than a song of praise for one special place.

CALDECOTT AWARD ACCEPTANCE

by *Robert McCloskey*

THANK you very much, Mr. Melcher and Children's Librarians, for awarding me the Caldecott Medal a second time.

I must tell you that in awarding *Time of Wonder* a prize, you are really awarding a prize to May Massee. It is her book, almost as surely as if she had held the brush in her hand. Without her it never would have been done. Without May Massee I should never have dared think in terms of so much color and so much paper. Without her patience and faith, I might never have finished the job.

As you are librarians, I think that you know enough about how picture books are made, so I've decided to say something that needs saying right now.

" What this country needs " is a phrase that keeps popping up. What this country needs is more exercise, or more religion, or a good five cent cigar, or, as of the moment, better education and more scientists.

With everyone clamoring for more scientists, I should like to clamor for more artists and designers. I should like to clamor for the teaching of drawing and design to every child, right along with reading and writing. I think it is most important for everyone really to see and evaluate pictures and really to see and evaluate his surroundings.

Stop for a moment and think how much time we all spend looking at and learning from or being influenced by pictures: pictures in magazines, pictures in newspapers, pictures in books, pictures that move, in movies or on TV. Think how much our lives are influenced by these pictures! We read these pictures. They add to and even supplant the written and spoken word. The widely quoted saying " A picture is worth a thousand words " may be true, but a picture is really worth only as many ideas or words as someone puts into it with his brush or pen or snap of a shutter.

Suppose we could produce a picture worth ten thousand words. It is of little use to the person who views it if he hasn't enough visual sense or experience to absorb what the picture-maker put into it. It is important that we develop people who can make worthwhile pictures, and it is important that we teach people to "read" these pictures. That is why, in my opinion, every child, along with learning to read and write, should be taught to draw and to design.

But, you answer, every child has Art classes now; you are asking for something we already have. What I am proposing is NOT Art; it is drawing and design. It is not Art any more than learning to write is Literature. This would be a course of study to teach design and to develop a visual sense. All too often our Art classes are used for occupational therapy and to help keep Johnny busy because he can't read. Clay modeling, finger painting, weaving, daubing and dribbling and expressing oneself, all have a place in this program, but teaching people to draw, to design, and to really see would be the object of my proposed course.

You may be sitting back in your seats and saying, "What nonsense! I certainly *can* see, and I know *what* I'm seeing when I see it!" Since you are an audience predominantly of ladies, let me give you this example. In a recent issue of a national magazine there was a double-page spread of seemingly casual photographs of a woman who had lost pounds and pounds of weight with the help of a jiggling machine. And in every one of these pictures the lady was altered about the middle by a retoucher's brush. In almost every issue of the magazine section of a large eastern newspaper, there are ads for "foundation garments" and other ladies' clothing. No woman alive ever had armpits such as appear in some of these photographs. Some are missing half their rib cages, and some have waists and hips that outside an altered photo would send a woman to the hospital. This same newspaper would never dream of printing in words something so misleading and so far from the truth as the photos in these ads.

About ten years ago I knew a sculptor who eked out a living

making manikins for displaying women's clothing. Along came one of those new looks that always seem to be coming our way from Paris. And with the clothes came new proportions to be used in making the new-look manikins — a necessary precaution so that the clothes would fit.

You say this doesn't mean anything? How many women do you know who diet and thump and jiggle and take pills, trying to match the impossible? You can take a special lens and photograph a woman to make her look taller and thinner — a handy little bit of equipment; you can turn it at right angles and photograph a car to make it look lower and longer. Or you can have an artist slice a low-priced car in half on paper and add three feet across the middle, making this modest piece of transportation look like the luxury car. The auto makers in Detroit have managed to make their products match the picture.

Watching a candidate for election deliver a speech on television, would you know that cunningly contrived lighting and camera angles were responsible for making the poor man look like a bug-eyed monster?

Do we know when someone is fooling us with pictures? With so many of our ideas being formed by pictures, it is important that we know.

I should like to speak for a moment about design. What are some of the elements of design? *Repetition:* as in a tree of apples, a herd of horses, a pattern of like marks made by a man with a brush or by a weaver in the cloth. As like as peas in a pod — alike, yes, but are they *exactly* alike, such as articles punched out by a machine? *Rhythm:* the rhythm of seasons, of growing shells and plants, of waves on the water and of grass in the wind. Is it the rhythm of pistons and machines? *Color:* as in the rainbow, the rocks and hills, the sea and sky and flowers, the colors of nature. Is it the color of neon lights and the colors that fluoresce? *Texture:* the textures of wood, of clay, of sand and stone, and of natural fibers. Are these like the textures of plastic, chromium and cellophane, made by machine? *Form:* the forms of plants and animals, the forms made by natural forces of wind and water, contrasting with the forms suggested by the machine — what the machine can make quickly and easily. *Space relationship:* how all of these various elements are used in relation to each other. This is the most important part of design and I should like to elaborate.

As you are librarians, I will start with a printed page. The design of a printed page of type is the relationship of the area occupied by the type to the margins, or the space around the type. The type has texture; we consider that, and if it is in color, that too influences our design. If this relationship is not well thought out, we shall have a page that is not pleasing to the eye. The area *around* the type is as important as the type itself. This page is a two-dimensional design.

Now let us consider a three-dimensional design — a picture that has height and width and also depth, a picture, let us say, of a child in a library. The three-dimensional space *around* this child is as important to the success of our picture as the child himself.

Now consider a sculptor designing a pair of lions to be placed before a library. He considers carefully the site for his lions and designs them accordingly. The space *around* the lions is as important to their success as the way the lions are sculptured. Think how carefully a museum displays its pictures and its sculpture. The space *around* these works of art is as important to the overall effect as the works of art themselves. If we were to cover a wall with old masters hung canvas to canvas, the visual effect would be much the same as that experienced looking at a comic strip.

"Interesting," you say, "but how does this affect my life?"

Until a few years ago, almost all design had its roots and inspiration in nature. But now there is another inspiration — the machine with its forms, its repetition, and its rhythm. Modern chemistry is providing new colors; electricity is providing new light sources. Every day there is a new material, a new texture to add to a long list. A generation of designers has been influenced by the machine and what the machine can do. Artists, architects, landscape architects, sculptors, painters, and even choreographers and musicians have been influenced by the machine. A generation of industrial designers has been busy designing furniture, gadgets, houses, filling stations, knives and forks, and skyscrapers that are easy for the machine to make. A generation of highway designers has been busy altering the look of our land with the help of machines, bulldozers and earthmovers, to make it easy for cars and trucks to speed from place to place.

I'm beginning to fear that with our machines, and machine-made materials, we are designing nature right out of our environment. In this country we have been designing, building, making things with machines, without paying the vaguest attention to the space around what we've produced.

How is a car designed? In secret, off by itself like a tremendous piece of mechanized jewelry. How do the ads show them? *One* car, zooming up the road with hardly another car in sight, or *one* car, before a velvet backdrop. How do they look bumper to bumper? How do they look side by side in a parking lot? Like the toy counter in the ten cent store on a grand scale. They look like hell!

Consider the Ranch type, Cape Cod, Salt Box, Williamsburg, Spanish Colonial, Modern house rendered on the architect's drawing board. Consider it in the photos and drawings in the magazines. The renderings: one house, carefully designed in relation to the page it is rendered upon; in the photos and pictures of the magazines, carefully selected, arranged and designed *in relation to the size of the page.* Sometimes there is a car in the garage. Have you ever wondered where the people are, in these pictures of houses, in these " machines for modern living "? And how do the houses look, lined up row after row, aerial to aerial in the housing development of an unimaginative builder? They look like hell.

What do you think of the shopping centers, used-car lots, motels, gas stations, drive-in theaters, all lined up, elbow to elbow, neon lights blazing out over acres of asphalt, glass, plastic, cement, wires, tubes, chromium, aluminum, cars, trucks, blinkers, flashers, signs, traffic circles, overpasses, underpasses, and development after development of houses with picture window after picture window facing the highway? What do you think as these things spread out from the cities until they meet? Do you shed a bitter tear, not from the noxious smell of truck exhaust, but because you deplore what is happening to the look of America?

We're designing things without designing the space and the area around them. We are building an environment unfit for human beings to live in. Our land with government of the people, by the people, for the people is fast acquiring an environment of machines, by machines, for machines.

Yes, I think every child ought to study design and drawing right along with reading, and writing, and arithmetic. I can't think of a scientist, minister, politician, bulldozer-operator or any other professional man or job-holder who would not be a better citizen for having had this training.

I get mad when I see this important part of life shoved way over to one side in our curriculum and labeled " Art." You cannot look at the face of our country without being painfully aware of the result.

We need a number of new professions: scientist designer, politician designer, anthropologist designer, social-scientist designer. Let us teach design, and let us get it out of the museums, let us get it off the pages and drawings boards and let us put it to work.

BIOGRAPHICAL NOTE

by *Margaret McCloskey*

Robert McCloskey

ROBERT MCCLOSKEY was born in Hamilton, Ohio, on September 15, 1914. He went to the public schools there and remembers that from the first, art was a major interest, closely followed by music, dismantling clocks and inventing things. This combination of talent led to an after-school job at the YMCA, during high school years, teaching hobbies. He taught other boys how to play the harmonica, and shepherded them to concerts at churches, grange meetings, lodge meetings and such. These experiences contributed to the creation of *Lentil, Homer Price,* and *Centerburg Tales*. Besides teaching the harmonica, he worked with a group of boys making model airplanes, and taught another to do soap carving. They met in the shower room once a week and the chips fell unhindered.

In high school, he played oboe in the orchestra, made drawings and wood engravings for the school paper and yearbook. During his senior year, he won one of the nation-wide Scholastic Awards, choosing a scholarship to the Vesper George School of Art in Boston. After three winters of study in Boston and three summers of counselling in a boys' camp near Hamilton, he moved to New York and called on May Massee, editor of Junior Books at the Viking Press, to show samples of his work. She told him to go back for more training and really learn to draw.

For two years he studied at the National Academy in New York, with summers of painting in Provincetown on Cape Cod. Again he went to Miss Massee, this time with the story and drawings for his first book, *Lentil,* which she accepted and published in 1940. In addition to doing the book, McCloskey had worked on two mural commissions, one of which was in Boston. During his second stay there, he came across the story of the peripatetic ducks and from that came the Caldecott winner, *Make Way for Ducklings* (Viking, 1941). In the previous year, he had married Margaret Durand, daughter of Ruth Sawyer, well-known writer and story-teller. World War II had just begun, but before he went into the army, he wanted to finish another book. It was *Homer Price* (1943) and it was written for older children than the picture books he had done before.

His next three years were spent making visual aids for the infantry at Fort McClellan, Alabama. Of this experience he says, "My greatest contribution to the war effort was inventing a machine to enable short second lieutenants to flip over large training charts in a high breeze." With army discharge in hand, the McCloskeys headed for Maine. They were now three, counting Sally who was born in 1945. They have been in Maine off and on for ten years, leading an amphibious life on an island in Penobscot Bay. The island and the sea around and the villages and farms on the coast have provided background for several books. *Blueberries for Sal* was published in the fall of 1948. Second daughter Jane was born in 1948, too, just in time for the family to sail for a year in Italy where McCloskey had a studio at the American Academy in Rome. Primarily, he studied the making of mosaics.

Centerburg Tales, or the Further Adventures of Homer, was published in 1951, and *One Morning in Maine* came out in 1952. The last few years have been spent in illustrating *Journey Cake Ho!* by Ruth Sawyer and *Junket* by Anne White, and in creating *Time of Wonder.*

Bob McCloskey, Inventor

by *Marc Simont*

SHOULD the recession get serious, a good inexpensive way for a tired man to find release from his tensions would be to go for a spin in Grampa Hercules' Hide-a-Ride Machine.

Bob McCloskey's talent for devising mechanical contraptions is topped only by his ability to turn out books that carry off the Caldecott Medal. I think there's a great book in a collection of Robert McCloskey Inventions.

This flair of Bob's for mechanical contraptions was very hard on his mother when, as a youngster, he came up with a machine for whipping cream. Being a generous boy, he didn't spare the juice, so when this whirling monster came in contact with the cream, it splattered a milky-way pattern around all four kitchen walls.

Time of Wonder is a poetic, pictorial record of his island home in Maine. But what the pictures in the book don't show is the staggering amount of equipment that it takes to turn a house on an island into a comfortable home. Bob is caretaker and up-keeper of electric generators, water pumps, winches, boat engines, etc., but the amazing thing is that he still has enough humor left to indulge in such refinements as hi-fi sets (which require special generators) and electrically run roasting spits.

In 1947 I was able to benefit from Bob's mechanical wizardry. I had just bought a car — a 1927 Pontiac — which had a good engine, I was told, and lots of dignity, which I could see. My wife and I borrowed the McCloskeys' car and went to pick it up. On the way back I drove the McCloskeys' car while my wife brought along the antique (as head of the family I can't afford to take chances). We proudly showed it off to the McCloskeys but when it was time to leave, it wouldn't start. I raised the hood and looked wise; Bob turned the crank a few times and listened. He removed a few bolts and a section of the fly-wheel housing came out. Then he reached in and pulled out the remains of a mouse nest. All the car needed (for him who could tell) was a little old-fashioned spring cleaning.

The motor started and we were on our way.

THE CALDECOTT MEDAL **1959**

Chanticleer
and the Fox

adapted and illustrated by BARBARA COONEY
written by GEOFFREY CHAUCER
published by THOMAS Y. CROWELL
1958

FORMAT

SIZE: 7⅝″ x 10″, 36 pp. (unfolioed)

ARTIST'S MEDIUM: Pre-separated art, black-and-white in scratch-board; four colors on Dinobase

PRINTING PROCESS: Offset lithography

ILLUSTRATIONS: Front matter, two-color pages in black-and-red interspersed with five-color pages (black, blue, green, red and yellow)

TYPE: Perpetua, Times Roman, and hand-lettering

BOOK NOTE

RETOLD from Chaucer's *Canterbury Tales*, this adaptation of "The Nun's Priest's Tale" has rhythmic style and humor in both text and illustration, as the rooster learns not to trust the flattery of a fox. Printed in bright clear colors emphasized with strong blacks, the illustrations have vigor, as well as the detail and flavor of the Chaucerian period.

CALDECOTT AWARD ACCEPTANCE

by *Barbara Cooney*

MR. MELCHER, our patron saint, my good friends, the librarians, and all the kind people who are here tonight, you must know that the honor you have given me is the pinnacle of my life as an illustrator. And I thank you with all my heart.

When I began illustrating, years ago, the first precept that I was taught was that a book is not a book until it is in print. I believe that this statement applies more to a picture book than to any other kind. While I was told not to be too humble tonight, I think that credit must be given where it is due. The Caldecott Award is given not only for the content of a book but for the visual qualities it possesses as well. Without fine bookmaking *Chanticleer and the Fox* would not have won this award. First, credit and thanks must go to Elizabeth Riley, my editor at Thomas Y. Crowell. A horse needs a good jockey in order to win a race. Next, I would like to thank Doris Barrett for her production skill. And then my thanks to the manufacturers of the book. If *Chanticleer and the Fox* is at all a beautiful book, credit should be given to all these people, not just to me. Last of all, my thanks to my dear and good friends the salesmen who sold the book to my dear and good friends the booksellers and the librarians who bought it. And now we have come a complete circle and I will start talking about myself and *Chanticleer*.

The question most generally asked me since the Caldecott Award was announced is how did I happen to do this book, what inspired me. That question is a little embarrassing because the answer is so simple. I just happened to want to draw chickens. Quite truthfully, I have not always drawn pictures simply because I loved my subject matter. When you have a large and lovely and impractical old house with a furnace the size of the boiler on the *Queen Mary* and children growing up and needing education, sometimes, shameful as it may seem, you work for money. On the other hand, when I am working with material that I love, I do work in a sort of passionate frenzy and then I am a proper unbusinesslike artist. Sometimes books that I have loved doing have not received so much attention as some of the more routine books. Then I feel the way a mother must feel when no one dances with her daughter. But tonight — if you can stand a mixed metaphor — *Chanticleer* is belle of the ball. And nobody could be happier than I that you have chosen a book that I loved working on.

To answer more exactly this question about what inspired me, I have tried to pinpoint the event that started the ball rolling. For years I have admired the work of Chinese and Japanese artists, in particular, their landscapes and their birds. But I think that the actual day that *Chanticleer* was conceived was three years ago one autumn day. I had been out in the woods picking witch hazel and was on my way home to cook supper. As I came out of the woods I passed a little barn that I had often passed before. But never at that time of day nor when the barn door was wide open. At that hour the sun was getting low and it shone right into the doorway. The inside of the barn was like a golden stage set. At that time of year the loft was full of hay, gold hay. And pecking around the floor of the barn was a most gorgeous and impractical flock of fancy chickens — gold chickens, rust-colored chickens, black ones, white ones, speckled ones and laced ones, some with crests on their heads, some with feathered legs, others with iridescent tails, and all with vermilion-colored wattles and combs. I don't know how their egg production was but they were beautiful. I think *that* was the beginning of this book.

Then I started casting around for a vehicle for my chickens. One day when I was in bed with the grippe — I do seem to get my best ideas when I'm slightly feverish — I was reading *The Canterbury Tales*. And there, in " The Nun's Priest's Tale," was my story. Besides chickens, I had a fourteenth century setting, a farm and children, animals and growing things. What more could I ask?

Of course, the story of Chanticleer and the Fox antedates

Chaucer, but I liked the pictures he conjured up in my mind and the way in which he told the story. Chaucer had a great time poking fun at human foibles, but at the same time he understood and loved people. For, of course, Chanticleer and Partlet and the other hens are people. Partlet is a bossy little woman who winds her husband around her finger. And Chanticleer is a rather puffed-up man who does not realize that he is being pushed around. I tried to convey in my pictures what Chaucer conveys in his words: that people — in this case, chickens — can be beautiful and lovable even when they are being ridiculous.

There is another reason too for *Chanticleer and the Fox*, and that is, I do think Chaucer is possible for children. Let me tell you a little story:

I have a bright young brother-in-law, named Stephen, who, at the age of eight, was found holed up in a corner reading *The Canterbury Tales*. A fond aunt, looking over his shoulder, was surprised to find that he was reading, not a translation but the *Tales* as Chaucer had written them, in Middle English. " Why, Stephen," she exclaimed, " how can you possibly understand that!" Stephen looked up at her and smiled. " Oh, I don't mind, Aunt Eleanor," he said, shrugging his shoulders. " I'm not such a good speller myself."

I believe that children in this country need a more robust literary diet than they are getting. *Huckleberry Finn* is a classic now, but I wonder how many editors today would allow the scene in which Huck's father has the " d. t. 's " — very graphic " d. t. 's " too — and chases Huck around the cabin with a clasp-knife. In my experience, which is limited compared to that of many of you, I find that children are not harmed by such scenes and that they will digest only as much as they are ready for. On the other hand, they have a greater capacity for accepting the world as it is than seems generally supposed. It does not hurt them to read about good and evil, love and hate, life and death. Nor do I think they should read only about things that they understand. " . . . a man's reach should exceed his grasp." So should a child's. For myself, I will never talk down to — or *draw* down to — children. Much of what I put into my pictures will not be understood. How many children will know that the magpie sitting in my pollarded willow in *Chanticleer and the Fox* is an evil omen? How many children will realize that every flower and grass in the book grew in Chaucer's time in England? How many children will know or care? Maybe not a single one. Still I keep piling it on. Detail after detail. Whom am I pleasing — besides myself? I don't know. Yet if I put enough in my pictures, there may be something for everyone. Not all will be understood, but some will be understood now and maybe more later. That is good enough for me.

Before I conclude, I want you to know that many times I have sat at my drawing board and watched the cars go by with skis strapped on top and wondered why I stayed home and who I thought I was to keep working away at my pictures. (Because drawing is work. The conception is pure pleasure but the execution is work.) After all, how burning was my message, really? And to whom, if anyone, was I talking? It was like the argument we used to have as children: If a cannon was shot off in the desert and there was no one there to hear it, would it make a noise? Well, it seems that someone was lurking in the sagebrush after all.

BIOGRAPHICAL NOTE

by *Anna Newton Porter*

Barbara Cooney

MY CLAIMS to distinction are few and frail. But that my daughter-in-law should love and trust me enough to ask me to write this sketch of her is surely one of them. When I told her I was neither an artist nor an intelligent critic, she said, " But you know about *me*." So I shall try my best. It is really not too easy.

Barbara is a small woman with a slim, compact and very strong body. She wears her blond hair straight and quite short. Her face is rather sharply cut and it is, somehow, not really a modern face. It is sensitive and vulnerable, like many of Da Vinci's faces. She can look, at times, perfectly lovely, at others almost plain. Her great beauties are her long slim artist hands and her dreaming eyes.

Maine, where she spent the happy summers of her childhood, gave her a love for rocky shores, pearl-gray fog, and the flash of blue water. As a child she shared these summers with three brothers and countless cousins. Her mother is an artist and I suppose that even then Barbara was drawing and painting. She goes back to Maine every year, like a pilgrim to Mecca, and still finds it magical.

I had not known her well until she married my eldest son, so I will not try to talk about her earlier years. Talbot is a tall, quiet, dark man with a deep voice which must reassure his patients as it has always reassured me. He is blessed with a sense of humor which every doctor needs. It must stand him in good stead as he watches the sudden and unpredictable activities of his always amusing wife.

Barbara's nervous energy is enormous and her capacity for the

sensuous enjoyment of life is inexhaustible. She is many people —
a conscientious wife for a busy doctor; a fiercely loving mother,
enjoying — and spoiling — her babies with passionate devotion;
an ambitious and excellent cook; an ardent gardener, and a serious
dedicated artist.

When, nearly six years ago, my son was in California waiting to
be sent to Korea, Barbara could not go west with him for the very
good reason that her fourth child, Phoebe, was about to arrive.
As soon as possible after this event, she flew out with the four
children and stayed until Talbot sailed. A devoted friend made
the trip to California to drive east with her and her lively family,
ranging in age from ten years to eight months. Under those
circumstances, most women would, I think, have gone home by
the quickest route they could find. But not these two! "The
children may not have such a chance again," said Barbara. So all
the national parks and historic sites which could be found were
duly seen and explored. Before the blue station wagon returned
to Pepperell it had traveled twice as far as the distance across the
continent.

After the birth of the two younger children, Barbara's older
son, who had been "the baby" for quite a long time, seemed to
feel a bit left out of things. She solved this common sibling problem by rising at six instead of seven so that she and Barney could
have an hour alone together before the rest of the family got up.
This seems to my lazy self the ultimate in motherly devotion.

Her younger son had reading difficulties in the first grade, as so
many of today's children do. Barbara undertook to teach him,
and by so doing not only got him into the "advanced reading
group" but became very much interested in the phonetic method
of teaching.

When my son gave his family a television set, his wife accepted
it as perhaps a necessary evil. But, becoming increasingly dis-
gusted with what the children were hearing and seeing all day
long, she made a rash offer. "If you will let me put it away," she
promised, "I will read to you as much as you want me to." So the
TV went into a closet, behind a number of large, unwieldy ob-

jects, and Barbara settled down to three or sometimes four hours of daily reading. " I got a sore throat from reading so much," she told me, " but they'll never be such slaves to *that* thing again." Eventually the TV set emerged from banishment but it now gets only reasonable use.

The Porters live in a large, rambling, early nineteenth-century house. While Talbot was still in Korea, it was bought by Barbara after much correspondence and some trepidation and most lovingly restored to its original dignity and beauty. One could lose oneself in it — in fact I do. But does it have a studio to which she may retire? No indeed. She works in the room where the family most love to gather, except perhaps for the big brown kitchen. Her long work-table faces the fireplace. Her drawing boards and brushes and half-finished sketches are always about and seem, miraculously, to be left undisturbed. There is no separation of her creative life from her everyday domestic activity. That is perhaps because she lives as creatively as she works. The children who run and dance across her pages run and dance across her life.

Barbara is very serious about her work. A " deadline " is a sacred thing, even if she has to wait until everyone has gone to bed to get on with her pictures. If she likes a book, she lives in it while she is illustrating it. When she did *Little Women* she even wore a bun. Though none of her family felt it was really her style, it may have helped her to understand Miss Alcott's immortal sisters. She went to Concord and sketched the houses where the Marches and " Aunt March " and Laurie may have lived. She drew the kind of furniture they must have used and walked on the streets where Jo may have strolled with Laurie.

When she did *Grandfather Whiskers M.D.*, a cage of mice stood near her work-table to the delight of her children. *Chanticleer* meant a pen of chickens loaned by a neighbor. But more than that, it meant the Middle Ages and with scrupulous and loving care she studied the period of Chaucer until it came alive for her. Indeed, I think there is something a bit medieval in much of her work, a perception of the beauty of humble flowers or tiny, peering animal faces which the illuminators of old missals felt.

Dürer expressed the same feeling in the delicate foregrounds of many of his etchings and in his water colors of common weeds and grasses. I have noticed that when Barbara takes a walk in the woods she seldom returns without great armfuls of ferns or branches. She will show you, perhaps, some strange mosses or gray-green lichens or the pale untimely bloom of witch hazel.

I asked her once which of her books she liked the best — she has illustrated fifty! She thought a bit and said, " Well, *Christmas in the Barn* and *Where Have You Been?* by Margaret Wise Brown, *American Folk Songs for Children* by Ruth Crawford Seeger, *Grandfather Whiskers M.D.* by Nellie M. Leonard, *Peter's Long Walk* by Lee Kingman, and *Chanticleer*."

Peter's Long Walk, the story of a very small boy's adventure, gave her an opportunity to draw the country scenes around Pepperell to the surprise and delight of her neighbors. Like all good artists, she gives meaning and poetry to ordinary things. But if she never touched a brush again, she would still bring color and meaning and humor into her everyday living and into the lives of those she loves, for she lives so ardently.

She is always trying to do something different with herself. Once she decided to change her handwriting completely and adopt an early Italian style. Even Barbara gave this up! Nor has she been able to turn her tennis-playing husband into a trout fisherman. Last winter she thought her mind was getting rusty and that the way to cope with this unfortunate condition might be to learn Russian. Always practical, she had a large blackboard put up where she must often see it, and wrote down all the strange sounds to study in odd moments. When I last saw the blackboard, however, the Russian had been erased and her fifteen-year-old daughter had written in its place, in her very best printing, " Laud and honor to thee, O Caldecotted Creature."

Her garden was a new enterprise of two or three years ago. A winter of planning and a spring and summer of very hard work resulted in a really beautiful, bloom-filled, formally laid-out square, sheltered by an ell of the house and boasting small brick walks and a little statue. She said it was a triumph almost beyond bearing to see four children and two dogs decorously walking on the paths she meant them to walk on and not crushing the flowers. It was a dream come true — and she, somehow, makes dreams come true.

I think no one but Barbara would contemplate taking four children with her and Talbot to Washington so that they can see her receive the Caldecott Medal. It is as if she were giving them part of the credit for her achievement. Perhaps they deserve it. For she has always used them as models for her book children and through loving them has learned to love and understand all childhood.

THE CALDECOTT AWARD 1960

Nine Days
to Christmas

illustrated by MARIE HALL ETS

written by MARIE HALL ETS and
AURORA LABASTIDA

published by THE VIKING PRESS 1959

FORMAT

SIZE: 8″ x 11″, 48 pp.

ARTIST'S MEDIUM: Pencil on Dinobase — four colors

PRINTING PROCESS: Offset lithography

ILLUSTRATIONS: Front matter, four-color pre-separated art, seven single-page drawings and sixteen doublespreads, mixed

TYPE: Century

BOOK NOTE

AFTER Ceci chooses a beautiful star-shaped clay *piñata* for her first *posada*, she is heart-sick at the thought it must be broken to shower her friends with candy. But when she finds her *piñata* has become a new star in the sky, her first Christmas *posada* takes on special meaning. The pencil drawings with their gray and black tones make Ceci and her Mexican way of life quite realistic. White, reds, golds, and purples are used for emphatic highlights.

CALDECOTT AWARD ACCEPTANCE

by *Marie Hall Ets*

NINE DAYS TO CHRISTMAS is a book many people helped to make. Mexicans, as I learned after living in their country for some time, have long resented our children's books on Mexico. The beautiful May McNeer-Lynd Ward book, *The Mexican Story* (Ariel), outlining their history, is an exception. The Mexicans say that since almost half of their people live in cities, it isn't fair that we always show them as poor village Indians.

I tried to explain to Aurora Labastida, children's librarian in the Benjamin Franklin Library in Mexico City, who first told me of this, that we do more or less the same thing with all countries. We like to point out the picturesque and exotic, to emphasize the differences in costume and customs of children everywhere, but at the same time to show that they are all very much alike in their joys and their sorrows, in love of their families, their friends, their pets, in their goodness and their naughtiness. And it may be that we choose the poor because our sympathy is with them and we can more easily gain the sympathy of our readers.

I had not gone to Mexico to do a children's book and I did not want to do a book on the Mexican city child, showing that he uses bathtubs and gas stoves like ours. So when Aurora Labastida suggested it, I said that this was the story *she* should write. She said she'd like to, but how was she to start? How should she go about it? Where could she get an idea? I told her that if she wanted ideas to come, she would have to start thinking. And to think first of a good ending.

Some weeks later she came to me in great excitement. She had had an inspiration: a star *piñata* could become a real star. I thought this a fine idea and told her to write the story leading up to it. But that proved a more difficult task.

When I returned to New York, I brought our problem to May Massee at the Viking Press. And somehow, with Aurora Labastida's consent, I found myself writing this story of the little city child in Mexico, using her idea of the star *piñata* as the climax. This was not too difficult, but when Miss Massee read it she said, "Fine, if you will go back to Mexico to do the pictures."

I had many reasons for not wanting to go back at this time. But I have learned in the last twenty-five years that when it comes to children's books, May Massee knows what is necessary and right. So I went.

Some years earlier, in doing *My Dog Rinty*, whose purpose was to show a normal family life in Harlem, May Massee had decided that photographs were safer than drawings. With photographs we could not be criticized for bias and distortion. Remembering this, I decided that my drawings of Mexicans must be so photographically realistic that the people could recognize themselves and each other.

I started *first* to search for a little girl who was to be our main character. (The real Ceci was too large, and she was too blond to be typical.) I never could find the right child. But as I searched, the child I was looking for became so real in my mind that I finally used my mind's child. Everyone accepted her as real, though they couldn't quite place her. All other characters *are* real and they have been delighted to recognize themselves and each other in the pictures. They are only amused to see themselves in places where they have never been and with people they do not know. (What I didn't foresee was that the children *not* in the book would feel slighted and hurt.)

Drawing in public in Mexico was a bit difficult. Sunday afternoon in Chapultepec Park I sat on the ground next to a tree near the lake where I thought no one would notice what I was doing. But I hadn't been there many minutes when people started crowding around, watching and asking questions. Trying to understand their Spanish and answer in the few words I knew while still drawing was bad enough. But then all the boats I was sketching came crowding up to shore to learn what was going on.

The public market was still worse. Though I stood with my back to a blank wall, as much out of the way as possible, a small

crowd soon gathered to watch and ask questions. I was just drawing the fountain when an unsuspecting old woman and little boy
came and sat down on the edge of it. Quickly I sketched them in,
too. The laughter and delight of my audience at this joke on the
old woman attracted so much attention that in minutes I had a
mob around me. Soon two policemen came pushing their way
through to find out what was happening. I expected to be chased
away as a public nuisance, but the words, " Just a picture for a
children's book," in my painful Spanish, seemed to work magic.
Instead of chasing *me* away, the police cleared away the mob in
front of me so I could see. One of my arms was cramping and both
hands were asleep from drawing so long with no rest, but with the
police beside me holding back the people, I had to keep on drawing
at full speed. One must go through a great deal, I thought, for a
children's book.

Those words, *children's book*, seemed to work magic everywhere. When the owner of the little home factory for *piñatas*
hesitated about letting me draw it, I had only to say, " Just a
picture for a children's book," to get his consent. I know he
wondered why I went out to the middle of the street to draw it,
but I didn't have enough Spanish to explain. I wanted to show
the aerials on the roofs beyond so that children in the States could
see for themselves that Mexicans, too, have television.

And now my reward for all the torture and embarrassment of
drawing in public — the Caldecott Award — which should help
more than anything else to accomplish the purpose of the book. For
this I am most grateful. My thanks to Mr. Melcher and to Miss
Elizabeth Burr, Chairman, Newbery-Caldecott Awards Committee, to her committee and to all the children's librarians, not
only for myself and my editor and designer but also for Aurora
Labastida and all the friends in Mexico who did so much to help.
Thank you very much.

BIOGRAPHICAL NOTE

by *May Massee*

Marie Hall Ets

GLIMPSES of the child that was can often show the character and talents of the woman that is. So we tried to make Marie Ets remember. She was the fourth of six children, three boys and three girls, all spread four or five years apart. When she was little there were her own sisters and brothers. " I'll never forget the first time I was allowed to rock my baby brother to sleep. We were shut off in a room by ourselves, and I hardly dared breathe as I sat at the head of the cradle and rocked. And I was happy for days remembering how he had gone off to sleep the same as he did for the grown-ups."

When she was older there were the children of her older sisters and brothers. There are always children around her though she has none of her own; she has never been without intimate contact with them. She has never forgotten what it is to be a child.

There were plenty of outdoor games, boisterous play, Pom Pom Pullaway, Andy Andy Over. " That was my favorite group game. I loved the suspense which came from not knowing whether the group on the other side of the barn had caught the ball or not. If there was absolute silence you could guess they *had* caught it and were sneaking around the barn to catch *you*."

Another picture: pigtails flying straight back, Marie is running for a path that leads into the woods near their summer home. She is running to get away from her older brother, an inveterate tease — about freckles, about being a girl, about not taking dares — he gave her no peace. But she has found her refuge. Out of sight in the woods she slows down and walks quietly not to disturb her friends, the animals and birds that live there. She loves to climb a favorite tree and stretch out on a branch growing over a deer trail. There the young artist can watch " for the deer with their fawns, for porcupines and badgers, and turtles and frogs and skunks and huge pine snakes and sometimes a copperhead." Then she will run home and draw what she has seen and thought about.

She knew the woods and the creatures that live there, and she knew the farms round about and the characters who made friends of their animals. And with a vivid imagination and maturer years it is not surprising to meet Mister Penny and find his animals reciprocating his friendship when he needed their help. And the cobbler in *Mr. T. W. Anthony Woo* is right out of an old-fashioned cobbler's shop in a Wisconsin village. Mrs. Ets says she thought that story gave the children the chance to laugh at a grown-up and that was good for them.

Marie made pictures from the time she could hold a pencil or a brush. Her drawings were so good that when she was in the first grade the art supervisor asked for the " privilege " of having Marie in her class for adults. Thus began Marie's formal instruction in art and from that time on she was always drawing or painting in her spare time, much to the disgust of the older brother who was thus deprived of a victim — and doubtless of a much-loved companion. Ever since then Marie has worked at her drawing and painting in various art schools in San Francisco, Chicago, New York, and Europe.

Marie hip-hopped through the grades and high school — into high school from the seventh grade and through it in three years. Then to Lawrence College where, Marie writes, " I had my first bout with what I thought Social Injustice. I was rushed by several sororities, especially by the one to which my sisters had belonged. But a newly made friend, a drab girl from the country who had to earn her way, was entirely ignored. The idea of sororities seemed cruel and unjust and I would have nothing to do with them, in spite of my outraged sisters. (And I still think I was right.)" Marie's mother was once heard to say that she never had known a child as sensitive as Marie and then added, " or one as stubborn." The child was to need both these traits when she grew up.

After a year at Lawrence Marie decided she was wasting time — she wanted to be an artist and she should be going to an art school. She finally persuaded her parents and arrived at the art school in New York to find that no one under eighteen was allowed in life classes. So she enrolled in Interior Architecture and Decorating. At the end of a year she had a two-year diploma and a job in San Francisco, where she made sketches for three decorators who couldn't make their own. Two happy years in San Francisco and one in Los Angeles, and then tragedy ended that phase of her life. She was engaged to a young engineer, Milton Rodig, while they were both volunteer English teachers in Little Italy in San Francisco. It was during World War I, and Mr. Rodig was given a furlough from camp before going overseas. They were married and had two weeks together in a little cabin on a cliff overlooking the ocean at La Jolla. Then he went back to camp, to measles and pneumonia and death before Marie reached him. Some of the camp personnel, in an effort to help her through her sorrow, suggested that she volunteer for war work. She was sent to do protective work for girls at the Great Lakes Naval Training Station with headquarters in Waukegan. During the year that she worked there her superiors discovered that she had a gift for social work. They arranged for her to live at the Chicago Commons, a justly famous social settlement where she did volunteer work while she took her degrees at the University of Chicago, and at the School of Civics and Philanthropy. But she never lost sight of children. She writes, " Of all my volunteer work at the settlement house I think I liked best my classes in toy-making and street games with little children." That's probably where she excelled, because it used her understanding of the child's world and her inventive genius — perhaps inherited from her grandfather who was author, doctor, minister, and inventor of the first automobile, made in 1873.

After work in various sections of this country Marie was sent to Czechoslovakia to help establish child-health clinics. " But this year in Europe ended my social work, since the experimental

shots given to protect me from all the possible diseases I might encounter – one set given twice by mistake – ended my health. So
when I returned to Chicago I went back to studying art.

"When or where the idea of doing children's books came to
me, I don't know. Perhaps from my sister's five children. It was
while playing with a little nephew who loved 'smashups' that I
decided a little story with pictures might save his toys, so I made
him a cloth book. It was *Little Old Automobile*. He wore it
threadbare, but it never occurred to me to try to do it for publication until years after I had started doing picture books. Summers,
at the cottage, the children spent all their time with the animals
at a nearby farm, and I used to go up and draw. The farmer and his
children and his animals were all our good friends, but the young
bull grew too fast. One day when I had my back to him, sketching
pigs, he made a running leap and butted me into the brook."

Marie had known Doctor Harold Ets when she was living at the
Chicago Commons. He too was a volunteer worker there while
he was teaching at Loyola University Medical School. When she
came back from Czechoslovakia they were married and lived
in a charming house in Ravinia which was then in the woods on the
North Shore beyond Chicago. Marie's health grew worse, and she
spent the next few years back and forth between the Mayo Clinic
in Rochester, Minnesota, and Chicago, trying to do children's
books at the same time. During one spell of treatment she says
she "needed some comic relief and got it by the story of *Oley the
Sea Monster*."

Loyola University had made for the Century of Progress Fair
in Chicago an exhibit of the human embryo from "a life too small
to be seen at all" through the months of growth to the baby's
birth. Doctor Ets helped make the exhibit, and Mrs. Ets worked
on it as a volunteer attendant. She said that it never failed, groups
would come in talking and laughing but as soon as they looked
around them they would quiet down and by the time they left
they would go almost on tiptoe – so under the spell of the wonder
and the beauty revealed to them. So Mrs. Ets made exquisite,
accurate drawings and simple text for a picture book from "a life

too small to be seen at all to a baby's first smile." And thousands of children who could never see the exhibit have pored over the book and have been shown with reverence and truth how a baby grows within its mother's body.

Anyone as ill as Marie might easily make a career of it, but there is never a hint of it in her children's books.

Doctor Ets enjoyed them with her. He used to love to tell people that he was her model for the pig caught under the fence in *Mister Penny*. But Doctor Ets was taken ill while they lived in Ravinia. By this time Marie was well enough to care for him while she was making *In the Forest*. Two years later, when the doctor died, Marie brought her memories to New York and has lived there ever since except for periods in Rochester, New York, the backwoods of Alabama, in Mexico — and last summer following the circuses in Wisconsin.

I think my favorite of all her books is *Play with Me*. That is a perfect little girls' book and a nice thing about it is that little boys like it just as much as little girls, because it is a universal experience — the child first becoming aware of the world outside of home — always supposing that she lives where she can have " the green grass growing all around." The joy in the face of that little girl when she realizes that if she stays perfectly still all the little animals will come to her is one of the most delightful moments in the picture-book world. The fact that it is vicarious experience for thousands of children who love it just means that, thank goodness, we're still born with an instinctive love of Nature and the desire to know that we belong.

Marie Hall Ets is a brave and delightful woman with a wonderful sense of humor and play, great talent as artist and writer, and just plain genius, the greatest and most demanding gift of all.

THE CALDECOTT AWARD 1961

Baboushka and the Three Kings

illustrated by NICOLAS SIDJAKOV
written by RUTH ROBBINS
published by PARNASSUS PRESS 1960

FORMAT

SIZE: 7″ x 6½″, oblong, 25 pp. (unfolioed)
ARTIST's MEDIUM: Tempera and felt-pen in four colors
PRINTING PROCESS: Photo lithography, four colors in halftone
ILLUSTRATIONS: Front matter, combination of doublespreads and
    full pages — four colors throughout
TYPE: ATF Invitation, hand-set, photographically enlarged

BOOK NOTE

BABOUSHKA, the peasant woman in this Russian folk tale, greets
the three kings, but refuses to accompany them into the stormy
night to search for the Christ Child. But on the next morning and
ever since, she goes about seeking Him. Type face, drawings and
color all combine to give a compelling quality of mystery and
dignity to a simple tale.

CALDECOTT AWARD ACCEPTANCE

by *Nicolas Sidjakov*

AN ARTIST has to protect himself against routine, monotony, and the resulting sterility. Only by keeping flexible, away from the beaten paths and clichés, can he expect to maintain originality and freshness of approach. Otherwise, he gets to be strictly a technician, or a bore, or both. This dreadful prospect accounts for the enthusiasm I felt when the opportunity presented itself to work on my first children's book. A refreshing new medium to work with seemed like a welcome shot-in-the-arm. It turned out to be more like a revolution, resulting in more pioneering than I had ever expected. Accustomed as I was to working with a single piece of art, a new dimension, the thickness of a book — in other words continuity — was a new experience for me. The cover, end paper, title page, typography — all these many ingredients had to form an aesthetic unit. One wrong factor could ruin the whole project.

The Friendly Beasts, my first book, surprisingly enough withstood these laboratory-stage manipulations of mine reasonably well. To a great extent this is due to an almost boundless patience on the part of Ruth Robbins, who led me along, pointing out all the numerous pitfalls I was so eager to tumble into.

After a suitable recovery time, not discouraged a bit, Ruth came up with *Baboushka and the Three Kings*. This time I felt more at ease with the medium and its problems. I even had some energy left to give a thought or two to child psychology, as my four-year-old son was ever present when I worked on the illustrations. This contact with him on a literary and artistic plane proved to be extremely fruitful. We approached each other with a reticent caution, not being sure that we spoke the same language. I soon found out, indeed, that we did not, and had to realize with apprehension how adult I was. It is difficult to remember how wide open everything is for children of that age. They start out from scratch, feeling their way along, relying on bits of information they are being fed or that they pick up. By putting these pieces of a puzzle together, they arrive at their own conclusions with a marvelous logic that is inaccessible to adults.

One day, perhaps being tired of hearing, "When you grow up you can do this . . . ," and "When you grow up you can do that . . . ," my son replied, "When I grow up and you will be a little boy. . . ." It took me a while to realize that it seemed quite probable to him that as some people are growing taller, others must be getting shorter — to keep things balanced, I suppose. Now this type of reasoning would seem very valid to us, *if* we could forget everything we know or have experienced. It occurred to me that our adult reasoning and taste are based on an almost axiomatic acceptance of certain rules. It is impossible for an adult to break down this barrier. All this is to say that I realized how vain an attempt to foresee a child's reactions would be. Any condescending effort to conform to a child's tastes or beliefs would seem doomed to failure. So I did the only thing left to do . . . I forgot all about children while trying to do the best I could and something I would be satisfied with, and then, hoping for the best, submitted the final drawings to my son and his friends for approval. This method proved to be satisfactory to all parties, and when, after having manifested a quite pleased reaction to my efforts, but not wanting me to get away with it too easily, Nicolas asked me why Baboushka *always* wears tennis shoes, I merely explained patiently that this is the kind of shoe that all Russian peasants used to wear. A fact he readily accepted.

This is one little detail that happens to be true. I did, however, take some liberties with authenticity concerning Baboushka's surroundings and her clothes, despite the extensive documentation that Ruth had gathered for me. A stricter application of reality, I felt, would make it more difficult for me to get the mood I sought. Loose interpretation is quite a dangerous thing, considering the love for accuracy and detail most children seem to have. Fortunately, the story is too far removed in time and space for them to check up on me. I will add, though, that my conscience is quite clear, since I believe that a Russian feeling has been given the book through color and style. Being Russian by birth I should know something about it. Even though I have never lived in Russia, my family was as Russian as can be — pre-Revolution, of course. Since this " Baboushka " seems to have all the pre-Revolutionary characteristics, I can claim my experience as valid.

Anyhow, having won the Caldecott Award gives me the assurance that whatever reasons I had for doing whatever I did, I was on the right track and nothing I can say will express adequately my gratitude for this encouragement.

When Miss Merrill called me announcing the good news, I was, naturally, quite pleased, but, frankly, I did not even come close to realizing what it was all about. It is embarrassing to admit that I was pretty vague about the Caldecott or, for that matter, if Mr. O'Dell will forgive me, the Newbery Award. Ruth called me shortly afterwards, and when I heard her tremulous whisper and sounds of elation, I began to get suspicious. Nevertheless, knowing the tremendous enthusiasm that the Scheins express in their work, and doubting their objectivity, I was still reticent to believe the proportions of it all. That state did not last long. From that day on things began to happen, and they kept happening, and they are still happening. I have met many wonderful people — librarians, reviewers, and others — and have discovered that enthusiastic dedication to high standards in this field is not the prerogative of Mr. and Mrs. Parnassus Press exclusively. Ruth and Herman Schein deserve a big slice of this medal. Two people doing what they are doing the way they are doing it in this time of big organizations is a refreshing exception. The hardships of being a small publisher are largely compensated, I believe, by the finished product that has a feeling of direct concern and taste; every one of their books is a personal involvement, exhausting, but rewarding. May Parnassus Press stay small forever.

I would like to add that it is the most gratifying experience to see that the hard effort, the long, painful, and exciting work put into our book, not only did not go by unnoticed, but has been acknowledged with the greatest honor there is. Thank you very much.

BIOGRAPHICAL NOTE

by *Ruth Robbins*

Nicolas Sidjakov

NICOLAS SIDJAKOV was born in Riga, Latvia, of Russian parents who had fled their homeland during the Revolution. As a young child he listened to stories of " home " told to him by his own *baboushka*. And so it was a personal satisfaction for him to picture this land, some thirty years later, in *Baboushka and the Three Kings*.

Nicolas Sidjakov was a young man alone in Paris at the end of World War II, having lost his family during the shattering world events of the previous years. Now, a new life began. His first serious thoughts of pursuing an art career took form as he studied painting at the Ecole des Beaux Arts in Paris. Later he became interested in the reviving postwar motion picture industry, and this led to early work as a designer of posters and other publicity material for the new French films, Orson Welles' *Othello* among them.

During the next several years, Nicolas Sidjakov traveled in Italy, Switzerland, and Germany, living and working in each country for months at a time. Between sojourns he always returned to Paris, which was home. The changing scene provided stimulation for this artist who was constantly exploring new ideas in the world of graphic arts. His travels also provided the incentive and the opportunity to learn five languages. He is still more at ease speaking and reading French than English.

In 1954, Nicolas met a young American girl, Jean McFarland, who worked in the economic branch of the United States Embassy in Paris. Soon after their meeting, Jean became Mrs. Sidjakov, and the newly married couple returned to the United States. Since Jean's home was on the West Coast, they decided to settle in the San Francisco Bay area. The Sidjakovs, with their four-year-old son, Nicolas, Jr., now live in Sausalito; Nik's studio is in San Francisco, across the Golden Gate.

Once again, Nicolas Sidjakov plunged into a new life in a new country. It was a challenge, not only to adjust to a different pattern of living, but, at the same time, to make headway in the highly competitive field of advertising art. Very soon he began to make his way. He brought to San Francisco a fresh, vibrant style and new concepts in visual expression. His work started to gain national recognition.

My first meeting with Nik was early in 1957, when he called at Parnassus Press to discuss his desire to illustrate a book for children. Already very busy as a commercial artist, he would, nevertheless, welcome the opportunity and experience of doing a picture book. For him it would be a new medium, a new dimension to explore. Soon after this meeting I was able to give Nik the opportunity he was seeking. We had just accepted the manuscript, *The Friendly Beasts*, which seemed to be a suitable story for Nik's talent. Nik thoroughly enjoyed illustrating his first book for children. He found that it was more demanding and more rewarding than he had anticipated. The book was well received, and we were thrilled when *The Friendly Beasts* was selected by the *New York Times* as one of the ten best illustrated children's books in 1957. Nik was not only gratified, but eager to do another picture book.

Perhaps the most important decision an art director or editor has to make — the very essence of success of a picture book — is the selection of the *right* artist for the *right* story. Early in 1960, the Russian folk tale of Baboushka came to my attention, and I immediately felt it would be a stimulating theme to present to Nik. After several weeks of toil and torture I came up with what some people thought was an acceptable adaptation. When Nik called me, after reading *Baboushka and the Three Kings* in manuscript, and said, "It's wonderful! I would love to do this book!", I felt that one of our greatest difficulties was over.

I soon learned that part of Nik's great enthusiasm for the Baboushka story stemmed from his nearness to the subject. For example, as the drawings of the old woman progressed, I learned from Nik that his peasant woman would never carry a basket, but rather a sack or bag which she could sling over her shoulder, leaving her arms free for her work in the fields. Thus, the word " basket," which I had used in the story was changed to " sack."

Working with Nik on *Baboushka* taught me the art of being patient. As days and weeks went by, and deadlines began to loom, the only assurance I had that work was progressing was a verbal one from Nik. " Things are going fine," he told me repeatedly; " we'll get together and look at something soon." More time passed. I finally saw *one* drawing of the old woman, Baboushka, in her hut. But for Nik this drawing symbolized the whole book. He had thought through the sequence of illustrations page by page. Now, transferring this sequence from his " head " on to paper would be no problem. I tried to relax. After the book was completed, I reflected on Nik's way of working. Remembering that he was an ardent chess player, I understood better why he is a person who *thinks* for a long time before he makes a move. This is not to say he is a slow worker, because once he does put his brush to paper the illustrations appear in a burst of enthusiasm and sureness.

The printing of a picture book today is a complex technical process. The work of many craftsmen comes into play between the finished illustrations and the printed page. Nicolas Sidjakov has a thorough understanding of the process, and constantly applies this knowledge in planning and carrying through his work. It allows him a freedom of style and technique which is sometimes daring, because he knows that the art he is creating at his drawing board may be a challenge to the printer, but still within the printer's capabilities to reproduce faithfully. In this way he is able to realize the fullest potential inherent in modern lithography. In his style and use of color in *Baboushka and the Three Kings*, Nik used his knowledge to excellent advantage.

To Nicolas Sidjakov the creation of a book is far more than drawing the illustrations alone. We were both concerned about the selection of a suitable typeface; one that would integrate well with the mood of the book. When we did discover such a typeface, we were dismayed to learn that it had become obsolete and was not easily available. We both felt, however, that this particular type was so important to the successful design of the book that it *had* to be found. Finally, after an extensive and exhaustive search, a sufficient number of fonts was found in the basement of an old San Francisco compositor to hand-set *Baboushka* a page at a time. This typeface — called "Invitation" — because it blends so well with the primitive Russian atmosphere of the illustrations, undoubtedly gave the book a special feeling which could not otherwise have been achieved.

Nik's enthusiasm for his work is infectious. Each project he undertakes is a new challenge and a new opportunity for fresh expression. He abhors the stereotype and the trite. Only by giving every assignment his whole mind and heart does he feel that he can produce a work that is meaningful, and thereby grow as an artist. I believe the final result of all his work transmits this inspired attitude to those who see it. In this way, Nicolas Sidjakov can open new doors of visual pleasure to the young reader. It is gratifying that this sincere dedication to the creative arts has been rewarded with the highest possible honor, the Caldecott Medal.

THE CALDECOTT AWARD 1962

Once a Mouse . . .

illustrated by MARCIA BROWN
written by THE ILLUSTRATOR
published by SCRIBNER'S 1961

FORMAT

SIZE: $9\frac{3}{16}''$ x $9\frac{7}{16}''$, 32 pp. (unfolioed)
ARTIST'S MEDIUM: Woodcuts in two and three colors
PRINTING PROCESS: Offset — separations reproduced by contact
ILLUSTRATIONS: Front matter, single page in three colors, double-spreads in two and three colors, alternating, single page in two colors
TYPE: Albertus

BOOK NOTE

A SIMPLE fable from ancient India tells of the hermit who rescues a mouse from a crow and to save him from other attackers changes him from small mouse to stout cat to big dog to royal tiger. But in the tiger's dislike of being reminded he was once a mouse, lies his undoing. The texture and grain of the woodcuts, as well as the bold shapes and designs, give primitive strength to a basic tale.

CALDECOTT AWARD ACCEPTANCE

by *Marcia Brown*

Big and Little

SEVEN YEARS AGO I was in the same predicament of trying to express adequately to you my appreciation of your recognition of my work. Seven was always magical; but when the seven comes between one and two, the magic has been more than doubled.

In 1932 Luigi Pirandello wrote to his friend Bontempelli: " Can I say something to you in confidence? I know that you are a judge in the Premio Viareggio. I read the list of contestants . . . and already the problem of the young winner gives me anguish. To be born is easy; to be born in art was always less so. The great venture of every artist is, on the contrary then, when he is born, to live; — to continue to live."

Seven years can bring a person to a time in which the initial impetus that started him in his career has altered in direction or intensity, when his understanding and experience are greater, but his energy is undeniably less, and all the clocks run faster. When I was working on *Once a Mouse* . . . , I suspected that it might be my best book to date. To have you recognize it is more than doubly precious to me.

I had wanted a big subject, with few words, that would say something to a little child, and in which I could immerse myself fully. Since I had been making colored wood blocks, I wanted a theme to which colored woodcuts would add another dimension. All fall of 1960 I had been drawing at the Bronx Zoo, magnetized particularly by the tigers in the Lion House and the monkeys. Then a friend sent me a collection of animal fables, published in Italy. Here I found the ancient Indian fable of " The Hermit and the Mouse," and my big subject for little children. The very fiber of wood might say something about a hermit and animals in a jungle.

I have always felt that a good book comes from an individual sensibility, or from one of those blessed unions when two act as one. But a finished book can hardly be the work of one person, especially the trade book with a rigid production budget for whatsoever book of the same size. For reasons known only to their creators, some books are not at all "whatsoever" to the person who is making them; and he is fortunate indeed if his editors recognize this, too.

When I showed my usual little dummy to Morrell Gipson, I received that most precious of go-aheads from any editor, complete liberty to develop the book as I felt it. Margaret Evans, art editor of Scribner's, believed in the book. How can one be grateful enough to work with one who, having control over the ultimate look of a book, demonstrates a will to integrity in everything she touches, which generally means everything to do with the physical book? You who make books know how challenging and often dismaying it is to work within the limits of the trade book today. Almost every desire to communicate on a plane other than that of words and pictures is thwarted. I am very grateful to my publishers, Charles Scribner's Sons, for many things, but especially for their trying their utmost to maintain a high standard in book production. Design still includes the whole book, and not just the inside pages. Some librarians have expected all things of all books, confusing books for leisure reading with textbooks, have made almost impossible demands for stronger bindings, out of all proportion to the normal use of a book and to the strength of the paper on which it is printed. Costs, naturally, have risen; and librarians have met the publisher's complaints of distress with protests at the cost of his books. Unless these demands are tempered, and sights are set, not on technical details such as durability of bindings, but on the life of a book in the mind and heart of a child and not only in his hands, the book as we have been privileged to make it, to use it, to share it, will cease to exist. It is disappearing fast. Like the Pobbles, we shall probably have no toes, and possibly taste will be so degraded that few will know the difference. But the effect will have been felt by the children.

The " will to integrity " was a Gibralter. Margaret Evans has a craftsman's patience with things, but is an artist, with an artist's quick comprehension of another's intent. For some time we had wondered what could be done if an illustrator might work on his own plates at the printers. Reehl Lithographers could not have given us more friendly co-operation. In order to preserve the texture as well as the outline of the blocks, the book was finally printed from contact plates made from my prints on very thin tissue.

Painters today have unlimited freedom in the choice of techniques, and an almost fetishistic interest in sensuous materials. But no matter how fascinated an illustrator is by techniques, illustration must still be that — a servant charged with elucidating the idea of the book. It involves a very different mental process from painting and arises from a different level of sensibility. A little child's own art is emblematic, but often falls short of the ideal in his mind. Recognition of species only — man with two legs, dog with four — is not enough to stimulate his awakening sense of personality. The child will have to make his home in the astonishing world of the future that is beginning to erupt about us. How complete is the personality that he takes from us into that future? His books help to make it.

Can you listen once more to a very free retelling of the fable of the hermit and the mouse?

You could call it *Once a Hermit* . . .

A long time ago, before the days of " togetherness " in the literary jungle, most publishers were hermits — meditative, often mighty at magic, and, once in a while, mighty at prayer. Some wore beards, all wore at least a loin cloth, and green was the color of the leaves of the trees. The hermit publisher lived in comparative peace in the jungle, amid the lions, the dogs, the jackals, and the nightingales.

But in a corner of the publishing hut there was a little mouse that the hermit had rescued — rescued from "peeps" and "glimpses" and "little excursions" into little-known places. The hermit nourished him with fresh experiences and fed him with fantasy, and the little mouse grew.

But look! One night, down the highroad and over the bridge to the crossroads, hovered the shadow of three owls, with their sights set high, and their great eyes focused — straight on the hermit-publisher's mouse.

When he looked up and saw the danger threatening his little pet, the hermit said, among other things, a little prayer, and toughened his mouse. It became a stout cat (with a future in millions and billions and trillions of kittens).

Days and nights came and went. The cat grew handsome (on good paper and good typography), grew playful, grew wise, possessed a normal vocabulary of purrs, but also knew how to use its claws. Children who came to play often went away wiser.

By now the forest was full of owls. Many, fortunately, were still flying high, but some had set their sights lower, and were becoming more expert all the time. They blinked more during the day, saw some things double and many things not at all — or at least much less clearly than their three ancestors. Some became shortsighted and were apt to swoop on the first thing they saw. The cat had a horrid feeling that they were after his skin! They were a real challenge to the cat and his master.

Then one night a cash register was heard to jingle in the jungle. The cat ran under the bed, but the publisher opened one eye. Then they both listened, and they liked the sound. And the hermit, who hadn't quite arrived at thinking about big, thought less about little. "Expand!" he cried; and the cat became a big dog. Now, when the dog barked, it was the cash register that listened.

Then an explosion shook the world, and the jungle felt the reverberations. Hungry hucksters prowled in the jungle, seduced some of the painters and nightingales, bedazzled or silenced forever some of the owls, and then leaped on the dog.

The hermit was already unnerved by the hootings of fearful owls. He lost his head. He forgot who he was and why he was.

He also forgot what was his dog. With a gesture to improving him, he changed the dog into a handsome tiger.

Superficially, the tiger resembled the cat, but he was much more blown up. His coat was brilliant, decorated by the most publicized artists. But he was hamstrung; his legs moved in only one direction — ahead. He roared in yelps to beginners beginning to be beginning. He frightened no one though, for the hermit, remembering that the cat's claws had made careful children cautious, had filed the claws of the tiger down to the pads. And every time he stepped off the path, the owls descended on him like hawks.

But you don't have to imagine the pride of the tiger. It was quite apparent. He fed on firsts and mosts and bests. He littered in so many new series a year that he couldn't always give much thought to the last of his litters. He lorded it over the other animals, because those taller than he had all been cut down.

People who came to look marveled at his size. "And to think that that tiger was once a mouse!" they said. The tiger was humiliated at this. He decided to destroy the hermit. But the hermit saw red. Quickly consolidating his forces and funds, he ceased altogether to be a hermit, leaped on the tiger's back, and rode him off into the jungle.

As for the children, they too had been hypnotized by all that brightness, charmed by those roars. Around a pool in the forest, many sat all day, gazing at their own reflections. They called into caverns, listening for the sound of their own voices. Many couldn't get over their beginning. They passed with averted faces the pens where the hobbled heroes were kept — the cages of the eagles with clipped wings, the soiled swans — to enter their private tunnels through the undergrowth. Because they had so little time for wandering, they liked their tunnels straight. And the tunnels often emptied into deserts, from which they could set their sights on distant stars, having lost interest in their own.

And now, at the end of the spring, there is a great gathering of birds in the palms by the sea at the edge of the jungle: hawks and magpies, warblers and crows, larks and doves. They plan, they sing, they celebrate. But the owls that have not turned ostrich, the owls that think ahead to the fall and winter, that have seen the retreat of the hermit, ask each other, " Is it partly our fault that he rides his tiger deeper and deeper into the jungle? Can he remember any more how it was to be a hermit? Can he ever stop thinking about big – to think once more about little?"

BIOGRAPHICAL NOTE

by *Helen Adams Masten*

From Caldecott to Caldecott

IT HAS BEEN only seven years since Marcia Brown won the Caldecott medal for her *Cinderella*. Comparing the exquisite little *gouache* drawings for *Cinderella* with the strong and rhythmically beautiful woodcuts for *Once a Mouse* . . . , one realizes that this artist has come a long way in seven years.

An artist grows by living, by traveling, studying, reading, looking with a seeing eye, drawing and painting everything that comes his way. What he does when he is *not* working on a book often determines not only the nature of his future work but also the quality of it.

A trip to Europe in 1956, which culminated in nearly a year spent in Paris and, later, almost three years living in Venice, opened up a whole new world to an artist whose eyes are quick to take in beauty of form, line, and color. During her years in Italy, Marcia studied Italian, which she now speaks and writes very well. While there the year before last, she did a good deal of research in the Marciana and Querini-Stampaglia Libraries for a prospective book for children somewhat older than the picture-book age.

Marcia uses her large collection of art books as one does an art gallery, for refreshment and study. She usually leafs through a book after breakfast until she finds something she wants to study. Reading, listening to music, and playing the flute are very important to her; but, when she is working on a book, almost nothing is allowed to interfere with her work, except the telephone. Sometimes even its persistent ringing is ignored.

Everywhere Marcia goes — whether it is Brittany, Denmark, Holland, or Spain — she sketches people, in the parks, on the subways, at the ballet, the circus or the beach. Many days are spent sketching at the zoo: goats, the big cats, birds, scenes through the trees. In her sketchbooks are some of the best drawings she has made. Later, some of these sketches form the basis for paintings in oil. Sometimes they are unintentional preparation for drawings for books.

The Three Billy Goats Gruff sprang onto the pages so fast that the artist's dummy was completed in five days. To create an entire picture book in a few days is only possible when an artist has lived with a story a very long time, when each picture is crystal clear in the mind's eye. *The Three Billy Goats Gruff* was always a favorite story with Marcia and it has proved to be the children's favorite as well.

In a story hour at The New York Public Library, I had the pleasure of using the artist's dummy with the children. There was never any doubt in the minds of the children, from the moment the goats appeared on the Norwegian hillside, that they would get the better of the troll. Little moans of pleasure and anticipation could be heard as I turned the page and they saw the Big Billy Goat Gruff fairly bursting with energy and confidence, sending forth his challenge to the troll. At the end of the story hour every child was clamoring to take home the artist's copy. No other book would satisfy them. For weeks they returned to the Library to ask for *The Three Billy Goats Gruff*, " the one with all the pictures." The drawings for this book are in crayon and ink. Marcia's conception of the troll is based on nature — fog, rocks, earth, and the roots of trees. One sees in the drawings small, rocky islands, some of the hundreds that dot the Norwegian coast. They are the troll after the Big Billy Goat Gruff has disposed of him.

Anne Carroll Moore's obvious delight in the artist's drawings settled the matter of the dedication, which reads, "To Anne Carroll Moore and the Troll." Miss Moore had a deep love of Norway following a visit there years ago.

All during the fall and through the winter of 1956 Marcia worked on *The Flying Carpet*. Being one of the more complicated and sophisticated of the Arabian Nights stories, *The Flying Carpet* is seldom included in editions intended for children. After research into translations and versions, the threads of the story were rewoven by Marcia to make a cohesive story, understandable to children. The original drawings for the book have great beauty. Unfortunately, some of this is lost in the printing, because the artist — always eager to experiment with new technical processes — used a combination of gold dust and gum arabic in making color separations. This combination allowed less light to filter through than was intended, with the result that a sky, spangled with stars and filled with beauty, became ominous with black clouds. In spite of the difficulties of printing, it is a beautiful book, greatly enjoyed by older children. Much of its distinction comes from the beautiful typography of Margaret Evans. Marcia has been most fortunate in her association with Margaret Evans, who has given of her time and knowledge of printing and design in the making of distinctive books. *Felice, Peter Piper's Alphabet,* and *Tamarindo!* were chosen by the American Institute of Graphic Arts for their Children's Book Show 1958-1960. The New York Society of Illustrators selected *Felice* and *Once a Mouse . . .* for their shows.

Marcia has been fortunate, also, in her long association and friendship with her editors, Alice Dalgliesh and Margaret McElderry. The latter she met the very first day she came to work in the Library. The understanding and respect of her editors have given her the necessary freedom to work.

One St. Nicholas Eve in the Central Children's Room, Anne Carroll Moore read aloud *Peter Piper's Practical Principles of Plain and Perfect Pronunciation.* Miss Moore's reading of the rhyme was inimitable. It brought out all the wit and humor in the verses. Marcia immediately saw the possibilities of the rhyme as a picture book. Almost at once the pictures began to evolve. When the book was more than half completed, Tip-Toe Tommy turned Turk and went right off on a carpet. Marcia apparently went off on a carpet, too, for she dropped *Peter Piper* and nothing more was seen of him until *The Flying Carpet* was off the presses.

When *Peter Piper's Alphabet* was finally completed in 1959, I went with Marcia to show it to Miss Moore, who had been very ill. Her laughter over the funny drawings, and her eagerness to keep the book for a few days to enjoy it further confirmed Marcia's feeling that the book really belonged to Miss Moore.

It is a delight to use this picture book in the picture-book hour, the story hour, or with class groups. All one needs to do is to read the witty " P-Preface," found in the first American edition, to send boys and girls off into gales of laughter and pursuit of the riddles in the pictures. The drawings have caught completely the ridiculous nonsense of the verses.

Marcia is always quick to see cats, wherever they are, as individuals with marked personalities. Most of her books have a cat somewhere in them. One night while she and I were exploring some alleys in Naples, we saw a cat quivering with anticipation, watching a darkened window high up in a wall. We stopped to watch; and in a few moments a light flashed on. A woman watching with us cried out " *Ecco!*" and out of the window came a basket on a long cord, lowered by an unseen hand. The cat raced across the alley, snatched a fish, and ran off with his supper. We stared at each other, delighted. Out of this incident *Felice* was born in Venice. Marcia's studio in Venice is on the same canal where the children swam in *Felice*. All winter long eight or nine stray cats were fed by her in the same way that Gino fed Felice.

From the moment Marcia saw Venice, she, like other artists, fell in love with it. Its decaying architectural beauty, its sparkling waters, tiny *campi*, and mysterious canals are there in *Felice* for children to enjoy and explore, along with the story of the homeless little cat. The original drawings are done in water colors. Margaret Evans and Marcia finally succeeded in getting this book printed from process plates, using the artist's own colors. It is a truly fine printing job.

In the spring of 1956 Marcia was in Sicily. The fields and hills were covered with daisies and poppies under the ancient, gray-green olive trees, the blossoming fruit trees, and the tall, black cypresses. Everywhere was beauty. Everywhere were big-eyed children and small, worn donkeys. Years before, a Sicilian friend had told Marcia of a childhood experience with a lost donkey. Now the story came alive for her once more as she saw for herself the Sicilian countryside and the village life so vividly described by her friend. The result was *Tamarindo!*, published in 1960. In the crayon-and-ink drawings the Sicilian landscape blossoms again in a happy story of four little boys and the lost donkey of her friend's childhood. The amusing and delightful pictures reveal many Sicilian ways. One has only to look at the picture of the *men* eating under the arbor to see that the *women* know their place.

It was while Marcia was working on *Tamarindo!* that she stopped long enough to help a friend by designing some charming stage sets, costumes, and a flyer. The designs were for a production of Eleanor's Farjeon's *The Glass Slipper* presented by The Pocket Players during the Christmas season.

In 1960 came also the publication of *Une Drôle de Soupe*, a French translation of *Stone Soup* made by Marcia's friend and teacher, Hilda Grenier Tagliapietra. *Une Drôle de Soupe* has been a welcome addition to the small collection of books which add interest to the learning of a new language.

On Marcia's return from Europe she drew and painted at the Art Students' League and other studios, sketched often at the Bronx Zoo, and worked on paintings in her own studio overlooking the East River. The paintings were abandoned when she became interested in an old legend from the Sanskrit.

The legend, " The Hermit and the Mouse," she found in a book sent from Italy. Marcia decided to rework the story and cut the pictures in wood. She had made wood carvings as a young student, using only a jackknife, and had cut *Dick Whittington and His Cat* in linoleum. Since, after studying with Louis Schanker, she had made many woodcuts, she came to the book with knowledge and skill. I think, however, she was unaware of the enormous amount of sheer physical labor the book was to exact from her. Since Marcia is a perfectionist, many blocks and prints were discarded. There were nights when she worked until two o'clock, carving, printing, proving the blocks. In July of 1961, after she had seen first proofs, Marcia sailed for Spain, exhausted and drained. Later, she returned to Venice and a studio to paint and draw for a year.

After she had sailed, I found in our wood basket some of the discarded blocks for *Once a Mouse.* . . . Since they seemed far too good and too interesting for kindling, they did not light my fire. *Once a Mouse* . . . has, in some of its pages, a Biblical quality. I have seen pictures of Moses which had less authority than the drawing of the hermit rebuking the tiger. There are fine composition, glowing color, humor, tenderness, and strength in this beautiful book which make it truly worthy of the Caldecott Medal.

THE CALDECOTT AWARD 1963

The Snowy Day

illustrated by EZRA JACK KEATS
written by THE ILLUSTRATOR
published by THE VIKING PRESS 1962

FORMAT

SIZE: 9″ x 8″, oblong, 32 pp.
ARTIST'S MEDIUM: Collage — cut papers and materials, some worked on with paint; some stamped with patterns cut in gum erasers
PRINTING PROCESS: Offset lithography
ILLUSTRATIONS: Front matter, full-color collage doublespreads throughout
TYPE: Aldine Bembo

BOOK NOTE

THROUGH a day of adventure and discovery, Peter finds all the joys and wonders of fresh-fallen snow in the city. Such a simple story is given excitement and strength by the sure and dramatic use of color and shapes.

CALDECOTT AWARD ACCEPTANCE

by *Ezra Jack Keats*

I AM very happy to be here to receive this great honor for a book which means so much to me, a book which led me into new avenues of expression.

I would like to tell you how *The Snowy Day* was done, and how I arrived at the technique used in it. However, it would be more accurate to say that I found myself participating in the evolvement of the book.

First let me tell you about its beginnings. Years ago, long before I ever thought of doing children's books, while looking through a magazine I came upon four candid photos of a little boy about three or four years old. His expressive face, his body attitudes, the very way he wore his clothes, totally captivated me. I clipped the strip of photos and stuck it on my studio wall, where it stayed for quite a while, and then it was put away.

As the years went by, these pictures would find their way back to my walls, offering me fresh pleasure at each encounter.

In more recent years, while illustrating children's books, the desire to do my own story about this little boy began to germinate. Up he went again — this time above my drawing table. He was my model and inspiration. Finally I began work on *The Snowy Day*. When the book was finished and on the presses, I told Annis Duff, whose guidance and empathy have been immeasurable, about my long association with this little boy. How many years was it? I went over to *Life* magazine and had it checked. To my astonishment they informed me that I had found him twenty-two years ago!

Now for the technique — I had no idea as to how the book would be illustrated, except that I wanted to add a few bits of patterned paper to supplement the painting.

As work progressed, one swatch of material suggested another, and before I realized it, each page was being handled in a style I had never worked in before. A rather strange sequence of

events came into play. I worked — and waited. Then quite unexpectedly I would come across just the appropriate material for
the page I was working on.

For instance, one day I visited my art supply shop looking for
a sheet of off-white paper to use for the bed linen for the opening pages. Before I could make my request, the clerk said, " We
just received some wonderful Belgian canvas. I think you'll like
to see it." I hadn't painted on canvas for years, but there he was
displaying a huge roll of canvas. It had just the right color and
texture for the linen. I bought a narrow strip, leaving a puzzled clerk wondering what strange shape of picture I planned to
paint.

The creative efforts of people from many lands contributed to
the materials in the book. Some of the papers used for the collage came from Japan, some from Italy, some from Sweden, many
from our own country.

The mother's dress is made of the kind of oilcloth used for
lining cupboards. I made a big sheet of snow-texture by rolling
white paint over wet inks on paper and achieved the effect of
snow flakes by cutting patterns out of gum erasers, dipping them
into paint, and then stamping them onto the pages. The gray
background for the pages where Peter goes to sleep was made by
spattering India ink with a toothbrush.

Friends would enthusiastically discuss the things they did as
children in the snow, others would suggest nuances of plot, or a
change of a word. All of us wanted so much to see little Peter
march through these pages, experiencing, in the purity and inno-
cence of childhood, the joys of a first snow.

I can honestly say that Peter came into being because we wanted
him; and I hope that, as the Scriptures say, " a little child shall
lead them," and that he will show in his own way the wisdom of
a pure heart.

BIOGRAPHICAL NOTE

by *Esther Hautzig*

Ezra Jack Keats

THE quality one immediately senses in Ezra Jack Keats is his genuine love for children. And what is more important, he not only loves children, he respects them, understands them, and *listens* to them. So many people love children, but, alas, so few really take the trouble to listen to them and understand them on their own level. Children have problems; they experience frustrations that seem unimportant to us as we look down on them from our Mount Olympus of adulthood; they take pleasure in things which may seem insignificant to us. But a sympathetic observer of children, and one who remembers his childhood as vividly and perceptively as does Ezra Jack Keats, knows instinctively, without deliberation and courses in child psychology, what the world of childhood is really like.

A snowy day, a beautiful, brisk snowy day can be a glorious experience for a child — and it is just that for Peter in the Caldecott Medal-winning book, *The Snowy Day.* The loss of a dog in a big, strange city can be a terrible and sad experience for a child, especially for a child who does not speak English, and it is just that for Juanito in *My Dog Is Lost!* (Crowell), which Ezra Jack Keats illustrated and wrote with Pat Cherr. That Peter is a Negro child and Juanito a Puerto Rican boy reflects Mr. Keats's desire to do books for all children.

Everything that concerns children interests him, be it the troubles of a young Puerto Rican neighbor like Juanito, who wanted a dog desperately but was not allowed to have one, or an appealing photograph of a boy just like Peter which he clipped from a magazine and saved for more than twenty years. When Mr. Keats decided to write and illustrate *The Snowy Day,* he found the clipping and put it in front of him because he felt that it would give him the feeling of ease and naturalness that the little boy had. When he showed the first few doublespreads of *The Snowy Day* to Annis Duff, his editor at Viking Press, he had alternate pages of full color and black and white. He says, " I'll be everlastingly grateful to Mrs. Duff because she asked me to do the whole book in full color, and while it made for an enormous increase in production costs, it was just the thing to have done! "

Ezra Jack Keats came to illustrating children's books after being a painter for a number of years. Following his discharge from the army at the end of World War II he made some full-color illustrations for the now-defunct magazine *Collier's*, and, having saved up enough money, he went to Europe for a year. He spent most of that time in Paris. When he returned to the United States he produced some book jackets for adult novels. One of them caught the attention of Elizabeth Riley, who asked Mr. Keats to do a jacket for a teen-age novel which was being published at the Thomas Y. Crowell Company. Shortly afterward Miss Riley suggested that Mr. Keats illustrate one of Elisabeth Hubbard Lansing's books, *Jubilant for Sure*, which is set in the hills of Kentucky. Mr. Keats recalls in detail the beginning of his career in the field of children's book illustration:

I liked *Jubilant for Sure* very much, and I wanted to do a good job, so I decided it was time for a trip. I didn't know anyone in Kentucky, but I knew remotely someone in Tennessee so I went down to the Smokies and decided to sketch there. One day I got a hitch on an ice truck and, as we were bumping along, I saw a really typical shack that had an old porch and a rocker. I asked the driver to stop and hopped off. As I was sketching I suddenly noticed on the righthand side of the porch a four-year-old girl, with a head of golden curls. She looked very boldly and calmly at me and kept shifting over so she was directly in front of me. I included her in my drawing and then showed it to her. She smiled but wasn't a bit surprised. She had never seen anyone draw! While I was talking with the child, her mother came out. She looked at the drawing and thought it very nice. She asked me to stay to lunch, which would be ready when the little girl's father and grandfather came home. So I joined them and we had a very nice lunch. When it was over, they invited me to stay with them for a few days. I could see that they weren't very well off, so I said that I would stay, but that I would like to pay for my share of the expenses. In that case, the father said, the invitation was off. So I accepted and spent a whole week with them, living right in the house with them, and what a marvelous experience it was. I had a wonderful time with that child!

Having a wonderful time with a child happened at the beginning of Ezra Jack Keat's distinguished career as a children's book illustrator, and his enjoyment of children's company has obviously not dimmed with the years. His own childhood was spent in Brooklyn, where he was the youngest of three children. He began to draw when he was very young; but, as he recalls it, he first became aware that his drawing meant anything to anybody when he was about nine or ten years old.

We had this kitchen table — it was enamel, with two drawers, one for silverware, the other for bread. Anyway, I proceeded to draw on the top of it, all the things kids draw pretty much, a profile of a lady with long lashes and a lot of curls. . . . I filled up the entire table with pictures of little cottages, curly smoke coming out of the chimneys, men's profiles, and kids. I drew an Indian and a Chinese with straw hat and pigtails. . . . I finished, the entire area was covered with sketches, completely covered with them. My mother came in and I expected her to say, " What have you been doing? " and " Get that sponge and wash it off! " Instead she looked at me and said, " Did you do that? Isn't it wonderful! " and she proceeded to look at each thing and clucked her tongue and said, " Now isn't that nice! " Then she said, " You know, it's so wonderful, it's a shame to wash it off." So she got out the tablecloth which we used only on Friday nights and she covered the whole little mural and every time a neighbor would come in, she'd unveil it to show what I had done. They'd all say, " Mmm, isn't that nice." They couldn't say anything else, Mother was so proud.

From the table-top mural, Ezra Jack Keats went on to other drawing. But his father did not look on the young artist's work with the same approval his mother had shown. Mr. Keats's father was a waiter in Greenwich Village when it was the Bohemia of America. He must have seen a great deal of deprivation and starvation there, for he constantly warned his son, " Never be an artist; you'll be a bum, you'll starve, you'll have a terrible life." But the boy painted nevertheless. When he heard his father coming up the stairs, he would hide everything as fast as he could under the long oilcloth cover of the sewing machine.

My father would come in and smell the paints and say, " You've been painting. Get out and play ball and stop making a fool of yourself." So I had to go out and play ball. . . . Then one day he came home and said, " If you don't think artists starve, well, let me tell you. One man came in the other day and swapped me a tube of paint for a bowl of soup." My father put down a brand-new tube of paint. I thought how lucky I was that the poor man had to make such a swap. The swap happened again and again, and one day my father brought home a package of brushes, very inexpensive brushes which no professional artist would have bought. It dawned on me that my father was buying this stuff for me and had a terrible conflict. He was proud of my paint-ing and he wanted to supply me with paint, but at the same time he lived in real dread of my living a life like that of the artists he had seen.

Mr. Keats's father continued to supply paints and brushes and he continued to complain. But once, when the boy made a sign for the candy store across the street from his home and got a quarter for it, his father was impressed. He said, " See, now you're using your head. You'll become a sign painter and you'll make a decent living, and you'll be a lot better off than these artists I see in the Village."

Once, a day Ezra Jack Keats remembers perfectly even now, his father took him to the Metropolitan Museum.

My father thought that the most important paintings in the world would be those of important people. He showed me Gilbert Stuart's painting of George Washington and Andrew Jackson's portrait and all the colonial paintings. . . . It was all very nice and it was all really dull, and I was getting tired. Suddenly I looked down the length of the corridor and at the other end was an arched doorway which opened to another gallery, completely bathed in sunlight. Framed in that arch-way was Daumier's *Third Class Carriage.* I never heard of Daumier and I knew nothing about his painting. . . . I felt a pounding in my heart and I just turned toward it and walked toward it as though hypnotized. As I got closer to it, it glowed more magnificently. . . .

The father lived to see his son become a professional artist, but he never uttered a word of praise when Ezra won a number of prizes upon graduation from Thomas Jefferson High School. After his father's death, Ezra Jack Keats found in a wallet tattered clippings about all the prizes he had won. " He never said a word to me about it, and when I looked into that wallet I looked into a different man."

Since those days, long ago, Mr. Keats has received words of praise from many sources. The books he has illustrated and those he has written have been praised by reviewers, educators, librarians, and, most of all, by children. Some months ago, my six-year-old daughter was showing her very best friend her well-worn copy of *The Snowy Day* and a picture of Ezra Jack Keats which appeared in *Publishers' Weekly* at the time of the announcement of the Caldecott Medal. " *My* friend Jack Keats wrote this book," she said with awe, " and it was picked as the best book in the world."

Ezra Jack Keats *is* her friend, as he is every child's friend, and *The Snowy Day is* undoubtedly " the best book in the world " to a multitude of children.

THE CALDECOTT AWARD 1964

Where the Wild Things Are

illustrated by MAURICE SENDAK

written by THE ILLUSTRATOR

published by HARPER & ROW 1963

FORMAT

SIZE: 10″ x 9″, oblong, 44 pp. (unfolioed)

ARTIST'S MEDIUM: India ink line over full-color tempera

PRINTING PROCESS: Offset lithography

ILLUSTRATIONS: Twenty full-color doublespreads

TYPE: Cheltenham Bold

BOOK NOTE

WHEN he is sent to bed without his supper, expressive Max discovers the place where the wild things are. With a magic look he tames them, only to discover that being the king of all wild things is lonely. His going home to eat supper is a happy ending. The wild imagination and humor combined make a fantasy well understood by many children. Max is a believable hero and the wild things gorgeously wild.

CALDECOTT AWARD ACCEPTANCE

by *Maurice Sendak*

THIS talk will be an attempt to answer a question. It is one that is frequently put to me, and it goes something like this: Where did you ever get such a crazy, scary idea for a book? Of course the question refers to *Where the Wild Things Are*. My on-the-spot answer always amounts to an evasive "Out of my head." And that usually provokes a curious and sympathetic stare at my unfortunate head, as though — à la Dr. Jekyll — I were about to prove my point by sprouting horns and a neat row of pointy fangs.

It is an incredibly difficult question. But if I turn to the work of Randolph Caldecott and define the single element that, in my opinion, most accounts for his greatness, then I think I can begin to answer it. Besides, this gives me an excuse to talk about some of the qualities I most enjoy in the work of one of my favorite teachers.

I can't think of Caldecott without thinking of music and dance. *The Three Jovial Huntsmen* beautifully demonstrates his affinity for musical language. It is a songbook animated by a natural, easy contrapuntal play between words and pictures. The action is paced to the beat of a perky march, a comic fugue, and an English country dance — I can hear the music as I turn the pages.

I am infatuated with the musical accompaniment Caldecott provides in his books, for I have reached for that very quality in my own. In fact, music is essential to my work. I feel an intense sympathy between the shape of a musical phrase and that of a drawn line. Sketching to music is a marvelous stimulant to my imagination, and often a piece of music will give me the needed clue to the look and color of a picture. It is great fun to look for just the right color on paper that Wagner found in a musical phrase to conjure up a magic forest.

No one in a Caldecott book ever stands still. If the characters are not dancing, they are itching to dance. They never walk; they skip. Almost the first we see of The Great Panjandrum Himself is his foot, and its attitude makes us suspect that the rest of his hidden self is dancing a jig. I remember my own delight in choreographing dances for picture-book characters; my favorite is a bouncy ballet some Ruth Krauss children danced to a Haydn serenade. I think Caldecott would have been sympathetic to such extravagances, for he was endowed with a fabulous sense of lively animation, a quality he shares with my other favorite illustrators: Boutet de Monvel, Wilhelm Busch, Hans Fischer, and André François. Characters who dance and leap across the page, loudly proclaiming their personal independence of the paper — this is perhaps the most charming feature of a Caldecott picture book. Think of his three clowning huntsmen, red in the face, tripping, sagging, blowing frantically on their horns, receding hilariously into the distance and then galloping full-blast back at you. It has the vivacity of a silent movie, and the huntsmen are three perfect Charlie Chaplins.

One can forever delight in the liveliness and physical ease of Caldecott's picture books, in his ingenious and playful elaborations on a given text. But so far as I am concerned, these enviable qualities only begin to explain Caldecott's supremacy. For me, his greatness lies in the truthfulness of his personal vision of life. There is no emasculation of truth in his world. It is a green, vigorous world rendered faithfully and honestly in shades of dark and light, a world where the tragic and the joyful coexist, the one coloring the other. It encompasses three slaphappy huntsmen, as well as the ironic death of a mad, misunderstood dog; it allows for country lads and lasses flirting and dancing round the Maypole, as well as Baby Bunting's startled realization that her rabbit skin came from a creature that was once alive.

My favorite example of Caldecott's fearless honesty is the final page of *Hey Diddle Diddle*. After we read " And the dish ran away with the spoon," accompanied by a drawing of the happy couple, there is the shock of turning the page and finding a picture of the dish broken into ten pieces — obviously dead — and the spoon being hustled away by her angry parents, a fork and a knife.

There are no words that suggest such an end to the adventure; it is a purely Caldecottian invention. Apparently he could not resist enlarging the dimensions of this simple nursery rhyme by adding a last sorrowful touch.

Caldecott never tells half-truths about life, and his honest vision, expressed with such conviction, is one that children recognize as true to their own lives.

Truthfulness to life — both fantasy life and factual life — is the basis of all great art. This is the beginning of my answer to the question, Where did you get such a crazy, scary idea for a book? I believe I can try to answer it now if it is rephrased as follows: What is your vision of the truth, and what has it to do with children?

During my early teens I spent hundreds of hours sitting at my window, sketching neighborhood children at play. I sketched and listened, and those notebooks became the fertile field of my work later on. There is not a book I have written or picture I have drawn that does not, in some way, owe them its existence. Last fall, soon after finishing *Where the Wild Things Are*, I sat on the front porch of my parents' house in Brooklyn and witnessed a scene that could have been a page from one of these early notebooks. I might have titled it " Arnold the Monster."

Arnold was a tubby, pleasant-faced little boy who could instantly turn himself into a howling, groaning, hunched horror — a composite of Frankenstein's monster, the Werewolf, and Godzilla. His willing victims were four giggling little girls, whom he chased frantically around parked automobiles and up and down front steps. The girls would flee, hiccuping and shrieking, " Oh, help! Save me! The monster will eat me! " And Arnold would lumber after them, rolling his eyes and bellowing. The noise was ear-splitting, the proceedings were fascinating.

At one point Arnold, carried away by his frenzy, broke an unwritten rule of such games. He actually caught one of his victims. She was furious. " You're not supposed to catch me, dope," she said, and smacked Arnold. He meekly apologized, and a moment later this same little girl dashed away screaming the game song: " Oh, help! Save me! " etc. The children became hot and mussed-looking. They had the glittery look of primitive creatures going through a ritual dance.

The game ended in a collapse of exhaustion. Arnold dragged himself away, and the girls went off with a look of sweet peace on their faces. A mysterious inner battle had been played out, and their minds and bodies were at rest, for the moment.

I have watched children play many variations of this game. They are the necessary games children must conjure up to combat an awful fact of childhood: the fact of their vulnerability to fear, anger, hate, frustration — all the emotions that are an ordinary part of their lives and that they can perceive only as ungovernable and dangerous forces. To master these forces, children turn to fantasy: that imagined world where disturbing emotional situations are solved to their satisfaction. Through fantasy, Max, the hero of my book, discharges his anger against his mother, and returns to the real world sleepy, hungry, and at peace with himself.

Certainly we want to protect our children from new and painful experiences that are beyond their emotional comprehension and that intensify anxiety; and to a point we can prevent premature exposure to such experiences. That is obvious. But what is just as obvious — and what is too often overlooked — is the fact that from their earliest years children live on familiar terms with disrupting emotions, that fear and anxiety are an intrinsic part of their everyday lives, that they continually cope with frustration as best they can. And it is through fantasy that children achieve catharsis. It is the best means they have for taming Wild Things.

It is my involvement with this inescapable fact of childhood — the awful vulnerability of children and their struggle to make themselves King of all Wild Things — that gives my work whatever truth and passion it may have.

Max is my truest and therefore my dearest creation. Like all children, he believes in a flexible world of fantasy and reality, a world where a child can skip from one to the other and back again in the sure belief that both really exist. Another quality that makes him especially lovable to me is the directness of his approach. Max doesn't shilly-shally about. He gets to the heart of the matter with the speed of a superjet, a personality trait that is happily suited to the necessary visual simplicity of a picture book.

Max has appeared in my other books under different names: Kenny, Martin, and Rosie. They all have the same need to master the uncontrollable and frightening aspects of their lives, and they all turn to fantasy to accomplish this. Kenny struggles with confusion; Rosie, with boredom and a sense of personal inadequacy; and Martin, with frustration.

On the whole they are a serious lot. Someone once criticized me for representing children as little old people worrying away their childhood. I do not deny that a somber element colors my vision of childhood, but I reject the implication that this is not a true vision. It seems a distortion, rather, to pretend to a child that his life is a never-ending ring-around-the-rosie. Childhood *is* a difficult time. We know it is a marvelous time as well — perhaps even the best time of all. Certainly all children's games are not therapeutic attempts to exorcise fear; often they are just for fun.

Max too is having fun, and not by playing hide-and-seek with Sigmund Freud. He is delighted at having conjured up his horrific beasts, and their willingness to be ordered about by an aggressive miniature king is for Max his wildest dream come true. My experience suggests that the adults who are troubled by the scariness of his fantasy forget that my hero is having the time of his life and that he controls the situation with breezy aplomb. Children do watch Max. They pick up his confidence and sail through the adventure deriving, I sincely hope, as much fun as he does. These are the children who send me their own drawings of Wild Things: monstrous, hair-raising visions; dream creatures, befanged and beclawed, towering King-Konglike over jungle islands. They make my Wild Things look like cuddly fuzzballs.

The realities of childhood put to shame the half-true notions in some children's books. These offer a gilded world unshadowed by the least suggestion of conflict or pain, a world manufactured by those who cannot — or don't care to — remember the truth of their own childhood. Their expurgated vision has no relation to the way real children live.

I suppose these books have some purpose — they don't frighten adults, those adults who cling to the great nineteenth-century fantasy that paints childhood as an eternally innocent paradise. These so-called children's books are published under false colors, for they serve only to indulge grownups. They are passed from adult to adult, for they could be loved only by adults who have a false and sentimental recollection of childhood. My own guess is that they bore the eyeteeth out of children.

The popularity of such books is proof of endless pussyfooting about the grim aspects of childlife, pussyfooting that attempts to justify itself by reminding us that we must not frighten our children. Of course we must avoid frightening children, if by that we mean protecting them from experiences beyond their emotional capabilities; but I doubt that this is what most people mean when they say, "We must not frighten our children." The need for half-truth books is the most obvious indication of the common wish to protect children from their everyday fears and anxieties, a hopeless wish that denies the child's endless battle with disturbing emotions.

Ursula Nordstrom has been a lifelong friend. I say "lifelong" because the best part of my life began when I was able to put my talents to use, and she was there to creatively guide me. She earned new respect from me when she confessed her squeamishness on seeing the first pictures for *Where the Wild Things Are*. This confession of misgivings and her realization that she was reacting in stereotyped adult fashion was a confession of utmost truth, and only she could have made it. This is how she put it recently: "And so we remembered once again, as so many times in the past, that the children are new and we are not." Her support and unflagging enthusiasm helped bring the book to a happy conclusion.

And I will not easily forget the pale face of Dorothy Hagen, art director, her sad, suicidal look at the prospect of examining yet another sheet of color proofs. I owe her much.

With *Where the Wild Things Are* I feel that I am at the end of a long apprenticeship. By that I mean all my previous work now seems to have been an elaborate preparation for it. I believe it is an immense step forward for me, a critical stage in my work, and your awarding this book the Caldecott Medal gives me further incentive to continue that work. For that I am especially grateful.

Where the Wild Things Are was not meant to please everybody — only children. A letter from a seven-year-old boy encourages me to think that I have reached children as I had hoped. He wrote: "How much does it cost to get to where the wild things are? If it is not expensive my sister and I want to spend the summer there. Please answer soon." I did not answer that question, for I have no doubt that sooner or later they will find their way, free of charge.

BIOGRAPHICAL NOTE

by *Leo Wolfe*

Maurice Sendak

" MR. SENDAK is a ' children's illustrator,' for people who want to pigeonhole things. He is, in fact, (to repigeonhole) a fantasist in the great tradition of Sir John Tenniel and Edward Lear." So wrote Brian O'Doherty, art critic of the New York *Times*, in his review of Sendak's first one-man show, a retrospective that encompassed drawings from *A Hole Is to Dig* (1952) and some sketches done a few weeks before the show opened last March.

Most people who concern themselves with children's books today would eagerly agree that Sendak's name can be pronounced in the same breath as Tenniel's or Lear's, and that mentioning both of them justly symbolizes the breadth of Sendak's work. For, like Tenniel, he has responded to distinguished manuscripts with pictures of distinction; and, like Lear, he has created both words and pictures for children's books born of a unique personal vision.

Maurice Bernard Sendak was born on June 10, 1928, the third child of Philip and Sarah, who emigrated from Poland before World War I. ("Sendak" comes from the Russian name of a particular kind of fish.) The Sendak children — Natalie is the oldest, Jack is five years older than Maurice — grew up in a quiet Brooklyn neighborhood where trees and grass were not unknown. Throughout childhood the three of them shared an intense affection that still survives.

One of Sendak's earliest memories dates, he believes, from the age of three or four. "I was convalescing after a long, serious illness. I was sitting on my grandmother's lap, and I remember the feeling of pleasant drowsiness. It was winter. We sat in front of a window, and my grandmother pulled the shade up and down, to amuse me. Every time the shade went up, I was thrilled by the sudden reappearance of the back yard, the falling snow, and my brother and sister busy constructing a sooty snowman. Down came the shade — I waited. Up went the shade — the children had moved, the snowman had grown eyes. I don't remember a single sound."

He credits both parents with helping to cultivate his appetite for fantasy. They communicated — unintentionally, by their very natures — a sympathy for the fantastical and the mythic that was natural to East European Jews. This ambience, familiar to any admirer of I. B. Singer or Chagall, was expressed most concretely in the stories Philip Sendak regularly told his children, improvisations on themes recollected from his childhood in a Polish *shtetl*.

Sendak first began writing his own stories when he was nine or so. He hand-lettered and illustrated them on uniform pages, then bound these with tape and decorated covers. In all of this, he was following his brother's example.

Sendak remembers that ". . . all during childhood I took pleasure in the feel of textured bindings, and sometimes judged a book by the smell and feel of its pages. I don't think this was a personal aberration. I've often seen children smell books, and that proves it's not unusual for them to be aware of such intangible niceties. My Robin Hood book positively smelled of Sherwood Forest."

At fifteen he had an after-school job drawing backgrounds (furniture, puffs of dust under running heels, etc.) for Mutt-and-Jeff comic books. These earnings bought him *Grimm's Fairy Tales*, illustrated by Fritz Kredel, and *Andersen's Fairy Tales*, illustrated by Arthur Szyk, the first books he coveted because of their illustrations and physical attractiveness. Around this time it became obvious to him that illustrating books was to be his life's work.

With the intention of showing publishers what he could do, he made, during his last two years in high school, suites of pictures for *The Snow Queen*, *Háry János*, *The Wind in the Willows*, and *Til Eulenspiegel*, as well as illustrated, " bound " editions of *The Happy Prince*, *The Luck of Roaring Camp*, *The Little Match Girl*, and his own retelling of *Peter and the Wolf*. In 1946 he graduated, ordered a business card ("Maurice Sendak, Illustrator," it announced), and for the next year or so doggedly made the rounds of New York children's book editors, who gave him mild encouragement but no commissions.

Because one of his high school teachers knew his work, his first book illustrations were published in 1947: they were diagrams and spot drawings for *Atomics for the Millions*, an adult book coauthored by that teacher. ". . . the many splendid drawings by Mr. Sendak . . . lend a touch of humor," the New York *Times* reported, and the Cleveland *News* said that ". . . the good-humored illustrations call for a bow." During this period he earned his living by constructing and designing papier-mâché figures for a window-display firm.

Around Christmas 1948 the Sendak brothers walked into F.A.O. Schwarz, the well-known New York toy store, with a collection of animated toys they had collaborated on. They learned that it would be impractical to manufacture their toys, but the decorations Maurice had painted on them got him a job working on the store's elaborate window displays.

For the next two years he also took evening classes at the Art Students League, his only formal art study. He was especially happy about his class with John Groth.

When Leonard Weisgard came to F.A.O. Schwarz to help with a special display for one of his books, he admired Sendak's work, and before long recommended him for a picture-book commission he was too busy to accept. The publisher, the United Synagogue Commission on Jewish Education, agreed to take a chance on him if Weisgard would credit himself as "art consultant," an honest designation since he had to teach Sendak the rudiments of pre-separated artwork before he could make his pictures. *Good Shabos, Everybody*, a book about the Sabbath, was published in 1951.

Sendak's talent, his wish to illustrate children's books, and his reluctance to take his portfolio to publishers a second time had also been recognized by Frances Chrystie, children's book buyer at F.A.O. Schwarz, and Richard Nell, the store's display director.

They arranged, without his knowledge, for Ursula Nordstrom of Harper to see his work. She immediately asked him to illustrate Marcel Aymé's *The Wonderful Farm*, published in the fall of 1951, and soon he was able to devote himself to children's books. *A Hole Is to Dig* followed the next year, and *Kenny's Window*, the first book he wrote, came out in 1956. Five Sendak books (*A Very Special House, What Do You Say, Dear?, Little Bear's Visit, The Moon Jumpers, Mr. Rabbit and the Lovely Present*) were runners-up for the Caldecott Medal before it was awarded to *Where the Wild Things Are*.

Sendak lives and works in a two-floor apartment on a quiet Manhattan street. There is a small, shady garden in back, where he tries to raise anything green that can survive city fumes and escape being eaten by Jennie, his Sealyham terrier. Jennie appears in most of the books he has illustrated over the past eleven years; early in *Where the Wild Things Are*, she is the dog Max is chasing with a fork.

The largest room in the apartment houses his library, which includes a large collection of rare children's books, mainly of the nineteenth century; a collection of books illustrated by Bonnard, Léger, Clavé, Picasso, Corinth, and others; and a nearly complete collection of Henry James first editions. There is also a vast record library dominated by Mahler, Mozart, Beethoven, Wolf, and Verdi.

THE CALDECOTT AWARD 1965

May I Bring a Friend?

illustrated by BENI MONTRESOR

written by BEATRICE SCHENK DE REGNIERS

published by ATHENEUM 1964

FORMAT

SIZE: 7¾" x 9½", 48 pp. (unfolioed)

ARTIST'S MEDIUM: Drawings on board in black with solid overlays (pink, yellow) and screened overlays (pink, yellow and black) on acetate

PRINTING PROCESS: Offset lithography

ILLUSTRATIONS: Front matter, combination of black-and-white pages, and full-color pages, some with screened overlay

TYPE: Benedictine Book

BOOK NOTE

INVITATIONS for every day of the week from a gracious King and Queen encourage the friendly hero of this short rhymed text to bring his unusual friends to call and to return the imperturbable royal hospitality with a merry party in the zoo. The sophisticated colors of this book add strikingly to its fanciful sense of fun.

CALDECOTT AWARD ACCEPTANCE

by *Beni Montresor*

I WILL begin by saying " Thank you with all my heart " for this wonderful prize. You have given me the prize; in return you've won my love. This is the simple truth, and I feel that I love all of you.

After the official announcement of the prize, some Italian journalists came to see me. Do you know how I described this award? I said, " It's the Nobel Prize of children's books! "

This is what I think, and you can imagine my feeling at having such an honor.

Now the only thing missing, after all the honor and the marvelous chance to talk to you, is to have forty-eight hours a day to devote to my work.

When people ask if I am happy or unhappy, I answer that these are old-fashioned questions. My only problem is how to invent a day forty-eight hours long in order to have enough time to put on paper the thousands of things that fill my head. There's no solution to the problem, of course; so, at least for now, let's put it aside.

Now sit back and get ready to listen to my talk with great patience. You'll need it. You know how much Italians like to talk. . . .

I recall in 1960 — I had just arrived in this country — somebody asked me, " Would you like to do children's books? " " Yes," was my quick reply. I must admit I didn't exactly know what they were. As a child I had never owned one, and besides, at that time in Italy there was only one book for children and that was *Pinocchio*. Today there may be a few more.

Still, the possibility of being involved in a new work seemed thoroughly natural to me; I felt quite simply that it would be a continuation of the things I had been doing all my life.

As a child, I was passionately and constantly involved in my own puppet theater. I searched out the most improbable objects, the most colorful materials, the most glittering pieces of metal, and I put them all together on my little stage to give shape to something within my head. What was it? An image; thousands of unconnected images that would cross my fancy. But aren't these what all children's minds are filled with?

Because I was an Italian child, the inspiration for my images very often came from what I saw in church, or around the church. In Italy (as everybody knows) there is a saint to celebrate every day of the year, but besides these there are special saints with special celebrations, and on such occasions the churches are adorned in particularly spectacular ways. Flowers, angels, halos, clouds, gilt, velvets, damasks . . . and then the scent of the incense and of the flowers . . . and then the music of the organ resounding under arches and cupolas.

How could this replendent *mise en scène* fail to touch the imagination of a child?

So it happened very often that I imagined myself protected under the opulent gold and silver mantle of the Madonna, or, in a more cheerful moment, traveling through the skies on the back of the Holy Spirit, something similar to what happens visually on the last page of my *Witches of Venice*. And when I came back to earth, I rushed home to my puppet theater, which was ready to be filled with all those images — and they fitted perfectly into it. It was the ideal place for them to come alive.

Interestingly enough, the theater in Italy was born in the churches, and this grand and resplendent relationship between theater and church has always existed in my native country. I love all this very much.

That is why, when after such a long time, and so far from that little puppet theater, I was asked, " Would you like to do children's books? " the answer, yes, seemed so natural to me. I felt I could find once more the little theater of my childhood, and I could again fill it with all the fancies that came into my head.

Of course, between that old little theater and the new little theaters, this time made of pages, there were many others. In the years between, I had spent ten years as costume and set designer for the cinema. But in films, the designer usually does not count much. I always felt, being a designer and not a director, that there wasn't enough room for me to express myself completely. I always had to leave too much of myself locked inside me. For this reason, I left the films, and now my theater work is primarily in operas and ballets and in theater shows with music. Music on the stage gives me the inspiration to create images with colors, lighting, action, and music. It is this that I find most exciting about working in the theater.

Exactly the same thing happens when I work on a children's book. For me there is no difference between these two things — in the methods, in the aims, or in the results. The blank page is like an empty stage that must be filled with scenes, costumes, movement, and theatrical crescendo. And the words and colors become the music.

People have already observed the similarity: they said that as each scene of *The Last Savage* appeared on the Metropolitan's stage, it was like looking through the pages of a children's book; on the other hand, upon looking at my books, they have the feeling that they are sitting through a theatrical spectacle.

The difference between working in the theater and on a book is that in the theater one is surrounded by hundreds of temperamental personalities; working on a book I have only one temperamental personality to deal with, myself, who, if nothing else, is much more restful to be with.

So my life has been a continual going on and off stages of various sizes and types. But now I can say that I have at last found my own real, definitive stage on which I feel I can best express myself.

My stage is called *picture book*. I didn't invent it, I know this, but I feel that I may have discovered something special about it. You can't imagine how much this excites me!

What is a picture book? A kind of book with many illustrations, people think. A kind of book with too many illustrations, the critics often write. In reviewing picture books, they give all the space to the text, leaving the last line to the illustrations.

Too many illustrations and too few words is the complaint I most often see. This, in other words, means that it is a book that does not nourish, and once quickly gone through can be laid down for always. Usually, one thinks, words demand a higher intellectual effort than drawings. *Reading* a book develops the mind; *looking at* a book is just a pastime.

Even the majority of editors, when working on a picture book, place all of their interest, or at least three-quarters of their interest, on the text. The text is everything. A book is made up of words.

This idea can be true of certain types of picture books. There are, for example, picture books that are stories *with* illustrations, or picture books that are lists of words to learn, where the task is made pleasanter and easier by adding a visual translation of the words. These are books that are *served* by the illustrations in a peripheral or didactic way. These are not the picture books I call " my stage," the picture book I intend to talk about.

For me *a picture book is a book whose content is expressed through its images*. This is a fact I find exciting. I think that very little exists so far in this field, and it is a field in which little has been explored. The things that we can discover may add something very important to the history of books.

I am old enough to remember the accusations that used to be hurled at the cinema: " Cinema is not Art because, unlike the theater, it does not express its content by means of words." But who worries about this any longer? We all know that the cinema is based on images, not words; it is these visual images that give the new art its reason for being.

Today, who can say, " A film makes audiences lazy because it is made of visual images " or " A film is intellectually inferior to a book or a play "? I'm speaking only of serious films. For example, Fellini's *8½*, I believe, is one of the most important artistic contributions of our time. Personally, I know that it told me, with force and great beauty, things about myself and my time that I hadn't found in any book or play.

Ours is a visual time, a time of great and fleeting visions because it is a time of speed. One rushes, speaking less and less. It is the image that represents this best, and it is the image to which we most naturally respond.

I have the impression that words as an art form will give us less and less, because we are becoming more and more visually oriented. The idea of the visual book, the book to look at, is an idea of today, and even more, of tomorrow.

Why, by the way, do you think television exists? *We* created it, and it expresses us. We don't yet know if it is a new art form. Perhaps it is too soon even to ask. But do you think, for instance, that when painting began, the making of art was a consideration? Do you think Cimabue and Giotto were painting because they wanted to make art? Certainly not. They painted to make something that would serve a purpose. They painted madonnas for believers who wanted to worship before them. That it was an art was discovered later.

But still there are people who feel that the visual image is inferior to the idea presented in words. What is the reason for this reluctance to grant a respectable place to the visual image? It's easy to give the answer. The word is the symbol of the adult world, which can speak and therefore must think. The image is the symbol of the infantile world, which does not speak and therefore seems not to think. Even civilizations in their infancy expressed themselves graphically, and only after growth made extensive use of words.

I have heard the theater criticized because it is too much to see and not enough to hear. But what is wrong about that? Think for a moment about the *commedia dell' arte*. The text barely existed; nearly everything was action, pantomime, ballet, sets, mechanical tricks, costumes, music. Basically everything was visual. And wasn't that one of the most inventive periods in the history of the theater?

Before the time of books, artists and sculptors filled walls and walls with images that told stories, wonderful stories, and all of this was art at the most sublime level — visual images conveying ideas, concepts, and adventures of the imagination. Since I had the good fortune to be born in Italy, this kind of art was one of my first experiences, the deepest, and the most formative, even if at the time I was unaware of it. I grew up seeing stories on the walls of many palaces and churches, and I know well that they permeated my being even at the earliest age. I know they made me become what I am.

In this way the picture book, of which I am speaking, was invented long before those favorite English illustrators of the nineteenth century created their books. The Trajan Column in Rome or the " Life of St. Francis " on Giotto's Assisi frescoes are excellent examples of the true picture book.

They were true picture books, created for people who didn't know how to read — not even a word. Just imagine what wonder and magic those pictures must have instilled in the people they were created for. And what wonder and magic is instilled by them today in people who can read — even in five languages!

The important point is this: *The story told with pictures has a language all its own: the visual language,* and therefore it is with this language that a picture book must express itself.

And it is in this direction that I will move with my work. This is the result of discoveries made during my first few years of working in children's books. But, as you now know, it is also the result of an instinct, formed over a long time and by many experiences, which has made me conscious of the necessity and the beauty of expressing oneself in images.

Some time ago at the Rizzoli International Bookstore in New York, there was a party for children to celebrate this year's Newbery and Caldecott Awards. For the occasion we dressed actors as a bullfighter and as a king and queen. During the party I overheard a young child exclaim to the king, " You know something? I never met a real king before! " And the little boy stood there wide-eyed and openmouthed. Certainly this will remain for that child one of his most important experiences. Santa Claus can be met on every street corner, but a real king is not so easy to meet.

More or less in the same period I was on the radio talking with another young child. I asked him what he liked best about my illustrations for *May I Bring a Friend?* He answered, " The pink elephant." I asked why. " Because before that I never saw a pink elephant! "

Characters never seen before and animals never seen before. As always, children in their direct and candid way give us *the answer*. It is an invitation to produce the never-seen-before, to look for the new, to hold oneself open to all possibilities. Because possibility is a door to poetry.

We have to be open to the marvelous adventure of books made of images, because it has already existed for a long time, and because now people are searching for it more than ever. At this time only one thing should occupy us: To work for images of the highest quality — full, rich, and provocative images that carry the imagination to new heights that will be launching pads for new and always more daring discoveries.

BIOGRAPHICAL NOTE

by *Velma V. Varner*

Beni Montresor

" MAGIC AND MYSTERY." "Sun-drenched." "Otherworldly." All of these are phrases that have been used to describe Beni Montresor's work in both children's books and theater design. In many ways, they describe him as a person too. For although anyone so totally involved in today's world can hardly be called otherworldly in the usual sense, there is a quality of mystery and magic about him that sets him apart. It is there even in the bare facts of his life.

Beni Montresor is thirty-nine years old. He grew up in Verona and Venice, where he attended art school and began working as a set designer for the movies and for the theater throughout Europe. In 1960 he came to New York for a Christmas vacation, and at the end of his first day here, knowing neither the English language nor any person in the city, he found himself sitting in a coffee shop waiting for curtain time at the ballet and writing his family in Italy, " This is the place to stay."

He did, and not long afterward at a party someone asked him if he would be interested in illustrating a picture book for children. The immediate answer was "yes," although Mr. Montresor had never seen a picture book ("We have in Italy only *Pinocchio* "). " I knew I was ready," he says.

Obviously, he was. Unlike many talented people who work a very long time to achieve eminence, Beni Montresor suddenly "burst" into children's books, first as illustrator and almost immediately afterward as author-artist (*House of Flowers, House of Stars*, Knopf, 1962). More important, the work he has done in this country has been done entirely on his own terms; nothing like it had appeared before, either in children's books or on the stage.

During the last four years, his output has been prodigious. The Caldecott Award winner, *May I Bring a Friend?* by Beatrice Schenk de Regniers, is the eleventh book he has illustrated, including a second book written by him as well, *The Witches of Venice* (Knopf, 1963). At the same time, he has won spectacular acclaim in the theatrical world for his sets and costume designs for, among others, the 1962 Glyndebourne Festival's production of Debussy's *Pelléas et Mélisande,* Gian-Carlo Menotti's opera *The Last Savage* at the Metropolitan Opera, the ballet *Raymonda* for Dame Margot Fonteyn and Rudolf Nureyev, and the current Broadway hit, Richard Rodger's *Do I Hear a Waltz?* At present, he is designing the sets and costumes for Rossini's *Cenerentola* (*Cinderella*), which will be the new Metropolitan Opera National Company's opening-night performance at the New York State Theater in November, 1965, and for Ponchielli's *La Gioconda,* to be performed next year by the Metropolitan Opera Company during its opening week in its new house at Lincoln Center.

Two books are also on the agenda for publication in the near future: a picture book of the libretto in English for *Cinderella,* written by Mr. Montresor and illustrated with his sketches for the stage designs, and a picture book for children by Stephen Spender of Mozart's *Magic Flute.*

Anyone who has had the good fortune to see Mr. Montresor's stage sets and costumes cannot help comparing them with his books, for although the mediums and techniques are different, the effects are the same: magic, mystery, and happiness. Gold and very rich yellow are Beni Montresor's favorite colors; sets and costumes glow with shimmering light and color achieved by using layer on layer of fabric of varying tones, overlaying each other and punctuated by touches of lace and gold in such a way that the observer feels caught up in reverberations of light.

The total effect is one of enchantment, as appealing to harassed adults as to children, and of grace without self-consciousness. There is no willfulness here, just as there is no nastiness or meanness in his children's book drawings. With this artist, both in his work and in his person, one comes face to face with a very cultured man who has assimilated his culture so well that he doesn't have to think about it. The details go together to become a whole. Beni Montresor is blessed with absolute, perfect taste.

The preoccupation with light shows itself in his picture books too, even in black and white. Here, he uses a fractured pen line, which I have been told by one of his friends was not in his previous work in Italy. And again, the total effect is one of shimmering light and warmth, of magic and enchantment.

Mr. Montresor's obsession with magic and mystery makes it easy to understand his devotion to the theater. "I was born liking the theater," he says. "It creates a new dimension." His earliest memories center on the altars of churches. With their angels and candles and glowing colors "they were the most beautiful stages of my childhood." Nor is it difficult to understand his affinity with picture books; even though such books written specifically for children were unknown to him until he came to this country, stories told by means of pictures were all around him in the frescoes, paintings, mosaics, and carvings of his native land. The concept of pictures as a means of conveying a story, an adventure, or an emotion ("Words sometimes scare me," he says. "Feeling in a picture or in life is for me more real and important, more true") was not new.

What is surprising — until one gets to know him — is the intense devotion this sophisticated, ferociously busy artist feels for children, especially American children. "They have the most gracious imaginations in the world," he says. "They bloom like flowers — until they begin to grow up, to conform. Then their state of grace is replaced by a kind of terror."

Beni Montresor himself grew up in a world at war. Although he rarely mentions it, hunger and cold and, once, "a human leg in the street" were part of his childhood. In his own books, both *House of Flowers* and *The Witches of Venice*, it is worth noting that in spite of the total effect of light and joy and beauty, at the end the children in each book go into the heavens. Beauty is magic, and transitory. Childhood is a state of grace, which is also transitory.

" A child's mind is crossed by thousands of images every day," says Mr. Montresor, " like a kaleidoscope. And at the same time he is filled with great liveliness and an unself-conscious ability for total involvement. It is possible for a child to create images, and to him they are beautiful. A child with a piece of wood may see it as the most beautiful doll in the world. The same child, given the most beautiful doll in the world, may abandon it. It is 'finished,' because there is nothing more left to be done by the child's own imagination."

These qualities are in Beni Montresor too. Whether he is working at home in the tiny, restricted space that is his studio — a table, a handful of pens and some ink, a small bookcase — or on a cavernous stage filled with people, he is totally involved and absorbed. He seems to know from the beginning what he is going to do and how to accomplish it. The same kind of energy goes into his friendships and his devotion to his brothers and nephews. He revels in the sun. Light streams through the windows of his studio, and his holidays are spent at the seashore.

Holidays are never merely holidays, however, for Mr. Montresor is really thoroughly happy only when he is working. He is profoundly aware that everything dies, that beauty and life are passing. One senses that his enormous energy and control stem from this knowledge.

Life is magic and mystery, and Beni Montresor sees no need to uncloak it. Instead he uses his talents to create beautiful images, full of warm color and shimmering light, joy, and enchantment. Is it any wonder that adults as well as children receive his gifts with delight?

Picture Books Today

by *Norma R. Fryatt*

LONG AGO the importance of pictures to children was established. Today the picture tube presents direct competition in many thousands of homes with the picture book. We hope and expect, therefore, that the Caldecott winners will reflect the best of contemporary art, as well as convey to children a warmth, color, action, clarity of thought, and boldness of conviction that the young child especially needs. A few years ago the fine artist Edward Ardizzone in talking of the creation of a picture book said, " Drawing is of paramount importance. The well-known picture book classics by Kate Greenaway, Randolph Caldecott, Beatrix Potter, William Nicholson and Jean de Brunhof are all impeccably drawn."

He went on to discuss characters and themes. They must have life, he said. " The child today is too much sheltered . . . Sorrow, failure, poverty, and, possibly even death, *if handled poetically*, can surely all be introduced without hurt." Hans Christian Andersen introduced many of these themes to his stories, and how sensitively have artists such as Erik Blegvad, Marcia Brown, Adrienne Adams interpreted his tales in pictures! In *Lullaby for Eggs* Betty Bridgman and Elizabeth Orton Jones urge the importance of fragile things. In *A Pocketful of Cricket* Rebecca Caudill and Evaline Ness show the wonders a farm boy finds in the natural world around him.

Randolph Caldecott was chosen as the inspiration for this medal because his work best represented the " joyousness of picture books as well as their beauty." Thus we look for joyousness in every Caldecott winner, whether inherent in the story itself or in the way the pictures are drawn so that one knows that the author and artist enjoyed the act of creating *that book*, with all their minds and hearts and skills.

The few woodcuts within John Newbery's flowered covers were only a faint premonition of the bright kaleidoscope of color and design now available to children. Because modern techniques, printing processes and materials are so abundant, there is all the more reason to develop and exercise discrimination and good taste in picture books.

In those produced abroad we often see a clarity, crispness and humor that is sometimes lacking in even the most expensively produced of our own picture books. Study, for example, the beautiful books of Alois Carigiet and Selina Chonz, *The Happy Owls* by Celestino Piatti from Switzerland, or John Burningham's rich palette in *Borka* from England. Even black and white line drawings have liveliness and style, as in Reiner Zimnik's *Jonah the Fisherman*.

With all our technology have we produced the kind of book the *child* delights in and learns from? Does the story have warmth, emotion, suspense, surprise and humor — often slapstick, that a child can appreciate? Will the child remember the book, want to share it and go back to it again? Can he understand what is happening if he has to rely on the pictures alone?

Apart from all these requirements, we call for unity and coherency in design and that " deft balance between text and pictures" which Esther Averill mentioned in her article "What Is a Picture Book? "*

Having these questions in mind, let us examine the ten picture books which have lately won the Caldecott Medal.

In *Frog Went A-Courtin'*, John Langstaff, an American ballad singer, and Feodor Rojankovsky, a Russian-born artist, have brought to life a sixteenth-century English ballad. " The Gentleman Frog " was known even before it first appeared in print in 1549. By 1781 it had become a popular nursery song. It easily leapt the Atlantic Ocean and clung to the balladry along the Eastern seaboard, with many variations. In this version for children, Mr. Langstaff included the " hmmm-mm," the humming

*Esther Averill, "What Is a Picture Book? ", *Caldecott Medal Books: 1938-1957*, pp. 307-314, The Horn Book, Inc., Boston.

sound of Miss Mouse's spinning wheel so that even the youngest children can participate in the rhythmic, singing lines.

In admiring Caldecott's drawing of the dish running away with the spoon in that old nursery rhyme, Kate Greenaway said, " You can't think how much he made of it." The same might be said of Rojankovsky's *Frog Went A-Courtin'*. With what exuberance the pictures tell the story! Mr. Frog sets forth from his log cabin in the marsh, mounts a dappled grey and off he rides to Mouse's Hall. Once Uncle Rat's consent is given to their wedding, a fantastic procession of wedding guests appears.

This artist's particular skill and imagination in the drawing of animals and insects have free play. And *play* is a quality that we are seeking in picture books. There is a sudden scary end to the wedding feast, but it had to end somehow — " if you want anymore, you must sing it yourself! "

The artist credits two events with determining the course of his childhood: He was taken to the zoo and at the same period was given a box of color crayons. These two events still strongly influence his work. This book was printed by offset lithography, a medium which gives the artist great freedom — to use line, tone, halftone and color, and Rojankovsky combines these for maximum effectiveness. How sparingly he uses the black in this picture book, yet the sparkling black figures and outlines provide the framework which holds the compositions together, without limiting or cramping the pages in any way.

In *A Tree Is Nice* by Janice Udry we have a set theme and a text very much like that in beginning readers. Such an illustrating assignment is a challenge to the artist's creativity and imagination. What has Marc Simont done with it? The pictures could have been tied to the seasons of the year or to the " life cycle " of a tree, and so the book would have had an over-all unity, but Mr. Simont chose a freer treatment, while adhering closely to the text. He depicts the many ways in which a tree provides shelter and comfort. The book becomes one of the most convincing sermons on conservation yet done for young children.

Doublespreads in full rich color alternate with those in monotone. Different kinds, sizes and ages of trees are pictured, while animals and humans in many postures lend variety to the composition of the pages.

This book, though it seems to lack the gaiety and zest of Simont's *Contest at Paca* or *Fish Head,* for example, pleases children because it has warmth of feeling and color and presents its theme in a way they can understand.

Time of Wonder by Robert McCloskey brings undiminished pleasure with each viewing, but requires for fullest appreciation an older child reader, — ideally one who has spent some time on the seacoast, sailed in a catboat or seen a storm come up. It holds the experience of a full summer in poetic words and pictures. Text and pictures are essential to each other, yet each composition is complete in itself.

Time of Wonder begins with a small white cloud over the islands of Penobscot Bay. Tremulous blues and shaded grays cast cloud-shadows on the islands in the second painting. The third is a shock, for " It's Raining on You! " The paleness of pearl comes next as a foggy morning dawns on the coast. Tones of brown in rocks and bright red in clothing bring needed warmth. As the fog lifts, sharp outlines return. The transparency of water color makes these diaphanous effects possible.

Action scenes follow, of sailing boats and swimming, diving children. Clear white, jade green, opaque blues, pink and yellow accents reflect the lighter, gayer tones under the summer sun.

In the impressionistic scene when the wind takes over and the storm is at its peak, details are still important, but now the main thing is to *feel* that wind, and you can almost feel and see it as it throws up the waves and wet spray, dashes through the house, sweeping books and papers and lamp before it. Particularly effective are the scenes inside the cottage at night, with their clever lighting and three-dimensional quality. Note especially the simplicity and peace in the painting of the two children going upstairs to bed. The storm is over and a white moon shines in at the window.

We feel a sense of wonder at these expressive pictures and of gratitude to the artist who has printed these scenes indelibly on our minds. Beauty and joyousness here — yes, Mr. Caldecott!

Barbara Cooney has perfected herself in the use of scratch-board. Her pictures for *Chanticleer and the Fox* are scrupulously drawn to achieve that crispness which the medium permits. She uses gay primary colors, also sharp and pure, in this retelling of one of Chaucer's *Canterbury Tales.* There is liveliness, from the parade of farmyard animals to Chanticleer strutting and his seven hens settling on their roosts. As you turn these pages, note the many ways in which seven hens can be arranged. In a dramatic night-dark scene, Fox enters. No color here. As he turns a smiling, beguiling face to Chanticleer, color again comes in to suggest bright sunlight and fair omens. But blackness returns as Fox shows his true purpose and makes off to the dark wood with Chanticleer by the throat! The dramatic possibilities in the tale are exploited gently but firmly, even turning the limitations of color printing into advantages.

Hours spent at the Cloisters and at the New York Public and Morgan Libraries have been repaid in the satisfaction of having the details correct: the costumes right for the period and every flower and grass just those that grew in England in Chaucer's time. The artist has placed the strawberry plant in the initial O of the first page as it might be seen in an illuminated book of the 14th century. There are other small delights for the eye in the clump of blue flag beside the woven fence, some mice playing with a spice pink far down in one corner. Generous white space sets off these details, and thought has been given to the book design as a whole, particularly shown in the calligraphy on the title page and in that beautifully plain copyright page — often a necessary but awkward hurdle in picture books!

Chanticleer and the Fox is retold with clarity, freshness and dedication to the task.

Nine Days to Christmas is a story of urban Mexico showing the strong contrasts of new and old to be found in many old cities today. Pencil drawings on a gray wash background show Dairy Queens and supermarkets near old-style outdoor markets where a fantastic array of colorful articles awaits shoppers. Ceci and her mother are in search of a *piñata*. Swinging on strings in the wind, the *piñatas* come to life for Ceci and urge her to choose. This scene is one of the gayest in the book with bright yellow, fuchsia pink, and orange highlighting the figures of penguins, zebras, ducks and clowns, owls and parrots, whose eyes turn appealingly toward Ceci. She chooses for her *piñata* a big shining gold star.

When the *piñata* has been filled with good things to eat and hung in the garden, Ceci leads the Christmas procession after sunset. Now the gray backgrounds deepen as night draws in and the bright glow of candles and a spotlight shine on the garden. White calla lilies and red roses emerge from the dusk with a special beauty.

Because the artist is allowed a limited number of colors, she has chosen them well for the exotic scenes at her disposal. She obviously knows and loves Mexico, yet the book gives the impression of insufficient planning. The gray backgrounds do heighten the intensity of the colors, but they have not been used consistently as a stage where the reader looks for the action. On certain pages, instead of cutting into the illustration, the text might have been printed on the gray or placed by itself on the opposite page. Not all of the drawings are well integrated with the text which is storybook length.

The first doublespread shows a most detailed street scene and the factory where the *piñatas* are made. The assembly line view of their *papier-mâché* figures and the skillful composition of the scene make it one of the best in the book. However, Marie Hall Ets's *Play with Me* and *In the Forest* more nearly fulfill the requirements for a Caldecott Medal.

Nicolas Sidjakov has worked in tempera on several successful picture books of which this is the second. The medium affords especially limpid colors with an effect of solidity and dryness. It most nearly resembles water color.

The jury of the American Institute of Graphic Arts included *Baboushka and the Three Kings* in their 1958-1960 Children's

Book Exhibit and commented: "A handsome book with strong, beautiful color drawings, original in conception. Title page is weak, and the music pages are not well planned. A more legible type might have been preferable."

However, others feel that the title page is neat and well-composed. As to the type, we sometimes feel that this large a type would stand out more effectively against wide margins. But this would mean a larger book, while this one is such a handy size.

From page one on, the reader is convinced that something unusual is going to happen! "As day turned into night, a trumpet call sounded on the wind." Then comes a procession led by three "splendid figures" in a sleigh drawn by three white horses. Three rigid, toylike men are shown — the three kings. Refusing Baboushka's invitation to share her warm hut, they disappear into the storm.

Precise line drawings give the impression of vast spaces of snow fields, of night and great snowflake-filled skies, a landscape of dark leafless trees and poor wooden villages. These pictures seem painted on parchment; they have a transparency like stained glass. We breathe the cold air of an ancient bitter country where there are both great riches and a grim poverty, the land of the Tsars, of Chekhov and Borodin. The drawings toward the end of Baboushka's search might seem gray and grim if one did not remember the words, the warmth inside these gray houses and the joy when Baboushka has left her few " poor but precious gifts." What might these be? It is something to ponder, for there is mystery and the sense of seeking and hope. Adults might interpret this as a fable for our time.

Children will find in it something unusual, perhaps too removed from their experience and the Christmas story as they know it, but certainly it is a book to which they should be introduced. The pictures create a mood and speak of something beyond the printed page, a quality achieved by such artists as Arthur Rackham, C. Lovat Fraser, Elizabeth MacKinstry, and André François.

Primitive colors, rigid vertical lines, stylized figures, an unusual typeface that satisfied both artist and designer, — this combination of graphic skills was an experiment and one which in the main succeeded.

Once a Mouse by Marcia Brown is quite different from the fairy-like delicacy of her *Cinderella* or the strong lino cuts used in her version of *Dick Whittington and His Cat.* She has turned to the discipline of woodcut, but now with ever greater skill and confidence. This is the India of wise hermits and magicians, of jungles and animals bold and fierce. In the fable of the big and the little is ancient wisdom from an ancient land. The pictures almost alone could tell the story. They have action, force, and a monumental quality despite the flat colors. Strong dark green contrasts with a mustard yellow and deep red in a wise economy of color that is the more effective and dramatic for being in low key. One color is added to another to create richness, depth, or drama — as the story requires. The red, used as a signal of danger or anger, builds excitement. Full advantage is taken of the medium, the texture or grain of the wood allowed to show where it adds movement or exciting patterns. The short text in jungle-green sans-serif block letters fits unobtrusively into the scheme.

After reading aloud five or six Caldecott-winning books, the mother of a young but actively reading family said of this: " My children liked this best of all. They had me read it several times. The beautiful wood cuts fascinated them, as did the magic element."

Chief characteristics of *The Snowy Day* by Ezra Jack Keats are great freedom and freshness — like breaking a path in new-fallen snow as the hero does in the story.

This artist introduces a new medium to the group of Caldecott-winning books, *papier collé* or collage. Great ingenuity is demanded of the artist working with this medium, especially in achieving a sense of depth and volume and of movement of the parts of the body. Yet this is very successful in *The Snowy Day*, with only small areas painted in — a line here and there and the face of the little boy. How much action and life is in that little red figure that hops, skips and jumps over the pages. How much scissor-skill and training it took to cut a figure so that the viewer feels the strain of its arm muscles or the pull on back and legs as the boy climbs the snow-hill.

The details are few, but heightened in importance because of that: the footprints in the snow, the stick, the soap bubbles in that delightful scene in the bath, the colored snowflakes at the end.

Color is used here with daring, with new juxtapositions and counterpoint, but with *knowing*. The eye longs to look long at this book. Like many things of beauty, it gives a sense of rest because there is so much satisfaction and pleasure in the viewing. Mr. Keats sees snow as radiating blues and pinks, mauve and yellow, and green. Compare this snow with Roger Duvoisin's in *White Snow, Bright Snow* or *The Big Snow* by the Haders, or with the soft dripping snow in Helen Sewell's *Blue Barns*. And what exciting skies Ezra Jack Keats mounts as background and contrast to the action — from early morning's pale, uncertain tones to deep turquoise, to dark green swirls on dark blue, to white spirals of cloud or flurries of snow on blue. Ezra Jack Keats has described his way of using collage in the June, 1964, issue of *The Horn Book*.

Crescendo-like, *Where the Wild Things Are* by Maurice Sendak quickly gains momentum, rises to a climax and falls to a quiet ending. It might be interpreted as a typical boy-runs-away-from-home theme, or the story of the angry little boy. The title page, with its bold figures of Max and the beasts outlined by ample white space, gives us a taste of things to come.

Max and his wild beasts are seen in a blue, moonlit world that is also a very private world for Max. It begins to grow up around him the minute he is confined to his room without supper. The moon shines on his white wolf-suit and a forest begins to surround him in his room. Then a private boat carries Max off suddenly to where the wild things are waiting to meet him on the shore. Here is another blue, moonlit jungle peopled by horned, scaly creatures like ogres and centaurs — a mixed-up world. Washes of pastel blue, yellow and pink produce the effects of moonlight, while crosshatching and many fine short lines make the shadows and hairy bodies of the beasts. It is almost impossible to miss the similarity of these leafy, moonlit jungles to those in Henri Rousseau's paintings.

Where the Wild Things Are is full of harsh, sharp edges — the pronged moon, sharp pointed teeth, horns, claws and beaks which seem about to prick and pierce. True to the young child's short attention span, when the wild experience is over, Max is glad to return home. The pervading blue tones and moonlit colors create the desired atmosphere of a private dream world, even in the flower-packed endpapers painted in the same colors. Text is subordinated to pictures in this book, but its thread is essential except at the climax. Here there are no words. Unfortunately the last five words were placed where you have to turn a page to find them.

This is truly an interesting picture book, which satisfies the requirements set forth at the beginning of this article — in an unexpected way.

Rich color, scenes of action, and a series of surprises build up to the climax in *May I Bring a Friend?* illustrated by Beni Montresor. But the first surprise is the greatest. Black and white drawings in pen and ink are overlaid with various colors, chiefly pink and yellow, in the scenes where king and queen entertain at tea, dinner, lunch, breakfast, through a whole week.

The pattern is complicated: An invitation page (black and white drawing of king and queen in various poses, in garden, dancing, fishing) faces a page with the words "So I brought my friend." The reader is in suspense until, turning the page, he sees a colored doublespread showing the friend, or friends, in action. This is followed by a page with a verse opposite a pen-and-ink illustration with colored background. The invited guests are a giraffe, a rhinoceros, a group of monkeys, an elephant, a pride of lions. This pattern of six pages is repeated six times until the conclusion when *all* the friends invite the king and queen to a very crowded tea at the City Zoo, their home.

There is humor, surprise and splendor in these scenes. Children enjoy the repetition and the suspense of wondering who the next guest will be. The adult critic, though appreciating the gaiety and richness, finds the pattern somewhat trying and wonders why a more inviting design for the title page might not have been achieved. Mr. Montresor's experience in stage setting is clear, but his charm and skill as a picture book artist have been more effective in, for instance, *House of Flowers, House of Stars*. In that, one feels a freedom and spontaneity lacking somehow in this winner of the Caldecott Medal.

It has been said that art is a reflection of the times in which we live. Yet in the ten picture books by contemporary artists just surveyed, there is only a little evidence of twentieth-century life and the influences on it: the city, machines, the discoveries of science. *Time of Wonder* shows some machinery: a motor boat, a sea plane, gasoline pumps, a truck, and electric light. *Nine Days to Christmas* includes television antennae, telephone wires, newspapers, trucks and automobiles. Is our environment too ugly to make suitable backgrounds for picture books, as Robert McCloskey finds, judging by the plea for education in design made in his Caldecott Award acceptance speech? What, in today's world, can the artist use to symbolize, dramatize, epitomize the good, the enduring or the beautiful?

In the ten books discussed the artists have created moments of wonder, exhilaration, triumph, satisfaction and hours of pleasure for children and all those who will read them, but four of these Caldecott winners turned for subject matter to another age or to legends; two stories are imaginative fantasy. Is the present scene devoid of interest, of materials, for the picture book artist?

As new generations use and read the Caldecott-winning books, along with other fine picture books not so honored, they will by their acceptance or rejection determine which will remain in print. Many books which ought to receive an award — if only that for long service — have been overlooked. But the satisfaction of having made a book widely enjoyed by children is accolade enough.

Winners and Honor Books for the Newbery and Caldecott Awards

List and notes prepared by Bonita E. Stecher, *Cooperative Children's Book Center*, Madison, Wisconsin.

I. NEWBERY AWARD: 1922-1965

1922 AWARD: *The Story of Mankind*, Hendrik Willem van Loon. LIVERIGHT.

HONOR BOOKS: *The Great Quest*, Charles Hawes. LITTLE, BROWN.
Cedric the Forester, Bernard Marshall. APPLETON-CENTURY.
The Old Tobacco Shop, William Bowen. MACMILLAN.
The Golden Fleece and the Heroes Who Lived Before Achilles, Padraic Colum. MACMILLAN.
Windy Hill, Cornelia Meigs. MACMILLAN.

1923 AWARD: *The Voyages of Doctor Dolittle*, Hugh Lofting. LIPPINCOTT.

HONOR BOOK: No record (Chairman, Elva Smith, Carnegie Library, Pittsburgh. C.L.S. voted by section membership.)

1924 AWARD: *The Dark Frigate*, Charles Hawes. LITTLE, BROWN.

HONOR BOOK: No record (Saratoga Springs, N. Y. A.L.A. established special selection committee.)

1925 AWARD: *Tales from Silver Lands*, Charles Finger. DOUBLEDAY.

HONOR BOOKS: *Nicholas*, Anne Carroll Moore. PUTNAM.
Dream Coach, Anne Parrish. MACMILLAN.

1926 AWARD: *Shen of the Sea*, Arthur Bowie Chrisman. DUTTON.

HONOR BOOK: *Voyagers*, Padraic Colum. MACMILLAN.

1927 AWARD: *Smoky, the Cowhorse*, Will James. SCRIBNER.

HONOR BOOK: No record.

1928 AWARD: *Gayneck, the Story of a Pigeon*, Dhan Gopal Mukerji. DUTTON.

HONOR BOOKS: *The Wonder Smith and His Son*, Ella Young. LONGMANS.
Downright Dencey, Caroline Snedeker. DOUBLEDAY.

1929 AWARD: *The Trumpeter of Krakow*, Eric P. Kelly. MACMILLAN.

HONOR BOOKS: *Pigtail of Ah Lee Ben Loo*, John Bennett. LONGMANS.
Millions of Cats, Wanda Gág. COWARD-MCCANN.
The Boy Who Was, Grace Hallock. DUTTON.
Clearing Weather, Cornelia Meigs. LITTLE, BROWN.
Runaway Papoose, Grace Moon. DOUBLEDAY.
Tod of the Fens, Elinor Whitney. MACMILLAN.

1930 AWARD: *Hitty, Her First Hundred Years*, Rachel Field. MACMILLAN.

HONOR BOOKS: *Daughter of the Seine*, Jeanette Eaton. HARPER.
Pran of Albania, Elizabeth Miller. DOUBLEDAY.
Jumping-off Place, Marian Hurd McNeely. LONGMANS.
Tangle-coated Horse and Other Tales, Ella Young. LONGMANS.
Vaino, Julia Davis Adams. DUTTON.
Little Blacknose, Hildegarde Swift. HARCOURT.

1931 AWARD: *The Cat Who Went to Heaven*, Elizabeth Coatsworth. MACMILLAN.

HONOR BOOKS: *Floating Island*, Anne Parrish. HARPER.
The Dark Star of Itza, Alida Malkus, HARCOURT
Queer Person, Ralph Hubbard. DOUBLEDAY.
Mountains Are Free, Julia Davis Adams. DUTTON.
Spice and the Devil's Cave, Agnes Hewes. KNOPF.
Meggy MacIntosh, Elizabeth Janet Gray. DOUBLEDAY.
Garram the Hunter, Herbert Best. DOUBLEDAY.
Ood-le-uk the Wanderer, Alice Lide and Margaret Johansen. LITTLE, BROWN.

1932 AWARD: *Waterless Mountain*, Laura Adams Armer. LONGMANS.

HONOR BOOKS: *The Fairy Circus*, Dorothy Lathrop. MACMILLAN.
Calico Bush, Rachel Field. MACMILLAN.
Boy of the South Seas, Eunice Tietjens. COWARD-MCCANN.
Out of the Flame, Eloise Lownsbery. LONGMANS.
Jane's Island, Marjorie Allee. HOUGHTON MIFFLIN.
Truce of the Wolf and Other Tales of Old Italy, Mary Gould Davis. HARCOURT.

1933 AWARD: *Young Fu of the Upper Yangtze*, Elizabeth Lewis. WINSTON.

HONOR BOOKS: *Swift Rivers*, Cornelia Meigs. LITTLE, BROWN.
The Railroad to Freedom, Hildegarde Swift. HARCOURT.
Children of the Soil, Nora Burglon. DOUBLEDAY.

1934 AWARD: *Invincible Louisa*, Cornelia Meigs. LITTLE, BROWN.

HONOR BOOKS: *The Forgotten Daughter*, Caroline Snedeker. DOUBLE-DAY.
Swords of Steel, Elsie Singmaster. HOUGHTON.
ABC Bunny, Wanda Gág. COWARD-MC CANN.
Winged Girl of Knossos, Erik Berry, *pseud.* (Allena Best). APPLETON-CENTURY.
New Land, Sarah Schmidt. MC BRIDE.
Big Tree of Bunlahy, Padraic Colum. MACMILLAN.
Glory of the Seas, Agnes Hewes. KNOPF.
Apprentice of Florence, Anne Kyle. HOUGHTON MIFFLIN.

1935 AWARD: *Dobry*, Monica Shannon. VIKING.

HONOR BOOKS: *Pageant of Chinese History*, Elizabeth Seeger. LONG-MANS.
Davy Crockett, Constance Rourke. HARCOURT.
Day on Skates, Hilda Van Stockum. HARPER.

1936 AWARD: *Caddie Woodlawn*, Carol Brink. MACMILLAN.

HONOR BOOKS: *Honk, the Moose*, Phil Stong. DODD, MEAD.
The Good Master, Kate Seredy. VIKING.
Young Walter Scott, Elizabeth Janet Gray. VIKING.
All Sail Set, Armstrong Sperry. WINSTON.

1937 AWARD: *Roller Skates*, Ruth Sawyer. VIKING.

HONOR BOOKS: *Phebe Fairchild; Her Book*, Lois Lenski. STOKES.
Whistlers' Van, Idwal Jones. VIKING.
Golden Basket, Ludwig Bemelmans, VIKING.
Winterbound, Margery Bianco. VIKING.
Audubon, Constance Rourke. HARCOURT.
The Codfish Musket, Agnes Hewes. DOUBLEDAY.

1938 AWARD: *The White Stag*, Kate Seredy. VIKING.

HONOR BOOKS: *Pecos Bill*, James Cloyd Bowman. LITTLE, BROWN.
Bright Island, Mabel Robinson. RANDOM HOUSE.
On the Banks of Plum Creek, Laura Ingalls Wilder. HARPER.

1939 AWARD: *Thimble Summer*, Elizabeth Enright. RINEHART.

HONOR BOOKS: *Nino*, Valenti Angelo. VIKING.
Mr. Popper's Penguins, Richard and Florence Atwater. LITTLE, BROWN.
"Hello the Boat!", Phyllis Crawford. HOLT.
Leader by Destiny: George Washington, Man and Patriot, HARCOURT.
Penn, Elizabeth Janet Gray. VIKING.

1940 AWARD: *Daniel Boone*, James Daugherty. VIKING.

HONOR BOOKS: *The Singing Tree*, Kate Seredy. VIKING.
Runner of the Mountain Tops, Mabel Robinson. RANDOM HOUSE.
By the Shores of Silver Lake, Laura Ingalls Wilder. HARPER.
Boy with a Pack, Stephen W. Meader. HARCOURT.

1941 AWARD: *Call It Courage*, Armstrong Sperry. MACMILLAN.

HONOR BOOKS: *Blue Willow*, Doris Gates. VIKING.
Young Mac of Fort Vancouver, Mary Jane Carr. CROWELL.
The Long Winter, Laura Ingalls Wilder. HARPER.
Nansen, Anna Gertrude Hall. VIKING.

1942 AWARD: *The Matchlock Gun*, Walter D. Edmonds. DODD, MEAD.

HONOR BOOKS: *Little Town on the Prairie*, Laura Ingalls Wilder. HARPER.
George Washington's World, Genevieve Foster. SCRIBNER.
Indian Captive: the Story of Mary Jemison, Lois Lenski. LIPPINCOTT.
Down Ryton Water, Eva Roe Gaggin. VIKING.

1943 AWARD: *Adam of the Road*, Elizabeth Janet Gray. VIKING.

HONOR BOOKS: *The Middle Moffat*, Eleanor Estes. HARCOURT.
"Have You Seen Tom Thumb?", Mabel Leigh Hunt. LIPPINCOTT.

1944 AWARD: *Johnny Tremain*, Esther Forbes. HOUGHTON MIFFLIN.

HONOR BOOKS: *These Happy Golden Years*, Laura Ingalls Wilder. HARPER.
Fog Magic, Julia Sauer. VIKING.
Rufus M., Eleanor Estes. HARCOURT.
Mountain Born, Elizabeth Yates. COWARD-MCCANN.

1945 AWARD: *Rabbit Hill*, Robert Lawson. VIKING.

HONOR BOOKS: *The Hundred Dresses*, Eleanor Estes. HARCOURT.
                The Silver Pencil, Alice Dalgliesh. SCRIBNER.
                Abraham Lincoln's World, Genevieve Foster. SCRIBNER.
                Lone Journey; the Life of Roger Williams, Jeanette
                Eaton. HARCOURT.

1946 AWARD: *Strawberry Girl*, Lois Lenski. LIPPINCOTT.

HONOR BOOKS: *Justin Morgan Had a Horse*, Marguerite Henry. RAND
                MC NALLY.
                The Moved-Outers, Florence Crannell Means.
                HOUGHTON MIFFLIN.
                Bhimsa, the Dancing Bear, Christine Weston. SCRIBNER.
                New Found World, Katherine Shippen. VIKING.

1947 AWARD: *Miss Hickory*, Carolyn Sherwin Bailey. VIKING.

HONOR BOOKS: *Wonderful Year*, Nancy Barnes. MESSNER.
                Big Tree, Mary and Conrad Buff. VIKING.
                The Heavenly Tenants, William Maxwell. HARPER.
                The Avion My Uncle Flew, Cyrus Fisher, *pseud.* (Dar-
                win L. Teilhet). APPLETON.
                The Hidden Treasure of Glaston, Eleanore Jewett.
                VIKING.

1948 AWARD: *The Twenty-One Balloons*, William Pène du Bois.
                VIKING.

HONOR BOOKS: *Pancakes — Paris*, Claire Huchet Bishop. VIKING.
                LiLun, Lad of Courage, Carolyn Treffinger. ABINGDON.
                The Quaint and Curious Quest of Johnny Longfoot,
                Catherine Besterman. BOBBS MERRILL.
                The Cow-tail Switch, and Other West African Stories,
                Harold Courlander. HOLT.
                Misty of Chincoteague, Marguerite Henry. RAND MC-
                NALLY.

1949 AWARD: *King of the Wind*, Marguerite Henry. RAND MC NALLY.

HONOR BOOKS: *Seabird*, Holling C. Holling. HOUGHTON MIFFLIN.
                Daughter of the Mountain, Louise Rankin. VIKING.
                My Father's Dragon, Ruth Gannett. RANDOM HOUSE.
                Story of the Negro, Arna Bontemps. KNOPF.

1950 AWARD: *The Door in the Wall*, Marguerite de Angeli. DOUBLE-
                DAY.

HONOR BOOKS: *Tree of Freedom*, Rebecca Caudill. VIKING.
The Blue Cat of Castle Town, Catherine Coblentz. LONGMANS.
Kildee House, Rutherford Montgomery. DOUBLEDAY.
George Washington, Genevieve Foster. SCRIBNER.
Song of the Pines, Walter and Marion Havighurst. WINSTON.

1951 AWARD: *Amos Fortune, Free Man*, Elizabeth Yates. ALADDIN.

HONOR BOOKS: *Better Known as Johnny Appleseed*, Mabel Leigh Hunt. LIPPINCOTT.
Gandhi, Fighter Without a Sword, Jeanette Eaton. MORROW.
Abraham Lincoln, Friend of the People, Clara Ingram Judson. WILCOX AND FOLLETT.
The Story of Appleby Capple, Anne Parrish. HARPER.

1952 AWARD: *Ginger Pye*, Eleanor Estes. HARCOURT.

HONOR BOOKS: *Americans Before Columbus*, Elizabeth Baity. VIKING.
Minn of the Mississippi, Holling C. Holling. HOUGHTON MIFFLIN.
The Defender, Nicholas Kalashnikoff. SCRIBNER.
The Light at Tern Rock, Julia Sauer. VIKING.
The Apple and the Arrow, Mary and Conrad Buff. HOUGHTON MIFFLIN.

1953 AWARD: *Secret of the Andes*, Ann Nolan Clark. VIKING.

HONOR BOOKS: *Charlotte's Web*, E. B. White. HARPER.
Moccasin Trail, Eloise McGraw. COWARD-MCCANN.
Red Sails to Capri, Ann Weil. VIKING.
The Bears on Hemlock Mountain, Alice Dalgliesh. SCRIBNER.
Birthdays of Freedom, Vol. I., Genevieve Foster. SCRIBNER.

1954 AWARD: *...and now Miguel*, Joseph Krumgold. CROWELL.

HONOR BOOKS: *All Alone*, Claire Huchet Bishop. VIKING.
Shadrach, Meindert DeJong. HARPER.
Hurry Home Candy, Meindert DeJong. HARPER.
Theodore Roosevelt, Fighting Patriot, Clara Ingram Judson. FOLLETT.
Magic Maize, Mary and Conrad Buff. HOUGHTON MIFFLIN.

1955 AWARD: *The Wheel on the School*, Meindert DeJong. HARPER.

HONOR BOOKS: *Courage of Sarah Noble*, Alice Dalgliesh. SCRIBNER.
                Banner in the Sky, James Ullman. LIPPINCOTT.

1956 AWARD: *Carry On, Mr. Bowditch*, Jean Lee Latham. HOUGHTON
                MIFFLIN.

HONOR BOOKS: *The Secret River*, Marjorie Kinnan Rawlings. SCRIBNER.
                The Golden Name Day, Jennie Lindquist. HARPER.
                Men, Microscopes, and Living Things, Katherine Shippen. VIKING.

1957 AWARD: *Miracles on Maple Hill*, Virginia Sorensen. HARCOURT.

HONOR BOOKS: *Old Yeller*, Fred Gipson. HARPER.
                The House of Sixty Fathers, Meindert DeJong. HARPER.
                Mr. Justice Holmes, Clara Ingram Judson. FOLLETT.
                The Corn Grows Ripe, Dorothy Rhoads. VIKING.
                Black Fox of Lorne, Marguerite de Angeli. DOUBLEDAY.

1958 AWARD: *Rifles for Watie*, Harold Keith. CROWELL.

HONOR BOOKS: *The Horsecatcher*, Mari Sandoz. WESTMINSTER.
                Gone-Away Lake, Elizabeth Enright. HARCOURT.
                The Great Wheel, Robert Lawson. VIKING.
                Tom Paine, Freedom's Apostle, Leo Gurke. CROWELL.

1959 AWARD: *The Witch of Blackbird Pond*, Elizabeth George
                Speare. HOUGHTON MIFFLIN.

HONOR BOOKS: *The Family Under the Bridge*, Natalie S. Carlson.
                HARPER.
                Along Came a Dog, Meindert DeJong. HARPER.
                Chicaro: Wild Pony of the Pampa, Francis Kalnay.
                HARCOURT.
                The Perilous Road, William O. Steele. HARCOURT.

1960 AWARD: *Onion John*, Joseph Krumgold. CROWELL.

HONOR BOOKS: *My Side of the Mountain*, Jean George. DUTTON.
                America Is Born, Gerald W. Johnson. MORROW.
                The Gammage Cup, Carol Kendall. HARCOURT.

1961 AWARD: *Island of the Blue Dolphins*, Scott O'Dell. HOUGHTON
                MIFFLIN.

HONOR BOOKS: *America Moves Forward*, Gerald W. Johnson. MORROW.
                Old Ramon, Jack Schaeffer. HOUGHTON MIFFLIN.
                Cricket in Times Square, George Selden, *pseud.* (George
                Thompson). FARRAR, STRAUS.

1962 AWARD: *The Bronze Bow*, Elizabeth George Speare. HOUGHTON MIFFLIN.

HONOR BOOKS: *Frontier Living*, Edwin Tunis. WORLD.
The Golden Goblet, Eloise Jarvis McGraw. COWARD-MCCANN.
Belling the Tiger, Mary Stolz. HARPER.

1963 AWARD: *A Wrinkle in Time*, Madeleine L'Engle. FARRAR, STRAUS.

HONOR BOOKS: *Thistle and Thyme: Tales and Legends from Scotland*, Sorche Nic Leodhas, *pseud.* (Leclaire Alger). HOLT.
Men of Athens, Olivia Coolidge. HOUGHTON MIFFLIN.

1964 AWARD: *It's Like This, Cat*, Emily Neville. HARPER.

HONOR BOOKS: *Rascal*, Sterling North. DUTTON.
The Loner, Ester Wier. MCKAY.

1965 AWARD: *Shadow of a Bull*, Maia Wojciechowska. ATHENEUM.

HONOR BOOK: *Across Five Aprils*, Irene Hunt. FOLLETT.

II. CALDECOTT AWARD: 1938-1965

1938 AWARD: *Animals of the Bible, A Picture Book.* Illustrated by Dorothy P. Lathrop. Text selected by Helen Dean Fish. LIPPINCOTT.

HONOR BOOKS: *Seven Simeons: a Russian Tale.* Retold and illustrated by Boris Artzybasheff. VIKING.
Four and Twenty Blackbirds . . . Illustrated by Robert Lawson. Compiled by Helen Dean Fish. STOKES.

1939 AWARD: *Mei Li.* Illustrated and written by Thomas Handforth. DOUBLEDAY.

HONOR BOOKS: *The Forest Pool.* Story and pictures by Laura Adams Armer. LONGMANS.
Wee Gillis. Illustrated by Robert Lawson. Text by Munroe Leaf. VIKING.
Snow White and the Seven Dwarfs. Freely translated and illustrated by Wanda Gág. COWARD-MCCANN.
Barkis. Story and pictures by Clare Newberry. HARPER.
Andy and the Lion. Written and illustrated by James Daugherty. VIKING.

1940 AWARD: *Abraham Lincoln.* Written and illustrated by Ingri and
               Edgar d'Aulaire. DOUBLEDAY.

HONOR BOOKS: *Cock-a-doodle Doo* . . . Story and pictures by Berta and
               Elmer Hader. MACMILLAN.
               Madeline. Story and pictures by Ludwig Bemelmans.
               VIKING.
               The Ageless Story. Illustrated by Lauren Ford. DODD
               MEAD.

1941 AWARD: *They Were Strong and Good.* Written and illustrated
               by Robert Lawson. VIKING.

HONOR BOOK: *April's Kittens.* Story and pictures by Clare Turlay
               Newberry. HARPER.

1942 AWARD: *Make Way for Ducklings.* Written and illustrated by
               Robert McCloskey. VIKING.

HONOR BOOKS: *An American ABC.* Text and pictures by Maud and
               Miska Petersham. MACMILLAN.
               In My Mother's House. Illustrated by Velino Herrera.
               Text by Ann Nolan Clark. VIKING.
               Paddle-to-the-Sea. Written and illustrated by Holling
               C. Holling. HOUGHTON MIFFLIN.
               Nothing At All. Story and pictures by Wanda Gág.
               COWARD-MC CANN.

1943 AWARD: *The Little House.* Written and illustrated by Virginia
               Lee Burton. HOUGHTON MIFFLIN.

HONOR BOOKS: *Dash and Dart.* Story and pictures by Mary and Conrad
               Buff. VIKING.
               Marshmallow. Story and pictures by Clare Turlay New-
               berry. HARPER.

1944 AWARD: *Many Moons.* Illustrated by Louis Slobodkin. Written
               by James Thurber. HARCOURT.

HONOR BOOKS: *Small Rain: Verses from the Bible.* Illustrated by Eliza-
               beth Orton Jones. Verses selected by Jessie Orton
               Jones. VIKING.
               Pierre Pidgeon. Illustrated by Arnold E. Bare. Text by
               Lee Kingman. HOUGHTON MIFFLIN.
               The Mighty Hunter. Story and pictures by Berta and
               Elmer Hader. MACMILLAN.
               A Child's Good Night Book. Illustrated by Jean Char-
               lot. Text by Margaret Wise Brown. W. R. SCOTT.
               Good-Luck Horse. Illustrated by Plato Chan. Text by
               Chih-Yi Chan. WHITTLESEY.

1945 AWARD: *Prayer for a Child*. Illustrated by Elizabeth Orton Jones. Written by Rachel Field. MACMILLAN.

HONOR BOOKS: *Mother Goose*. Illustrated by Tasha Tudor. WALCK.
In the Forest. Story and pictures by Marie Hall Ets. VIKING.
Yonie Wondernose. Written and illustrated by Marguerite de Angeli. DOUBLEDAY.
The Christmas Anna Angel. Illustrated by Kate Seredy. Written by Ruth Sawyer. VIKING.

1946 AWARD: *The Rooster Crows* . . . Illustrated by Maud and Miska Petersham. MACMILLAN.

HONOR BOOKS: *Little Lost Lamb*. Illustrated by Leonard Weisgard. Text by Golden MacDonald, *pseud.* (Margaret Wise Brown). DOUBLEDAY.
Sing Mother Goose. Illustrated by Marjorie Torrey. Music by Opal Wheeler. DUTTON.
My Mother Is the Most Beautiful Woman in the World. Illustrated by Ruth Gannett. Retold by Becky Reyher. LOTHROP.
You Can Write Chinese. Text and illustrations by Kurt Wiese. VIKING.

1947 AWARD: *The Little Island*. Illustrated by Leonard Weisgard. Written by Golden MacDonald, *pseud.* (Margaret Wise Brown). DOUBLEDAY.

HONOR BOOKS: *Rain Drop Splash*. Illustrated by Leonard Weisgard. Story by Alvin Tresselt. LOTHROP.
Boats on the River. Illustrated by Jay Hyde Barnum. Text by Marjorie Flack. VIKING.
Timothy Turtle. Illustrated by Tony Palazzo. Written by Al Graham. ROBERT WELCH PUB. CO.
Pedro, the Angel of Olvera Street. Text and illustrations by Leo Politi. SCRIBNER.
Sing in Praise: a Collection of the Best Loved Hymns. Illustrated by Marjorie Torrey. Stories of hymns and musical arrangements by Opal Wheeler. DUTTON.

1948 AWARD: *White Snow, Bright Snow*. Illustrated by Roger Duvoisin. Written by Alvin Tresselt. LOTHROP.

HONOR BOOKS: *Stone Soup*. Told and illustrated by Marcia Brown. SCRIBNER.
McElligot's Pool. Written and illustrated by Dr. Seuss, *pseud.* (Theodor Seuss Geisel). RANDOM HOUSE.
Bambino the Clown. Text and pictures by George Schreiber. VIKING.

Roger and the Fox. Pictures by Hildegard Woodward. Text by Lavinia Davis. DOUBLEDAY.

Song of Robin Hood. Designed and illustrated by Virginia Lee Burton. Selected and edited by Anne Malcolmson. HOUGHTON MIFFLIN.

1949 AWARD: *The Big Snow.* Written and illustrated by Berta and Elmer Hader. MACMILLAN.

HONOR BOOKS: *Blueberries for Sal.* Written and illustrated by Robert McCloskey. VIKING.

All Around the Town. Illustrated by Helen Stone. Text by Phyllis McGinley. LIPPINCOTT.

Juanita. Written and illustrated by Leo Politi. SCRIBNER.

Fish in the Air. Story and pictures by Kurt Wiese. VIKING.

1950 AWARD: *Song of the Swallows.* Written and illustrated by Leo Politi. SCRIBNER.

HONOR BOOKS: *America's Ethan Allen.* Pictures by Lynd Ward. Story by Stewart Holbrook. HOUGHTON MIFFLIN.

The Wild Birthday Cake. Illustrated by Hildegard Woodward. Written by Lavinia R. Davis. DOUBLE-DAY.

The Happy Day. Pictures by Marc Simont. Story by Ruth Krauss. HARPER.

Bartholomew and the Oobleck. Written and illustrated Dr. Seuss, *pseud.* (Theodor Seuss Geisel). RANDOM HOUSE.

Henry Fisherman. Written and illustrated by Marcia Brown, SCRIBNER.

1951 AWARD: *The Egg Tree.* Written and illustrated by Katherine Milhous. SCRIBNER.

HONOR BOOKS: *Dick Whittington and His Cat.* Told and illustrated by Marcia Brown. SCRIBNER.

The Two Reds. Illustrated by Nicolas, *pseud.* (Nicolas Mordvinoff). Written by Will, *pseud.* (William Lipkind). HARCOURT.

If I Ran the Zoo. Written and illustrated by Dr. Seuss, *pseud.* (Theodor Seuss Geisel). RANDOM HOUSE.

The Most Wonderful Doll in the World. Illustrated by by Helen Stone. Written by Phyllis McGinley. LIP-PINCOTT.

T-Bone, the Baby Sitter. Story and pictures by Claire Turlay Newberry. HARPER.

1952 AWARD: *Finders Keepers.* Illustrated by Nicolas, *pseud.* (Nicolas Mordvinoff). Written by Will, *pseud.* (William Lipkind). HARCOURT.

HONOR BOOKS: *Mr. T. W. Anthony Woo.* Story and pictures by Marie Hall Ets. VIKING.
Skipper John's Cook. Written and illustrated by Marcia Brown. SCRIBNER.
All Falling Down. Illustrated by Margaret Bloy Graham. Written by Gene Zion. HARPER.
Bear Party. Written and illustrated by William Pène du Bois. VIKING.
Feather Mountain. Written and illustrated by Elizabeth Olds. HOUGHTON MIFFLIN.

1953 AWARD: *The Biggest Bear.* Written and illustrated by Lynd Ward. HOUGHTON MIFFLIN.

HONOR BOOKS: *Puss in Boots.* Illustrated and translated from Charles Perrault by Marcia Brown. SCRIBNER.
One Morning in Maine. Written and illustrated by Robert McCloskey. VIKING.
Ape in a Cape: An Alphabet of Odd Animals. Text and pictures by Fritz Eichenberg. HARCOURT.
The Storm Book. Illustrated by Margaret Bloy Graham. Written by Charlotte Zolotow. HARPER.
Five Little Monkeys. Story and illustrations by Juliet Kepes. HOUGHTON MIFFLIN.

1954 AWARD: *Madeline's Rescue.* Written and illustrated by Ludwig Bemelmans. VIKING.

HONOR BOOKS: *Journey Cake, Ho!* Illustrated by Robert McCloskey. Text by Ruth Sawyer. VIKING.
When Will the World Be Mine? Illustrated by Jean Charlot. Written by Miriam Schlein. W. R. SCOTT.
The Steadfast Tin Soldier. Illustrated by Marcia Brown. Story by Hans Christian Andersen, trans. by M. R. James. SCRIBNER.
A Very Special House. Illustrated by Maurice Sendak. Written by Ruth Krauss. HARPER.
Green Eyes. Story and pictures by A. Birnbaum. CAPITOL PUB.

1955 AWARD: *Cinderella, or the Little Glass Slipper.* Illustrated and translated from Perrault by Marcia Brown. SCRIBNER.

HONOR BOOKS: *Book of Nursery and Mother Goose Rhymes.* Illustrated by Marguerite de Angeli. DOUBLEDAY.

Wheel on the Chimney. Illustrated by Tibor Gergely. Written by Margaret Wise Brown. LIPPINCOTT.
The Thanksgiving Story. Illustrated by Helen Sewell. Text by Alice Dalgliesh. SCRIBNER.

1956 AWARD: *Frog Went A-Courtin'*. Illustrated by Feodor Rojankovsky. Text retold by John Langstaff. HARCOURT.

HONOR BOOKS: *Play With Me*. Story and pictures by Marie Hall Ets. VIKING.
Crow Boy. Written and illustrated by Taro Yashima. VIKING.

1957 AWARD: *A Tree Is Nice*. Illustrated by Marc Simont. Written by Janice May Udry. HARPER.

HONOR BOOKS: *Mr. Penny's Race Horse*. Written and illustrated by Marie Hall Ets. VIKING.
1 Is One. Story and pictures by Tasha Tudor. WALCK.
Anatole. Illustrated by Paul Galdone. Written by Eve Titus. MC GRAW-HILL.
Gillespie and the Guards. Illustrated by James Daugherty. Written by Benjamin Elkin. VIKING.
Lion. Written and illustrated by William Pène du Bois. VIKING.

1958 AWARD: *Time of Wonder*. Written and illustrated by Robert McCloskey. VIKING.

HONOR BOOKS: *Fly High, Fly Low*. Story and pictures by Don Freeman. VIKING.
Anatole and the Cat. Illustrated by Paul Galdone. Written by Eve Titus. MC GRAW-HILL.

1959 AWARD: *Chanticleer and the Fox*. Adapted from Chaucer's *The Canterbury Tales* and illustrated by Barbara Cooney. CROWELL.

HONOR BOOKS: *The House that Jack Built: La Maison Que Jacques A Batie*. Text and illustrations by Antonio Frasconi. HARCOURT.
What Do You Say, Dear? Illustrated by Maurice Sendak. Written by Sesyle Joslin. W. R. SCOTT.
Umbrella. Story and pictures by Taro Yashima. VIKING.

1960 AWARD: *Nine Days to Christmas*. Illustrated by Marie Hall Ets. Written by Marie Hall Ets and Aurora Labastida. VIKING.

HONOR BOOKS: *Houses from the Sea.* Illustrated by Adrienne Adams. Written by Alice E. Goudey. SCRIBNER.
The Moon Jumpers. Illustrated by Maurice Sendak. Written by Janice May Udry. HARPER.

1961 AWARD: *Baboushka and the Three Kings.* Illustrated by Nicolas Sidjakov. Written by Ruth Robbins. PARNASSUS PRESS.

HONOR BOOK: *Inch by Inch.* Written and illustrated by Leo Lionni. IVAN OBOLENSKY, INC.

1962 AWARD: *Once a Mouse.* Retold and illustrated by Marcia Brown. SCRIBNER.

HONOR BOOKS: *The Fox Went Out on a Chilly Night; an Old Song.* Illustrated by Peter Spier. DOUBLEDAY.
Little Bear's Visit. Illustrated by Maurice Sendak. Written by Else H. Minarik. HARPER.
The Day We Saw the Sun Come Up. Illustrated by Adrienne Adams. Written by Alice E. Goudey. SCRIBNER.

1963 AWARD: *The Snowy Day.* Story and pictures by Ezra Jack Keats. VIKING.

HONOR BOOKS: *The Sun is a Golden Earring.* Illustrated by Bernarda Bryson. Text by Natalia M. Belting. HOLT.
Mr. Rabbit and the Lovely Present. Illustrated by Maurice Sendak. Written by Charlotte Zolotow. HARPER.

1964 AWARD: *Where the Wild Things Are.* Written and illustrated by Maurice Sendak. HARPER.

HONOR BOOKS: *Swimmy.* Story and pictures by Leo Lionni. PANTHEON.
All in the Morning Early. Illustrated by Evaline Ness. Text by Sorche Nic Leodas, *pseud.* (Leclaire Alger). HOLT.
Mother Goose and Nursery Rhymes. Illustrated by Philip Reed. ATHENEUM.

1965 AWARD: *May I Bring a Friend?* Illustrated by Beni Montresor. Beatrice Schenk de Regniers. ATHENEUM.

HONOR BOOKS: *Rain Makes Applesauce.* Illustrated by Marvin Bileck. Written by Julian Scheer. HOLIDAY HOUSE.
The Wave. Illustrated by Blair Lent. Written by Margaret Hodges. HOUGHTON MIFFLIN.
A Pocketful of Cricket. Illustrated by Evaline Ness. Text by Rebecca Caudill. HOLT.

Index of Titles Mentioned

American Folk Songs for Children, 206
The American Practical Navigator, 4, 13, 18
And Both Were Young, 126
. . . and now Miguel, 90

Baboushka and the Three Kings, 8, 10, 217-224, 275
The Big Snow, 278
Blue Barns, 278
The Blue Teapot, 29
Blueberries for Sal, 195
Borka, 271
A Boy's First Book of the Stars, 18
Boys' Life of Will Rogers, 54, 65
The Bronze Bow, 3, 5, 10, 109-115, 160

Calico Captive, 73, 81
Call It Courage, 157
Camilla Dickinson, 126
Carry On, Mr. Bowditch, 10, 13-30, 160
Centerburg Tales, 194, 195
Chanticleer and the Fox, 10, 198-202, 206, 274
Charlotte's Web, 135
Christmas in the Barn, 206
Cinderella, illustrated by Beni Montresor, 267
Cinderella, illustrated by Marcia Brown, 232, 277
Contest at Paca, 273
Country of the Sun, 107
Curious Missie, 41, 45

Daniel Boone, 172, 173
Dick Whittington and His Cat, 236, 277

The Evening and the Morning, 37

Felice, 234, 235
Fish Head, 273
The Flying Carpet, 233
The Friendly Beasts, 218, 222
Frog Went A-Courtin', 7, 9, 165-170, 171, 172, 173, 175, 271, 272
Frou, 173

Good Luck Duck, 183
Good Shabos, Everybody, 256
Grandfather Whiskers M.D., 205, 206
Gray Bread, 29

The Happy Day, 183
The Happy Owls, 271
Hey Diddle Diddle, 248
Hill of the Hawk, 107
A Hole Is to Dig, 254, 257
Homer Price, 194
House of Flowers, House of Stars, 266, 268, 280
The House Next Door, 45, 46
How to Have Fun With Arithmetic, 18

In the Forest, 216, 275
Invincible Louisa, 120
Island of the Blue Dolphins, 5, 10, 97-108, 155, 156
It's Like This, Cat, 6, 10, 129-139, 159

Jonah the Fisherman, 271
Journey Cake Ho!, 195
Jubilant for Sure, 242
Junket, 195

Kenny's Window, 257

Lentil, 194
Letters of a Portuguese Nun, 127
Little Bear's Visit, 257
A Little Lower Than the Angels, 45
Little Old Automobile, 215
Little Women, 205
The Lovely Summer, 184
Lullaby for Eggs, 270

Magic Flute, 267
Make Way for Ducklings, 195
Many Heavens, 45
Market Day for Ti André, 151
Mary Poppins, 46
The Matchlock Gun, 60
May I Bring a Friend?, 9, 258-265, 267, 279
Medals for Morse, 28
Meet the Austins, 126

The Mexican Story, 209
Mimi, 184
Miracles on Maple Hill, 5, 10, 31-49,
  160
Mister Penny, 216
Mon Chat, 173
The Moon by Night, 126
The Moon Jumpers, 257
Mr. Rabbit and the Lovely Present,
  257
Mr. T. W. Anthony Woo, 213
My Dog Is Lost!, 241
My Dog Rinty, 210

The Nightmare, 29
Nine Days to Christmas, 8, 10, 208-
  216, 274, 275, 280

Odyssey of Courage, 145, 152
Oklahoma Kickoff, 65
Old Doc, 17, 29
Oley the Sea Monster, 215
Once a Mouse, 8, 10, 225-231, 232, 234,
  237, 277
One Morning in Maine, 195
Onion John, 6, 7, 9, 82-96, 160
Opera Soufflé, 185

Panache, 173
Peter Piper's Alphabet, 234
Peter's Long Walk, 206
Plain Girl, 46
Play with Me, 216, 275
The Plumber out of the Sea, 184
A Pocketful of Cricket, 270
Polly's Oats, 184

Regarde, 173
Rifles for Watie, 4, 10, 50-68, 160

Señor Freedom, 29
Shadow of a Bull, 4, 7, 140-152, 155,
  157
The Small Rain, 126
The Snowy Day, 8, 10, 238-240, 277
Sports and Games, 65
Stone Soup, 236
The Story of Eli Whitney, 22, 28

The Tall Book of Mother Goose, 175
Tamarindo!, 234, 236
The Thirteen Clocks, 182
This Dear-Bought Land, 28
The Three Billy Goats Gruff, 233
The Three Jovial Huntsmen, 247
Time of Wonder, 7, 10, 187-193, 195,
  273, 280
Trail Blazer of the Seas, 28
A Tree Is Nice, 7, 10, 176-179, 182,
  183, 184, 272

Une Drôle de Soupe, 236

A Very Special House, 257

What Do You Say, Dear?, 257
Where Have You Been?, 206
Where the Wild Things Are, 9, 246-
  257, 278, 279
White Snow, Bright Snow, 278
The Witch of Blackbird Pond, 5, 10,
  69-81, 112, 160
The Witches of Venice, 260, 267, 268
The Wonderful Farm, 257
The Wonderful O, 182
A Wrinkle in Time, 6, 10, 116-128,
  135, 159

Index by Author
of Books Mentioned

Alcott, Louisa May, *Little Women,* il. by Barbara Cooney,
                             Crowell (1955)   205
Averill, Esther, *Daniel Boone,* il. by Feodor Rojankovsky,
                             Domino (1931)   172
Aymé, Marcel, *The Wonderful Farm,* tr. from the French by
  Norman Denny, il. by Maurice Sendak, Harper (1951)   257

Baker, Laura Nelson, *The Friendly Beasts, il. by Nicolas*
             Sidjakov, Parnassus (1957)   218, 222
Beucler, André, *Mon Chat,* il. by Nathalie Parain, Nouvelle
               Revue Française (1930)   173
Bowditch, Nathaniel, *The American Practical Navigator,* First
                published 1802   4, 13, 18
Bridgman, Elizabeth Klein, *Lullaby For Eggs,* il. by Elizabeth
           Orton Jones, Macmillan (1955)   270
Brown, Marcia, *Cinderella, or the Little Glass Slipper,* trans.
  from Perrault and illustrated by the author, Scribner (1954) 232, 236, 277
  Dick Whittington and His Cat, il. by the author, Scribner
                       (1950)   236, 277
  Felice, il. by the author, Scribner (1958)   234, 235
  The Flying Carpet, il. by the author, Scribner (1956)   233
  Once a Mouse, il. by the author, Scribner (1961)
           8, 225, 226, 232-237, 270, 277
  Peter Piper's Alphabet, il. by the author, Scribner (1959)   234
  Tamarindo!, il. by the author, Scribner (1960)   234, 236
  Three Billy Goats Gruff, il. by the author (1957)   233
  Une Drole de Soupe, il. by the author, trans. by Hilda Grenier
            Tagliapietra, Scribner (1960)   236
Brown, Margaret Wise, *Christmas in the Barn,* il. by Barbara
            Cooney, Crowell (1952)   206
  Where Have You Been?, il. by Barbara Cooney, Hastings
     (1963) (First published by Crowell in 1952)   206
Burningham, John, *Borka,* Random (1963)   271

Caldecott, Randolph, *Hey Diddle Diddle Picture Book,* il. by
      the author, Routledge (1883) 247, 248, 270
  The Three Jovial Huntsmen, il. by the author, Warne (1880)   248
Caudill, Rebecca, *A Pocketful of Cricket,* il. by Evaline Ness,
                 Holt (1964)   270
Cherr, Pat. See Keats, Ezra Jack
Colette, *Regarde,* il. by Méheut, Deschamps (1929)   173
Cooney, Barbara, *Chanticleer and the Fox,* adapted and il. by the
  author from the story by Geoffrey Chaucer, Crowell (1958)
       8, 112, 198, 199, 203-207, 274

DeJong, Meindert, *Good Luck Duck,* il. by Marc Simont,
                 Harper (1950)   183

de Regniers, Beatrice Schenk, *May I Bring a Friend?*, il. by Beni
  Montresor, Atheneum (1964)   9, 258, 267, 279

Edmonds, Walter D., *The Matchlock Gun*, il. by Paul Lantz,
                            Dodd (1941)   60
Ets, Marie Hall, *In the Forest*, il. by the author, Viking (1944)   216, 275
  Mister Penny, il. by the author, Viking (1935)   216
  Mr. T. W. Anthony Woo, il. by the author, Viking (1951)   213
  Oley the Sea Monster, il. by the author, Viking (1947)   215
  Play With Me, il. by the author, Viking (1955)   216, 275
Ets, Marie Hall and Labastida, Aurora, *Nine Days to Christmas*,
  il. by Marie Hall Ets, Viking (1959)   8, 208, 209, 212-216, 274, 275, 280
Ets, Marie Hall and Tarry, Ellen, *My Dog Rinty*, il. with
  photographs by Alexander and Alexandra Alland, Viking
                            (1946)   210

Fritz, Jean, *Fish Head*, il. by Marc Simont, Coward (1954)   273

Hader, Berta and Elmer, *The Big Snow*, il. by the authors, Mac-
                            millan (1948)   278

Joslin, Sesyle, *What Do You Say, Dear?*, il. by Maurice Sen-
                            dak, W. R. Scott (1958)   257

Keats, Ezra Jack, *The Snowy Day*, il. by the author, Viking
                    (1962) 8, 238, 239, 241-245, 277, 278
Keats, Ezra Jack and Cherr, Pat, *My Dog Is Lost!*, il. by the
                            authors, Crowell (1960)   241
Keith, Harold, *Boys' Life of Will Rogers*, Crowell (1936)   54, 65
  Oklahoma Kickoff (pub. by the author) (1948)   65
  Rifles for Watie, Crowell (1957)   50, 53, 63-68, 160
  Sports and Games, Crowell (1941)   65
Kingman, Lee, *Peter's Long Walk*, il. by Barbara Cooney,
                            Doubleday (1953)   206
Krauss, Ruth, *A Hole is to Dig*, il. by Maurice Sendak, Harper
                            (1952)   254
  The Happy Day, il. by Marc Simont, Harper (1949)   183
  A Very Special House, il. by Maurice Sendak, Harper (1953)   257
Krumgold, Joseph, *. . . and now Miguel*, il. by Jean Charlot,
                            Crowell (1953)   90
  Onion John, il. by Symeon Shimin, Crowell (1959)   9, 82, 85, 90-96, 160

Lansing, Elizabeth Hubbard, *Jubilant for Sure*, il. by Ezra Jack
                            Keats, Crowell (1955)   242
Langstaff, John, *Frog Went A-Courtin'*, il. by Feodor Rojan-
                    kovsky, Harcourt (1955) 165, 171, 175, 271, 272
Latham, Jean Lee, *Carry on, Mr. Bowditch*, il. by John O'Hara
                    Cosgrave II, Houghton (1955) 13, 16, 25-30, 160
  Medals for Morse, il. by Douglas Gorsline, Aladdin (1954)   28
  The Story of Eli Whitney, il. by Fritz Kredel, Aladdin (1953) 28
  This Dear-Bought Land, il. by Jacob Landau, Harper (1957)   28
  Trail Blazer of the Seas, il. by Victor Mays, Houghton (1956) 28

L'Engle, Madeleine, *And Both Were Young*, Lothrop (1949)   126
   A Wrinkle in Time, Farrar (1962)   6, 116, 119, 124-128, 135, 159
   Camilla Dickinson, Simon and Schuster (1951)   126
   Meet the Austins, Vanguard (1960)   126
   The Moon by Night, Farrar (1963)   126
   The Small Rain, Vanguard (1945)   126
Leonard, Nellie Mabel, *Grandfather Whiskers M.D.*, il. by
   Barbara Cooney, Crowell (1953) (Earlier edition, 1919, called
                       Granddaddy Whiskers, M.D.)   206

McCloskey, Robert, *Blueberries for Sal*, Viking (1948)   195
   Centerburg Tales, Viking (1951)   194
   Homer Price, Viking (1943)   194
   Lentil, Viking (1940)   194
   Make Way for Ducklings, Viking (1941)   195
   One Morning in Maine, Viking (1952)   195
   Time of Wonder, Viking (1957)   7, 187, 188, 194-197, 273, 280
McNeer, May, *The Mexican Story*, il. by Lynd Ward, Farrar
                              (1953)   209
Meigs, Cornelia, *Invincible Louisa*, Little Brown (1933)   120
Minarik, Else H., *Little Bear's Visit*, il. by Maurice Sendak,
                           Harper (1962)   257
Montresor, Beni, *House of Flowers, House of Stars*, il. by the
                    author, Knopf (1962)   266, 280
   Witches of Venice, il. by the author, Knopf (1963)   260

Neville, Emily, *It's Like This, Cat*, il. by Emil Weiss, Harper
                 (1963) 6, 129, 131, 137-139, 159
O'Dell, Scott, *Hill of the Hawk*, Bobbs (1947)   107
   Island of the Blue Dolphins, Houghton (1960)   5, 97, 99, 105-108, 155, 156

Piatti, Celestino, *The Happy Owls*, Atheneum (1964)   271

Robbins, Ruth, *Baboushka and the Three Kings*, il. by Nicolas
             Sidjakov, Parnassus (1960)   217, 218, 221, 275
Rodman, Maia (see also Wojciechowska, Maia), *Market Day
   for Ti André*, il. by Wilson Bigaud, Viking (1952)   151
Rojankovsky, Feodor, *Frou the Hare*, il. by the author, trans-
   lated from the French by Rose Fyleman, The Pere Castor
   Wild Animal Books, George Allen & Unwin (1938)   173
   Tall Book of Mother Goose, Harper (1942)   175

Sawyer, Ruth, *Journey Cake Ho!*, il. by Robert McCloskey,
                       Viking (1953)   195
Seeger, Ruth Crawford, *American Folk Songs for Children*,
                       Doubleday (1948)   206
Sendak, Maurice, *Good Shabos, Everybody*, il. by the author,
   United Synagogue Commission on Jewish Education (1951)   256
   Kenny's Window, il. by the author, Harper (1956)   257
   Where the Wild Things Are, il. by the author, Harper (1963)
                 9, 246, 247, 254-257, 278, 279

Sewell, Helen, *Blue Barns*, il. by the author, Macmillan (1933)   278
Simont, Marc, *The Contest at Paca*, il. by the author, Harper
                                                         (1959)   273
   The Lovely Summer, il. by the author, Harper (1952)   184
   Mimi, il. by the author, Harper (1954)   184
   Opera Soufflé, il. by the author, Abelard-Schuman (1950)   185
   The Plumber out of the Sea, il. by the author, Harper (1955)   184
   Polly's Oats, il. by the author, Harper (1951)   184
Smith, Red and Simont, Marc, *How to Get to First Base*,
                  il. by Marc Simont, Abelard-Schuman (1952)   184
Sorensen, Virginia, *A Little Lower Than the Angels*, Knopf
                                                         (1942)   45
   Curious Missie, il. by Marilyn Miller, Harcourt (1953)   41, 45
   The Evening and the Morning, Harcourt (1949)   37
   The House Next Door, Harcourt (1954)   45
   Many Heavens, Harcourt (1954)   45
   Miracles on Maple Hill, il. by Beth and Joe Krush, Harcourt
                                     (1956) 31, 34, 43-49, 160
   Plain Girl, il. by Charles Geer, Harcourt (1955)   46
Speare, Elizabeth George, *The Bronze Bow*, Houghton (1961)
                                         3, 5, 109, 111, 160
   Calico Captive, il. by W. T. Mars, Houghton (1957)   73, 81
   The Witch of Blackbird Pond, Houghton (1958)   5, 69, 72, 78-81, 160
Sperry, Armstrong, *Call It Courage*, il. by the author, Macmillan
                                                         (1940)   157

Thurber, James, *The Thirteen Clocks*, il. by Marc Simont,
                             Simon and Schuster (1950)   182
Tresselt, Alvin R., *White Snow, Bright Snow*, il. by Roger
                             Duvoisin, Lothrop (1947)   278

Udry, Janice May, *A Tree Is Nice*, il. by Marc Simont, Harper
                                         (1956)   7, 176, 272
   The Moon-Jumpers, il. by Maurice Sendak, Harper (1959)   257

White, Anne Hitchcock, *Junket*, il. by Robert McCloskey,
                                         Viking (1955)   195
White, Elwyn Brooks, *Charlotte's Web*, il. by Garth Williams,
                                         Harper (1952)   135
Wojciechowska, Maia (see also Rodman, Maia), *Odyssey of
Courage*, il. by Alvin Smith, Atheneum (1965)   145
   Shadow of a Bull, il. by Alvin Smith, Atheneum (1965)
                     xviii, 7, 140, 142, 147-152, 155, 157

Zimnik, Reiner, *Jonah the Fisherman*, il. by the author, tr.
from the German by Richard and Clara Winston, Pantheon
                                                         (1956)   271
Zolotow, Charlotte, *Mr. Rabbit and the Lovely Present*, il. by
                             Maurice Sendak, Harper (1962)   257